# BLACK TALK

# BLACK TALK

## Words and Phrases from the Hood to the Amen Corner

### GENEVA SMITHERMAN

Revised Edition

Houghton Mifflin Company
Boston   New York

For information about permission to reproduce selections from
this book, write to Permissions, Houghton Mifflin Company,
215 Park Avenue South, New York, New York 10003.

Library of Congress Cataloging-in-Publication Data

Smitherman, Geneva, date.
Black talk : words and phrases from the hood to the
amen corner / Geneva Smitherman. — Rev. ed.
p.    cm.
ISBN 0-395-96919-0
1. Afro-Americans — Languages Dictionaries.   2. English
language — United States Glossaries, vocabularies, etc.
3.  English language — United States — Slang Dictionaries.
4.  Black English — United States Dictionaries.
5.  Americanisms Dictionaries.   I.  Title.
PE3102.N4S65  2000
427'.089'96073 — dc21    99-40637    CIP

Book design by Anne Chalmers
Typeface: Minion; Clarendon and Lettres Éclatées display

Printed in the United States of America
QUM  10  9  8  7  6  5  4  3  2  1

Text credits appear on page 306.

For Anthony and Amber

# ACKNOWLEDGMENTS

THIS PROJECT WAS STARTED back in the 1970s when my editor at the time asked me to prepare a small glossary of terms and expressions for inclusion in *Talkin and Testifyin: The Language of Black America,* which was subsequently published by Houghton Mifflin in 1977. In the years since then, I have been gradually adding to that initial collection, and numerous people have helped to bring this project to fruition at last. Of course, any mistakes or shortcomings in this book are entirely my own.

First, a word of gratitude for language research in the hood done by hundreds of students in my courses over the years at Harvard University, Wayne State University, and Michigan State University.

For responding to my call for language surveys and sound advice, I am indebted to Ana Celia Zentella, Harry Allen, Corey Katsu Takahashi, Yusuf Nuruddin, and Milton Baxter of New York City; Sandra Wright of New Orleans; Police Chief Benny Napoleon of Detroit; Gregory Moore and Abdul Alkalimat of Chicago; Mashana (Deucette) and Milbrun (Deuce) Pearson, Sterling Beasley, and Kenny Snodgrass of Detroit; Gary Simpkins and Edward Boyer of Los Angeles; Nathan Magee of Stockton and the Bay Area in California; James Ward of Houston; Perry Hall of Chapel Hill, North Carolina, and Ronn Hopkins of Bath, North Carolina; Christianna Buchner of Munich, Germany; Ron Stephens of Philadelphia; Ezra Hyland of Minneapolis; and Bobby White of Detroit.

For helpful word lists, I thank John Rickford of Stanford, California; Hilton Morris of Fort Wayne, Indiana; Ronald Butters of Durham, North Carolina; Police Chief Robert L. Johnson of Lansing, Michigan; Kimara Sangster of Saginaw, Michigan; and Rafique Anderson of Detroit.

For steering me to legendary sources of language in the hood, I thank Henry (White Cap) Rupert and all of his Old School gangsta partners, but especially Lyin Willie of Chicago, Diamond Joe of Atlanta, Old Mose and Slick Trick of Los Angeles, Hustlin Arthur of Detroit, Slim Jim of Dallas, and the Bad Dudes of East St. Louis and Yazoo, Mississippi.

A shout out to Milbrun (Deuce) Pearson for pulling me aside back in the 1980s and making me give a serious listen to Hip Hop. And to Kofi Davis and Kwame Finn for introducing me to Underground Rap and serving as guides to the oral culture of Hip Hop. Thanks, Youngbloods.

My student research assistants, Kerry Rockquemore and Nicole Smith, deserve special recognition. In addition to processing data cards, typing and retyping and retyping, they assisted in the tedious process of tracking down permission rights and aided me in the thousand and one laborious and painstaking details necessary to complete this kind of dictionary. Thanks to Nicole for going above and beyond the call of duty in countless ways. Much appreciation to Kerry for being a diligent researcher and a stickler for details—and for tolerating my phone calls late in the midnight hour. Props to my secretarial assistant, Lorraine Hart, for her diligence and to my student researcher, Rachel Forbes-Jackson, who persevered through this new edition as she carried new life.

A project of this sort needs the guiding hand of a wise and understanding editor. Fortunately, I have had two such editors, Elizabeth (Liz) Kubik for the first edition and Suzanne Samuel for this new edition. I have benefited immeasurably from their advice and experience.

In writer and scholar Dr. Keith Gilyard I found a kindred spirit with a profound understanding of the cultural significance of and critical necessity for this kind of book. He continues to inform with poetic vision and mother wit.

Not least of all, I owe a debt of gratitude to the millions of African Americans who talk that Talk in the churches, at senior-citizen bingo games, in daylong hair-braiding gatherings of women, at family reunions, on the buses and subways, playing pickup basketball, in bars and comedy clubs, at house parties, dances and concerts, at community meetings and political rallies—and wherever Black people congregate. Actually, this entire country is indebted to Africans in America for enriching and enlivening Americans' daily conversation with words and phrases from the hood to the Amen Corner.

—GENEVA SMITHERMAN
June 1999

# CONTENTS

❖ ❖ ❖ ❖ ❖ ❖

# EXPLANATORY NOTES

THE WORDS/PHRASES in this dictionary are in current use by Blacks from all walks of life: blue- and white-collar workers, professionals and businessmen/women, preachers and other church folk, Hip Hoppers, political activists, musicians, hustlers and gangstas, senior citizens. Some words/phrases are more common in one context than another—that is, in the Traditional Black Church, or in Hip Hop Culture, or among Black women. The particular context is indicated in the definitions and examples that accompany such words/phrases.

Several methods were used in compiling this dictionary. Some words/phrases are from written language surveys and word lists completed by Black people from various age and social groups around the country. Other words/phrases were gathered from songs, hit recordings, and films. Still others were gathered using ethnographic methods: participating in and observing conversations and speakers; conducting informal face-to-face interviews, collecting words/phrases from community bulletins, leaflets, meetings, announcements, handwritten notes and letters, call-ins to radio programs; and occasionally even eavesdropping. In general, formal written or published sources were not consulted, and no words/phrases are included that have appeared only in formal writing. The various illustrative sentences accompanying the definitions are the actual spoken words of Africans in America.

Of course, what we linguists call my "native speaker competence," as a daughter of the hood who continues to work and socialize there, was very useful in pulling together this dictionary. However, no word/phrase is included whose use could not be verified by several Black speakers.

Unlike standard dictionaries, the definitions here do not usually include the origin, or etymological history, of a word/phrase, nor is there any attempt to identify who first used a word/phrase—these are risky propositions at best when dealing with an oral language such as African American Language. Instead, since Black Talk can be fully understood only within the Black context, this dictionary concentrates on the historical and contemporary significance of words/phrases in the context of African American Culture and the Black Experience. Such explanatory details accompany many of the definitions.

In many words/phrases in Black Talk, the authentic Black sound depends on use of the African American Language system of grammar and pronunciation. (Some of the rules governing this system are explained in the Introduction.) Where the authentic Black sound is important, a word/phrase is listed with the spelling that most closely approximates that sound. In some instances, the African American Language spelling produces a word that appears to be the same as an altogether different word in formal written English. Such words/phrases are listed with both the formal written spelling and the spelling that conveys Black Talk, but the definition is given only at the entry under the Black pronunciation.

If a word/phrase used in a definition appears in small capitals, it is listed elsewhere in the dictionary.

"Also" is used to indicate a word/phrase that is a synonym or near equivalent. "See also" is used to refer to words/phrases that will provide further information. Words and phrases following "Also" and "See also" appear in italics.

"Crossover" refers to a word/phrase in Black Talk that has moved beyond the African American context and is now in general use by

European Americans. Some crossover words/phrases are linked to African languages and have become so common in American speech that most people are unaware of their origin. (The African background of Black Language is discussed in the Introduction. Interested readers should also consult the references given there for more information on this aspect of Black Talk.) In many cases, however, the linguistic origin of crossover words/phrases is unknown. Such words/phrases were (and still are) used widely in the African American community before they entered into more general use among European Americans.

# INTRODUCTION

☒ ☒ ☒ ☒ ☒ ☒ ☒ ☒ ☒

## From Dead Presidents to the Benjamins¹: The Africanization of American English

LYIN and SIGNIFYIN...TALKin and TESTIFYin...MARINATin and PLAYA HATin...This is the dynamic language of U.S. slave descendants, more commonly known as AFRICAN AMERICANS. Terms for this language vary—Black Talk, African American Vernacular English, Black or African American Language, Black English, Black Dialect, Ghetto Speech, Street Talk, Ebonics, and others. This book favors the terms "Black" or "African American Language," "Black Talk," and "U.S. Ebonics" (more accurate than just "Ebonics" because there are other Ebonic languages, such as Jamaican). Speakers of U.S. Ebonics can be found in all sectors of African America, from senior citizens to HIP HOPpers, from preachers to politicians, from schoolgirls to GANGSTAS, from the AFRICAN-CENTERED to the E-LIGHT. Black Talk crosses boundaries of age, gender, region, religion, and social class because it all comes from the same source: the African American Experience and the oral tradition embedded in that experience. In this dictionary you will find words and phrases from all segments of the Black² community, with cultural history and experience that charts word meanings within the various contexts of Black life. And, to paraphrase the late writer James Baldwin, if the language spoken in these contexts isn't a language, then tell me what is.

In one sense, there is today greater diversity within the African American community than ever before in the history of U.S. slave descendants. Take just a simple thing like a SISTA's hairdo. There was a time when virtually all Black women straightened their hair, usually with a HOT COMB and/or HOT CURLERS. There was GOOD HAIR and BAD HAIR. The bad hairstyle (which in the 1960s would come to be celebrated as the NATURAL) was almost nonexistent; it was viewed as ugly and uncouth, a disgrace to the race. And braids, they wuhdn't even in the running! Today, African American women wear their hair in all variety of styles. There is the natural, in both long and short hair versions. There are DREADS, adopted from the RASTA-FARIAN Culture of the Caribbean, in both long and short hair versions. There are all kinds of braided styles, done up with and without EXTENSIONS, in ZILLIONS, GODDESS style, and the SENE-GALESE TWIST. There are PERMed hairstyles, RELAXED, JHERI-CURL, and WAVE NOUVEAU treatments. There are all sorts of WEAVES, including those that render an ultrathick hairdo. And there are still the older hot combed and hot curled treatments. Sometimes these styles are all worn by the same Sista at different periods of time.

In another sense, however, there is an underlying uniformity among Blacks, owing to the fact that race, meaning not just skin color, but also culture, history, and experience, continues to define African America. Contrary to what many assume, the language within the African American community goes beyond mere slang, encompassing words and phrases that are common to generations, social classes, and both males and females. True, Black slang is Black Language, but all Black Language is not Black slang. (And what is Black slang today often becomes mainstream American English tomorrow.) Black Language is much more inclusive and expansive than the label "slang" suggests. For one thing, slang refers to language that is transitory and that is generally used by only one group, such as teenagers' slang or musicians' slang. African American Language, however, has a lexical core of words and phrases that are fairly stable over time and are familiar to and/or used by all groups in the Black community. This dictionary attempts to capture the essence of this lexical core.

Africans in America have always pushed the linguistic envelope. The underlying tone of resistance in the language may explain why African American linguistic innovations are so often dismissed as slang. It's an easier concept to deal with than confronting the reality that the words represent. Slang, after all, is rather lighthearted and harmless, and it's usually short-lived—here today, gone tomorrow—but the social critique embodied in Black slang is SERIOUS AS A HEART ATTACK. For 1990s HIP HOPpers, fed up with the oppressive treatment of PEOPLE OF COLOR in the nation's major cities, it's not *New* York, it's *Zoo* York; it's not Los *Angeles,* it's Los *Scandalous.* In the 1960s, Malcolm X shocked white America by dubbing northern cities UP SOUTH, contending that these supposedly progressive areas were just a variation on the theme of racial domination that Blacks were experiencing DOWN SOUTH. In these and many other examples, Africans in America flipped the script, making an alien tongue their own by imbuing "ole massa's" language with their unique, African semantics. Words came to have double meanings as their definitions shifted according to the situation and were infused with irony, metaphor, and ambiguity. When it first came into use, THE MAN referred to the white man, or the white man's enforcer, the policeman. Today, of course, it is used to refer to any male of distinction and power. ANN is just a woman's name, but in the past as well as today in Black Talk, it represents an uppity, demanding, spoiled white woman. In one context, "Everbody talkin bout Heaben ain goin dere," an expression that dates back to enslavement, was an admonition to those Blacks not practicing the religion they sing and testify about; in another context, it referred to white Americans who preached Christianity but practiced enslavement. "I cain't kill nothin and won't nothin die" is still used as a BLUES metaphor from the survival-of-the-fittest animal world and is applied to times in a person's life when they are down on their luck.

Alice tells Humpty Dumpty in the Lewis Carroll classic that you can't make words mean what you want them to mean. Communication demands linguistic conformity, and so it has been said that words are our masters, otherwise there would be no communication. Yet it has also been said that we are masters of words, otherwise there would be no poetry. Although the "poetry" created in the Africanization of American English undoubtedly dates back to the seventeenth century,[3] perhaps the richest period of linguistic innovation was the last half of the twentieth century, particularly the 1960s and beyond. The emergence of the Black Freedom Struggle[4] marked a fundamental shift in linguistic consciousness as Black intellectuals, scholar-activists, and writer-artists deliberately and consciously engaged in an unprecedented search for a language to express Black identity and the Black condition. This era was in fact the first period in the history of U.S. slave descendants when there was a critical mass of highly educated Blacks. To cite just one example, 80 percent of all the doctoral degrees (Ph.D.s, Ed.D.s) in the entire history of Africans in America were awarded between 1960 and 1980.[5] And although a conscious call for Black pride had existed in other historical periods—for example, the Harlem Renaissance[6] of the 1920s—the era of the 1960s Freedom Struggle was the first to call for *linguistic* Black pride. It was a call characterized by the learning of African languages (notably Swahili), by efforts to reinvent the Africanized language of the Black community, and by other forms of linguistic experimentation. Poet Haki Madhubuti put it this way: "black poets [will] deal in...black language or Afro-American language in contrast to standard english...will talk of kingdoms of Africa, will speak in Zulu and Swahili, will talk in muthafuckas and 'can you dig it.'" This linguistic consciousness and the experimentation driven by it—particularly among intellectuals, writers, entertainers, activists, and, in more recent years, HIP HOP Culture—has continued virtually unabated.

This dictionary takes you beyond a word list. It is a cultural map that charts word meanings along the highways and byways of African American life. In order to understand idioms like H.N.I.C., FORTY

ACRES, and TRYIN TO MAKE A DOLLA OUTA FIFTEEN CENT,
and words like OFAY, VOODOO, and JOHNSON, we need to understand how this nation within a nation developed its unique way of
using the English language. Which brings us to history and the
importance of the past in understanding, and moving beyond, the
present.

## FROM AFRICAN TO AFRICAN AMERICAN

Just as we were called colored, but were not that...and then Negro,
but not that...to be called Black is just as baseless...Black tells you
about skin color and what side of town you live on. African American evokes discussion of the world.[7]

Names for the race have been a continuing issue since JUMP-
STREET, 1619, when the first slave ship landed at Jamestown. From
AFRICAN to COLORED to "negro" to NEGRO with the capital to
BLACK to AFRICAN AMERICAN, with side trips to AFROAMER-
ICAN, AFRIAMERICAN, AFRAAMERICAN, and AFRIKAN, what
are we Africans in America, today thirty-five million strong, "we peo-
ple who are darker than blue," as Curtis Mayfield once sang, to call
ourselves?

Debates rage. The topic is discussed at conferences. Among leaders
and intellectuals, as well as among everyday people, the issue is sometimes argued so hotly that folk stop speaking to one another! In 1904,
the *A.M.E. Church Review* sponsored a symposium of Black leaders
to debate whether the "n" of "negro" should be capitalized. However,
participants in that symposium went beyond the mere question of
capitalization to debate whether "negro" was the right name for the
race in the first place. In 1967, during the shift from "Negro" to
"Black," and again in 1989, during the shift from "Black" to "African
American," *Ebony* magazine devoted several pages to the question

"What's in a Name?" And the beat goes on...The status of Blacks remains unsettled. Name changes and debates over names reflect our uncertain status and come to the forefront during crises and upheavals in the Black condition.

Although African Americans are linked to Africans on the Continent and in the DIASPORA, the Black American, as James Baldwin once put it, is a unique creation. For one thing, other Diasporic Africans claim citizenship in countries that are virtually all-Black—Jamaicans, Bajans, Nigerians, Ghanaians, for example, are not minorities in their native lands. For another, not only are Blacks a distinct minority in America, but our status as first-class citizens is debatable, even at this late hour in U.S. history. As the SISTA said about Rodney King's beating in Los Angeles, the torching of a Black man by whites in Florida, and Malice Green's death in Detroit, "After all we done been through, here it is [the 1990s], and we still ain free." Some activists and AFRICAN-CENTERED Blacks have coined the term NEO-SLAVERY to capture the view that the present Black condition, with whites still powerful and Blacks still powerless, is just enslavement in another form.

Blacks are a minority amid a population who look distinctly different physically and who promote racial supremacist standards of physical attractiveness. This state of affairs has created a set of negative attitudes about skin color, hair, and other physical features that are reflected in the U.S. Ebonics Lexicon, in terms such as GOOD HAIR (which Zora Neale Hurston once described as "nearer my God to thee"), BAD HAIR, HIGH YELLA, LIVER-LIPS, and NAPPY. Because black skin color was so devalued at one time, to call an African person "black" was to CALL HIM or HER OUTA THEY NAME. It was: "If you white, you all right; if you brown, stick around; if you black, git back." Thus the necessity, during the Black Freedom Struggle of the 1960s and 1970s, of purging the racial label "Black" and adopting it as a name for the race in symbolic celebration of the changed status of Africans in America.

Back to GIDDAYUP. The British colonists, who would become Americans in 1776, called the Africans "free" (a few were, but most were not), "slave," or, following fifteenth-century Portuguese slave traders, *negro* (an adjective meaning "black" in Portuguese and Spanish). But the Africans called themselves "African" and so designated their churches and organizations as in the names African Educational and Benevolent Society, African Episcopal Church, and African Masonic Lodge No. 459. In those early years, the thought was Africa on my mind and in my MIND'S EYE. Enslaved Africans kept thinking and hoping, all the way up until the nineteenth century, that they would one day return to Mother Africa. Some hummed the tune "I'll Fly Away," believing that, like the legendary hero Solomon, they would be able to fly back to Africa. And especially after fighting at Lexington, Concord, and Bunker Hill in the Revolutionary War, they just knew they would be free to return home. Instead, the thirteen British colonies that became the United States tightened the reins on their African slaves, passing laws abolishing temporary enslavement and indentured servitude for Africans and making them slaves for life.

By 1800, several generations of Africans had been born on American soil, thousands had been transported from Africa, and the Black population numbered more than one million. Both the vision and the possibility of returning to Africa had become impractical and remote. Further, a movement had begun to abolish slavery and to make the Africans citizens. And both free and enslaved Africans were becoming critically aware of their contributions to the development of American wealth. In light of this new reality and in preparation for citizenship and what they thought would be opportunities to enjoy the national wealth they had helped create through two hundred years of free labor, enslaved Africans began to call themselves "Colored" (often spelled "Coloured" in those days), and the designation "African" declined in use.

"Colored" was used throughout much of the nineteenth century until the white backlash began. The year 1877 marked the end of Reconstruction and set the stage for "the Coloreds" to be put back in their place. The political deal cut in D.C. led to the withdrawal of the federal/Union troops that had been stationed in the South to ensure justice for the ex-enslaved Africans. Power and home rule were returned to the Old Confederacy. The "freedmen" (as they were called by the federal government and by whites) lost the small gains in education, citizenship, and political power that the Civil War and the Emancipation Proclamation had made possible. New forms of repression and torture began—lynch mobs, Ku Klux Klan, loss of voting rights, and the beginning of separate but (*un*)equal. By 1900, the quest was on for a new name to capture the new reality of being neither "slave nor free," as one ex-enslaved African put it.

Although some Colored had begun using and rallying for the label "negro," when the National Association for the Advancement of Colored People (NAACP) was founded in 1909, the COMMUNITY had not yet reached a consensus. The push for "negro" and for its capitalization hit its full stride during the period between the two world wars. With the U.S. campaign to "make the world safe for democracy," and with Colored soldiers shedding their blood for America, the community thought surely that the contradictory status of Africans in America would be resolved on the side of first-class citizenship and economic equity. Leaders such as Dr. W.E.B. Du Bois, editor of the NAACP journal, *Crisis,* launched a massive nationwide effort to capitalize and to elevate the Portuguese-derived adjective "negro" to a level of dignity and respect. The NAACP mailed out more than seven hundred letters to publishers and editors. Community newsletters addressed the issue, both sides debated it, and talks and sermons in the Traditional Black Church focused on it. By 1930, the major European American media were using "Negro" and capitalizing it. (The two glaring exceptions were *Forum* magazine and the U.S. Government Printing Office.) The *New York Times* put it this way: "[This] is not merely a typographical change, it is an act in

recognition of racial self-respect for those who have been for generations in the 'lower case.'"

"Negro" was the name until the 1960s when Africans in America
struggled to throw off the shackles of Jim Crow and embraced Black
Culture, the Black Experience, and black skin color. Again, conferences were held, many under the rubric of "Black Power," debates en-
sued, and yes, folk had hot arguments and DISsed one another about
abandoning the name "Negro" for "Black," which was "only an adjective," as those who favored "Negro" often put it. However, the motion
of history could not be stopped. The name change to "Black" and the
profound significance of this change in the language and life of
Blacks was captured in a 1968 hit song by James Brown: "Say It Loud
(I'm Black, and I'm Proud)."

The final period in the name debate (for now, at least) began in
late 1988 with a proposal from Dr. Ramona Edelin, president of the
National Urban Coalition, to call the upcoming 1989 summit the
African American, rather than the Black, Summit. She asserted that
this name change "would establish a cultural context for the new
agenda." Her view was that present-day Africans in America were facing a new reality—the erosion, since the late 1970s, of hard-won
progress; high unemployment; the rise of racism; the growth of
urban youth violence; the proliferation of crack (introduced, it continues to be widely argued in the Black community, by the CIA); and
the general deterioration of the community. The situation called for
a reassessment within the framework of a global identity, linking
Africans in North America with those on the Continent and
throughout the Diaspora.

As in previous eras, the name issue, this time the shift from "Black"
to "African American," has been debated at community forums and
conferences. It has been the topic of conversation and heated arguments at the barber and BEAUTY SHOP, at family reunions, social
gatherings, and at Church events. The change has not been as cata-
clysmic, though, as the shift from "Negro" to "Black" in the 1960s, be-

cause "African American" lacks the negative history of "Black." Further, "African American" returns us to the source, the "African" of early years, but with a significant dimension added: "American." This addition calls attention to four hundred years of building wealth in America and legitimates the demand for political and economic equity, or at least FORTY ACRES AND A MULE. This line of argument was put forth as long ago as 1829 by David Walker, one of the first RED, BLACK, AND GREEN BROTHAS, in his *Appeal, in four Articles: Together with a Preamble to the Coloured Citizens of the World, but in particular, and very Expressly, to those of the United States of America.* His *Appeal* was published during the era of "Colored." Calling for open rebellion against enslavement, and opposing the American Colonization Society's plan to resettle enslaved Africans in Africa, Walker wrote:

> Men who are resolved to keep us in eternal wretchedness are also bent on sending us to Liberia...America is more our country than it is the whites'—we have enriched it with our BLOOD AND TEARS.

To date, "African American" appears to have caught on throughout the community, although "Black" continues to be used also (and, to a lesser extent, the name "African"/"Afrikan"). In opinion polls about the name issue, Black youth are the strongest supporters of "African American," which is not surprising, given the African-Centered consciousness that has emerged in HIP HOP Culture. However, there are those—generally the parents and older siblings of youth—who still favor "Black" because this name generated an intense, long-overdue struggle around old, past scripts of racial self-hatred and because the eventual adoption of the name "Black" symbolized a victorious shift to the positive in the African American psyche.

The historical motion to reconfigure Black identity and Black Language, a movement launched in the 1960s and 1970s, can be viewed as the quest for Re-Africanization. The shift from "Black" to "African

American" was inevitable as Black Americans have now come full circle, back to where they had been from the JUMP in 1619: "African." The process of linguistic Re-Africanization continues today and is most evident in HIP HOP Culture and in the works of Black women writers such as Alice Walker, Toni Morrison, and Terry McMillan. Simultaneously, there is an emerging sense of a bilingual consciousness among middle-class Blacks (particularly those who are not yet middle-aged), who value both U.S. Ebonics and the Language of Wider Communication ("standard English"); this linguistic consciousness has set the stage for a developing level of linguistic experimentation as they incorporate the FLAVA of Black Talk into dialogue and discourse. The linguistic efforts of Black women writers and the HIP HOP NATION, in concert with the linguistic experimentation of young Black professionals, will eventuate in a new language, reflecting a dynamic blend of traditional and innovative linguistic patterns, as U.S. Ebonics enters the twenty-first century. Stay tuned.

## GRAMMAR AND PRONUNCIATION IN BLACK TALK

Although here we are concerned only with words and phrases in African American Language (AAL), there are correct ways of saying these words, of talking Black, that is, that depend on knowledge of the rules of grammar and pronunciation in U.S. Ebonics. Like the popular DJ said to a DUDE who phoned in a request for DJ Jazzy Jeff & The Fresh Prince's JAM "Summertime": "Okay, man, I'll play it for you, but see, it ain't summertime, it's summahtime." A complete inventory and analysis of the grammar and pronunciation is beyond the scope of this introduction. This Africanized style of speaking the English language is a complicated system, made even more complex by the existence of Euro-American patterns of English within the Africanized English system. Interested readers may consult Lorenzo Dow Turner's *Africanisms in the Gullah Dialect;* Molefi Kete Asante's "African Elements in African American English" in Joseph Holloway's excellent collection *Africanisms in American Culture;* J. L. Dillard's *Black English;* Mervyn Alleyne's *Comparative Afro-American;* my own *Talkin That Talk: Language, Culture, and Education in African America;* John Baugh's *Black Street Speech;* John Rickford's *African American Vernacular English (Ebonics): Features and Use, Evolution and Educational Implications;* Walter Wolfram and Nona H. Clarke's *Black-White Speech Relationships;* and William Labov's *Language in the Inner City.*

Listed below are only a few of the patterns of AAL grammar and pronunciation; these patterns are found in some of the words and expressions in this dictionary:

1. *Final and postvocalic "r."* The "r" sound at the end of a word or after a vowel is not heard in AAL. Instead, use a vowel sound, as in "summa*h*time," as that big-city DJ instructed his caller. The expression "Sure, you're right" becomes SHO YOU RIGHT. "Torn up" would be TOE UP. Use YO instead of "your." And HIP HOP Music's popular, if controversial, word HO is the AAL pronunciation of "whore" (not to be confused with "hoe," as the white teacher in the film *House Party* did when she asked her Black male student why he called another Black male student's mother a "garden tool").

2. *Final and medial consonants.* Reduce to a vowel sound or a single consonant sound. Thus, for example, "cold" is COAL in AAL. This can get a bit complicated if a word requires the operation of two rules simultaneously, as for example in the phrase "torn up," where the double consonant "rn" must be reduced while the "r" after the vowel sound is deleted. Applying the rules correctly gives you *toe,* not "ton," which is what one beginning student of AAL produced.

3. *Stress on first syllable.* For most words, put the stress, or emphasis, on the first syllable of the word. For example, AAL speakers say PO-leece, not po-LEECE, and DE-troit, not De-TROIT.

4. *Vowel sound in words that rhyme with "think" and "ring."* In AAL, this vowel is pronounced like the vowel in "thank" and "rang." Thus "sing" is rendered as *sang*, "drink" is pronounced *drank*, etc. This pattern produced the "thang" in "It's a Black Thang," and the "thang" of Dr. Dre's "Nuthin' but a 'G' Thang," from his 1992 album, *The Chronic*.

5. *Indicate tense (time) by context, not with an "s" or "ed."* For example, "Mary do anythang she want to" and "They look for him everywhere but never did find him."

6. *"Be" and "Bees" to indicate continuous action or infrequently recurring activity.* For example, "Every time we see him, he be dress like that." This rule produced "It bees dat way," which may be shortened to simply BEES.

7. *Initial "th" sound, if voiced as in "that" and "the," pronounced as "d."* This pattern accounts for the popular phrase DA BOMB.

8. *Final "th" sound, if voiceless, becomes "t" or "f."* This pattern gives us DEF, as in "Def Comedy Jam" from the 1970s expression DO IT TO DEF, with the final "th" in "death" pronounced as an "f." This is also where WIT, as in the HIP HOP phrase GIT WIT *you,* comes from, with the final "th" in "with" rendered as a "t" sound.

9. *Is* and *are* in sentences. These words aren't necessary to make full statements; nor are the contracted forms of these words (that is, the "'s" for "is" and the "'re" for "are"). This is the rule that allows WHAT UP? for "What's up?"

## "EBONICS" HERE TO STAY?

The term "Ebonics" entered the national consciousness in the midst of the controversy set off by the Oakland, California, School Board's Resolution on Ebonics, passed on December 18, 1996. The board's resolution was the result of months of deliberation and study about

the educational crises facing Oakland's Black students. The resolution cited the dismal facts about the educational achievement level of
these students—that they were 71 percent of the "special needs" but
only 53 percent of the total student population, that they were 80 percent of the suspensions, and that their grade point average was 1.8
(on a 4.0 scale) compared to the average for *all* students of 2.4. Given
this sorry state of affairs, the Oakland board's resolution called for a
plan of teaching its Black youth through their primary language,
Ebonics. This language was to serve as a vehicle for "maintaining the
legitimacy and richness" of the students' language and to "facilitate
their acquisition and mastery of English language skills." The board
based its plan on standard procedures for teaching students by using
their native language (the "mother tongue") to teach the three Rs,
and for maintaining that language while teaching the students English (and other languages as well). The Oakland board also based its
plan on the voluminous body of research that linguists and other
scholars have conducted on the language of African America, especially the work done since the 1960s.

Unfortunately, public discussion did not center on the serious lit-
eracy and educational issues facing Oakland's Black students, nor on
the deepening educational crises facing Black youth in all major
cities, not just Oakland, California. For instance, according to national data presented during the 1997 Senate hearings on Ebonics, at
age nine Black kids are 27 points behind in reading; at age seventeen,
they are 37 points behind. Instead of focusing public attention on
these critical educational problems, the Oakland resolution became
an emotional, symbolic issue in which racial attitudes and stereotypes, on the part of both Blacks and whites, took center stage. Some
Oakland School Board advocates argue that, in the context of a still-
racialized society, the sheer boldness of the resolution made its rejection inevitable. Here was a policy issued by a board comprised of
PEOPLE OF COLOR, who were daring to put forth a plan to em-
power Black youth while simultaneously preserving their language,

which also happened to be the language of their community. Other Oakland sympathizers contend that the negative reaction to the resolution resulted from initial misguided media coverage. From the outset, the majority of the media portrayed the resolution as a plan to teach Black students Ebonics instead of the Language of Wider Communication; thus they would be condemned to a future of poverty, illiteracy, and outsider status in American life. Of course, the resolution does not advocate Ebonics only, but consistently calls for Oakland's African American students to be taught "English proficiency" and "mastery of English language skills." Thus the students would become bilingual. However, by the time the press got the story right, the damage had already been done; people had formed negative opinions and seemed impervious to the truth.

Whether one agrees with Oakland's educational plan, the crux of the issue was, and remains, how best to teach and prepare Black youth for the future. A full-blown treatment of the racial dynamics and complex educational issues involved in the Oakland Ebonics controversy is beyond the scope of this introduction. Interested readers should consult Theresa Perry and Lisa Delpit's *The Real Ebonics Debate: Power, Language, and the Education of African American Children* (which includes an essay of mine); *Ebonics I and II* (special issues of *The Black Scholar;* one issue includes my article on the education of Black children "one mo once"); John Rickford's "Suite for Ebony and Phonics" in *Discover* magazine; Keith Gilyard and Nicholas Sitx's debate "Would Ebonics Programs in Public Schools Be a Good Idea?" in *Insight* magazine; the *Journal of English Linguistics* special issue on Ebonics (which includes my "Ebonics, *King,* and Oakland: Some Folk Don't Believe Fat Meat Is Greasy"); and a special issue on Ebonics in *Black Issues in Higher Education.*

As for the term "Ebonics" itself, even though it was Oakland, California, that showcased it to the nation at large in December 1996, the term has been in use by some Black scholars since 1973, the year it was coined by Black clinical psychologist Dr. Robert Williams at a confer-

ence on language and the urban Black child. The conference was convened in St. Louis by what was then the Institute of Black Studies. In
1975, Dr. Williams published the conference papers in his book *Ebonics: The True Language of Black Folks*. In the Preface and Introduction
to that book, Williams writes:

> A significant incident occurred at the conference. The Black confer-
> ees were so critical of the work on the subject done by white re-
> searchers, many of whom also happened to be present, that they
> decided to caucus among themselves and define Black Language
> from a Black perspective. It was in this caucus that the term **Ebon-
> ics** was created... [It] may be defined as "the linguistic and paralin-
> guistic features which on a concentric continuum represent the
> communicative competence of the West African, Caribbean, and
> United States slave descendant of African origin. It includes the
> various idioms, patois, argots, ideolects, and social dialects of Black
> people," especially those who have been forced to adapt to colonial
> circumstances. **Ebonics** derives its form from ebony (black) and
> phonics (sound, the study of sound) and refers to the study of the
> language of Black people in all its cultural uniqueness.

Dr. Williams and the other scholars who early on subscribed to the
term "Ebonics" clearly conceived of it as a broad term covering all of
the various African-European language mixtures that had developed
as a result of enslavement and contact between Africans and Europeans over the past several hundred years. The Ebonics spoken in the
United States is only one of the Ebonic languages. The term also
refers to the French-African language mixture spoken in Haiti, to the
English-African language mixture spoken in Jamaica, to the Dutch-
African language mixture spoken in Surinam, and so forth. As is the
case with all other languages, each of the Ebonic languages, including
that spoken here in the United States, has a grammatical structure, a
system of sounds, and a vocabulary.

"Ebonics" is no longer confined to the inner circle of a small group of Black scholars and educators; the term has gone mainstream. And although some linguists and other scholars continue to use the term "African American (Vernacular) English," what one hears outside the academy is "Ebonics." Perhaps in the public mind, the term doesn't shout "Race!" in the way that a term like "Black English" or "African American English" does. Or maybe folk just like the sound of the word—"pretty cool name for a language," one BLOOD remarked recently. In any event, while the Oakland, California, School Board, who brought the term "Ebonics" out into the public arena, has had its proverbial fifteen minutes of publicity and has faded from the national scene, "Ebonics" is enjoying widespread public use. A Traditional Black Church preacher used it in a recent sermon. Warning his congregation not to be "playin wit God," he said that "some of yall call yoself talkin in tongue and don't even know what it's all about, can't speak English or Ebonics." While some people now view the term as simply a neutral label for a Black style of speaking, others, especially those among the HIP HOP generation, loudly celebrate the term and the language. Late HIP HOP artist Big L., in his 1998 jam entitled *Ebonics,* gives a lesson in Ebonics, using a kind of Ebonics glossary with interlocking rhymes, flaunting his vocabulary SKILLZ and his ability to flow. The term "Ebonics" seems destined for a long linguistic life.

We cannot always determine the exact origin of words and phrases in African American Language as we are able to do with the term Ebonics. However, some understanding can be gleaned by looking at four critical forces that have clearly played a role in shaping the direction and evolution of Black Talk: 1) African languages and cultures; 2) the Traditional Black Church; 3) Black Music; and 4) servitude and oppression.

"WHAT IS AFRICA TO ME?"

What is Africa to me:
Copper sun or scarlet sea,
Jungle star or jungle track,
Strong bronzed men, or regal black,
Women from whose loins I sprang
When the birds of Eden sang?
One three centuries removed
From the scenes his fathers loved,
Spicy grove, cinnamon tree,
What is Africa to me?

Writer Countee Cullen posed this question in his poem "Heritage" (1925) during the Harlem Renaissance, but it is a question that continues to be raised in African America. Over the past three decades, there has been a decided emergence of AFRICAN-CENTERED consciousness, evidenced, for instance, in the wearing of KENTE cloth accessories; in the establishment of Africentric schools, teaching materials, and curricula; and in travel to Africa by church and school groups, professional organizations, and individuals. Still, many Black Americans feel a disconnect with Africa, making statements like those in a survey I conducted some years ago: "We are more American than African; we have been here too long" and "What do they mean about 'African American'? By now we have no African in us." On the other hand, there are also many Black Americans who feel and acknowledge a strong connection to Africa, what some Blacks in the same survey called "our origin and cultural identity."

As far as historians, linguists, and other scholars go, during the first half of this century it was widely believed that enslavement had wiped out all traces of African languages and cultures, and that Black "differences" resulted from imperfect and inadequate imitations of EUROPEAN AMERICAN language and culture. George Philip

Krapp, writing in the 1920s, is one linguist who held this view about the speech of Africans in America. In the 1960s these opinions came under close scrutiny and were soundly challenged by a number of experts, such as historian John Blassingame and linguist J. L. Dillard. Today scholars generally agree that the African heritage was not totally wiped out, and that both African American Language and African American Culture have roots in African patterns. (This view had also been advanced by anthropologist Melville Herskovits and linguist Lorenzo Dow Turner in the 1930s and 1940s, but they were a distinct minority in those days.) Over time, and after prolonged contact with European Americans, Africans in America adopted some Eurocentric patterns, and their African patterns of language and culture were modified—but they were not erased.

African American Language and Culture thus reflects a dual heritage, part African, part American. As Dr. W.E.B. Du Bois put it nearly a century ago in *The Souls of Black Folk,* "One ever feels his two-ness—an American, a Negro." However, Yoruba, Wolof, Efik, Mandinka, and other African languages did not survive enslavement intact. As linguist John Baugh has noted, Black Americans are the only racial/ethnic group in the United States in which the first generation did not speak its native tongue. (Pidgin and Creole English were spoken in the enslavement community.) Nonetheless, there are a few words of direct African origin that did survive; these have become household words, for instance: *tote* (to carry), from Kikongo, *tota; jazz,* from Mandinka, *jasi; banana,* fromWolof, *banana; cola* as in *Coca-Cola,* from Temne, *kola; juke,* as in *jukebox,* from Wolof, *dzug* (to misbehave), and Bambara, *dzugu* (wicked); *gumbo,* from Tshiluba, *kingombo,* and Umbundu, *ochingombo; banjo,* from Kimbundu, *mbanza;* and *Voodoo,* from Fon, *vodoun,* and Ewe, *vodu.*

Although exact African word survivals are few in number, there is a dominant African linguistic presence that survived in the African style of speaking; in other words, using English words with an African linguistic FLAVA. One such example is found in word meanings that have survived by way of what linguists call loan translations. These are words and phrases in which the literal *meaning* of the African language phrase is retained, but not the word itself. For example, in U.S. Ebonics, the word *bad* means "good." In Mandinka, the language spoken by the Mandingo people in West Africa, the phrase is *a ka nyi ko-jugu,* which means, literally, "it is good badly," that is, it is very good, or it is so good that it's bad! Another example of this kind of loan translation is in the good old American English word *okay.* Several West African languages use the form *kay,* which is added to a statement to mean "yes," "of course," or "all right." For example, in Wolof, the form is *waw kay;* in Fula, *eeyi kay;* in Mandinka, *o-ke.*

## "I Love the Lord, He Heard My Cry"

This is the opening line to an old familiar Dr. Watts hymn that dates back to the eighteenth century. Dr. Watts hymns involve a congregational style of singing in which the words to the song are "lined-out." A leader calls out each line, and the congregation responds by singing the line in long, drawn-out, plaintive notes. The hymns were passed on to enslaved Africans along with the Protestant form of Christianity after the American Revolutionary War. The lining-out style of singing also reflects the antiphonal nature of African work songs and the Black interactive style of communicating. In the Traditional Black Church[8] world, this type of hymn was named "Dr. Watts" after the pastor and composer of hundreds of such hymns, a white Englishman Isaac Watts (1674–1748). The fact that he did not have a doctorate is irrelevant; in the Traditional Black Church, preachers are designated "Doctor" or "Dr." because they administer to the spirit. The pattern of naming these old hymns after their creator is unique to the Black Church and typical of the Black Language tradition in which adaptations are made to Africanize borrowed language and culture.

The Black Church is one of the two significant forces that nurtured African cultural traditions and the Traditional African World View.⁹ (The other is Black Music.) Fundamental to this view is the unity of the sacred and secular worlds, the precedence of the spiritual over the material, the certainty that there's a God on high who may not move the mountain, but will give you strength to climb. Such are the fundamental tenets of the Traditional African World View transposed to the African American Judeo-Christian context in the United States. Yes, enslaved Africans adopted ole massa's religion, but they Africanized this religion into spirit-gittin, tongue-speakin, vision-receivin, amen-sayin, singsong preachin, holy-dancin worship.

The Church, with its preservation of Africanisms, has had an impact on Black Culture at large. When a soulful, moving Black musician or singer is really GITTin DOWN in a performance, members of the audience spontaneously respond by SHOUTin, that is, they show signs of being moved by the musical spirit—hollering, clapping hands, stomping feet, dancing frenziedly, and other kinds of emotional responses, in short, GITTin THE SPIRIT, as in the Church. This unity of the sacred and the secular is reflected in the number of musical artists who came out of the Black Church tradition, and in those who continue in both worlds—such as diva Aretha Franklin, who started singing and playing piano in her father's church at a very young age and went on to make record hits in the secular world, but returned to the church to record Gospel songs and albums (for example, *Amazing Grace,* with the late Reverend James Cleveland), and such as 1990s HIP HOP diva Faith Evans, who talks about her early years singing in church, where she began at the age of two.

Over the centuries, the Traditional Black Church has functioned as a social as well as a religious unit, and it has stood as a rich reservoir of terms and expressions in Black Language, like: ON TIME; SISTA and BROTHA (as generic terms for any African American); TELL THE TRUTH; proverbs such as GOD DON'T LIKE UGLY and WHAT GO ROUND COME ROUND; the ritual of SHOUTin and

GIT tin THE SPIRIT when moved by the musical "spirit" even at a secular concert. Undoubtedly a major reason for the paramount position of the Church in the Black Experience is that it is the only independent African American institution—an institution for Black folk which is solely supported by donations from the folk. This independence and autonomy has meant that it has not had to capitulate to the sociocultural pressure of Eurocentric culture and the language of white folk.

## The Musician Got Game Too

Music, dance, religion, do not have *artifacts* as their end products, so they were saved. These nonmaterial aspects of the African's culture were almost impossible to eradicate. And these are the most apparent legacies of the African past, even to the contemporary Black American...blues, jazz and the Negro's adaptation of the Christian religion all rely heavily on African culture.

—LeRoi Jones (now Amiri Baraka), *Blues People*, 1963

Black Music has always been central to Black reality and thus a major force in the formation and development of U.S. Ebonics's words and phrases. The pervasive influence and impact of HIP HOP Music today is therefore not a new phenomenon. The musicians' way of life, their lingo, their STYLIN AND PROFILIN, have always provided a kind of standard in the Black community. They become culture heroes whose COOLNESS and HIP consciousness are emulated. With their fast life—at times intermingled with wild, abandoned sex, drugs, lush drinking—Black musicians have always been outside the mainstream of white American values. Implicit in their outsider status is a rejection of the narrowness of mainstream white America, with its rigidity, provincialism, and racism that would stifle Black creativity.

In the 1960s, Motown, under the leadership of its founder, Berry

Gordy, sought to "cleanse" and "purify" the image of Black musicians, to make them acceptable to white audiences so they could cash in on million-dollar record and concert sales. Given the success of Diana Ross and the Supremes, the Temptations, and other Motown acts, Berry Gordy's strategy was overwhelmingly successful. However, classic Black musicians have typically not been squeaky clean, nor embraced by the white American mainstream. More importantly, their musical style has been Africanized to the core—funky beats, much drum and rhythm, blue notes, antiphonal melodies, and raw lyrics about love, sex, "empty-bed blues," and a man or woman "who done me wrong." From this historical perspective, BUSTIN RHYMES about hard times in the USG, life on the raw edge, RAppin "ruffneck," and GANGSTA lyrics over FUNKY beats locate HIP HOP squarely within the tradition of Black Music. The musician as BAD NIGGA rules, culturally and linguistically.

In the 1920s and 1930s, Blues singers on the CHITLIN CIRCUIT sang phrases like "The eagle flies on Friday," and these expressions gained renewed popularity in the COMMUNITY. For a few years during this time, THE DOZENS appeared in several Blues songs, by Speckled Red, Ben Curry, Leadbelly (whose 1935 "Kansas City Papa" song talks about two women playing THE DOZENS). Memphis Minnie (Minnie McCoy) showed that women had linguistic GAME in her 1930 recording "New Dirty Dozen," in which she rocked the house with lines like:

> I know all about yo pappy and yo mammy
> Your big fat sister and your little brother Sammy
> Your aunt and your uncle and your ma's and pa's
> They all got drunk and showed they Santy Claus.
> Slip you in the Dozens, yo poppa is yo cousin
> Yo momma do the Lawdy, Lawd.

Continuing this tradition, Ahmad, in his 1994 release "Back in the Day," RAPS:

Yall remember way back then
I think I was about ten
One of those happy little niggaz
Always tryin to rag
Sayin, "Yo momma black," "His momma this," "His momma that."

Old proverbs, popular for decades in the Black Language community, like "Actions speak louder than words" (recorded by Chocolate Milk, 1975) and "Smiling faces sometimes tell lies" (recorded by Undisputed Truth, 1971), were turned into hit song titles in the Rhythm 'n' Blues era of the 1950s to the 1970s. In 1990s HIP HOP, the old proverb "THE BLACKER THE BERRY, THE SWEETER THE JUICE" was incorporated into Tupac Shakur's repertoire of self-esteem RAPS. That old saying "TRYIN TO MAKE A DOLLA OUTA FIFTEEN CENT" found its way into MC Lyte's 1998 album *Seven & Seven,* as well as into Raps by Tupac and Master P, who remind us that they are "Just another Black man caught up in the mix, tryin to make a dollar outa fifteen cent."

A significant number of words and phrases are created and popularized by musicians. They often remain around long after the hit record fades away, extended to contexts beyond the song in which the musician originally used the phrase or word. The jazz tradition brought us words like GIG, FUNKY, CHANGES, and GOIN THROUGH CHANGES.

Two classic examples from the Rhythm 'n' Blues tradition are Aretha Franklin's 1967 "Respect" and James Brown's 1972 "Git on the Good Foot." In Sista Rea's jam, she spelled out the word that she was demanding: "R-E-S-P-E-C-T, that's what you got to give to me." The word entered everyday Black Language to emphasize the demand for respect; people articulated the word by spelling it out, letter by letter, as in the song. This linguistic innovation lasted for several years and can still be heard occasionally in conversations between middle-aged Blacks. In the Godfather of Soul's jam, he "preached" that you had to "git on the good foot," that is, correct whatever needs improving, straighten things out. GIT ON THE GOOD FOOT maintained linguistic currency for years after the record faded and can still be heard occasionally today.

In the HIP HOP era of contemporary times, there is, for instance, the expression "BRING THE NOISE," from Public Enemy's 1988 RAP, an exhortation from P.E. as everybody parties to the beat. This phrase served as the title of a 1991 book about Rap Music and Hip Hop (by Havelock Nelson and Michael A. Gonzales) and still enjoys a limited degree of linguistic currency today. It inspired the 1996 George C. Wolfe musical *Bring in Da Noise, Bring in Da Funk*. In the late 1990s, there was Master P's "Bout It," from his 1997 soundtrack to the video *I'm Bout It*, which he produced. For the past two years, BOUT IT, BOUT IT has maintained steady linguistic currency. Another Hip Hop phrase is "AIN A THANG," or "IT AIN A THANG," from the title of Rapper Jay-Z's 1998 jam featuring Jermaine Dupri: "Money Ain't a Thang." "Ain a thang" is a variation on the 1970s expressions "It ain no thang" and "It ain no big thang," and seems headed for a long linguistic life in U.S. Ebonics.

## "I-OWN KNOW WHAT DEM WHITE FOLK TALKIN BOUT — WE NEVER DID GIT OUR FORTY ACRES"[10]

Servitude and racial discrimination, or as African-Centered Blacks call it, enslavement and neo-enslavement, are critical forces in shaping African American Language, equal to the impact and influence of Black Music and the Traditional Black Church. Africans in enslavement were forced to use English—their version of English, that is—as a common language because the slaver's practice was to mix Africans from different ethnic-linguistic groups in order to foil communication and rebellion. However, enslaved Africans stepped up to the challenge and made English work for them by creating a new language using the English language vocabulary. This counter-language was formed by assigning alternate, and sometimes oppositional, meanings to English words. It was a coded language that allowed them to talk about Black business publicly and even to talk about ole massa himself right in front of his face. For example, *ofay,* an older term for a white person, was once highly negative, formed from a convergence of the pig Latin for "foe" and the word for "white" and "white man" in a number of West African languages ( *fe* in Bama, *fua* in Gola, extended form *ofaginzy,* literally "white man"). PECKA-WOOD and CHARLES (also CHUCK and MISTA CHARLIE) are other examples of this coded language of oppression. The Old Testament–based Negro Spirituals were as much about "dis heah" as "after heah." When the enslaved sang triumphantly "this train bound for Glory," they were talking about the "freedom train" that ran on the Underground Railroad, the network of escape routes and schemes devised to assist slaves fleeing to the "glory" of freedom in Canada and the North. "Moses" was one of the code names for the freedom fighter Harriet Tubman, the "conductor" of the Underground Railroad, who in her lifetime assisted more than three hundred slaves to escape.

The tradition of a coded language whose meaning is veiled from whites persisted through the post-Emancipation period and the advent of a new form of enslavement in the form of Jim Crow and Southern-style apartheid laws and policies. In this era, THE MAN and MISTA CHARLIE emerged to go along with OFAY. Terms symbolizing bonding with other Blacks, more crucial than ever, given the dispersion brought on by neo-enslavement, came into greater use: BLOOD, HOMES, MEMBER. In the urban north, to which Blacks had migrated in droves during the 1940s and 1950s, fleeing the Jim Crow South in search of the PROMISED LAND, the police became a force to be reckoned with. The term PIG was used to symbolize the inhumanity of the white police, who were perceived as animal-like in their brutality. And in the 1990s, with racial oppression more subtle, though no less insidious, the phrase "driving while Black" (DWB) was created to refer to traffic stops of motorists, particularly males, with no reason generally given, and often no ticket issued—all of which leads to the conclusion that the BROTHA's "offense" was simply his Blackness. In one highway area, Interstate 95 through Maryland, Blacks comprise 17 percent of the 111 million travelers each year, but make up 70 percent of the traffic stops.[11]

The origin of Black Talk's vocabulary in enslavement and the still unresolved status of Africans in America account for the constant changes in the Black Lexicon. Forms that gain widespread usage in the white American mainstream become suspect and are no longer considered relevant in the Black COMMUNITY. After all, a code is no longer a code if the foe/OFAY is hip to it. A new code word must be coined. Of course a lot of Black Talk gets picked up by European Americans, especially since the 1960s and the mass explosion of Black popular culture not only in this country but worldwide, a process made possible by the evolution of technology and mass media, which accelerated the linguistic assimilation of U.S. Ebonics. Nonetheless, the pattern persists: once a phrase or term is adopted by whites, a new one comes into play as a replacement. Which brings us to the complex process of "crossover" (linguistic borrowing, or what some folk call "theft").

## "WHY BLACK PEOPLE HAVE NO CULTURE"

The linguistic and cultural absorption of Blackness by the dominant white American culture has been dubbed "crossover" in this postmodern era. But this is an age-old process in American life. In his history of African American Language, published in 1972, J. L. Dillard traced borrowings from slave speech by young whites during and after enslavement. In the 1920s, when the "Negro was in vogue," whites flocked to Harlem clubs and cabarets, immersing themselves in Black Language and Culture; that "crossover" became so complete that one white writer published a novel about the glorious "Negro Renaissance" and entitled it *Nigger Heaven* (Carl Van Vechten, 1926). Norman Mailer wrote about the "white Negro" speaking the "language of Hip" back in the 1950s.

The 1960s was a defining moment in this cultural diffusion process, with Motown, on the one hand, crossing racial lines with its music, and the Civil Rights Movement, on the other, crossing racial boundaries with its language and rhetoric of protest and moral confrontation, all broadcast live on the eleven o'clock news. One of the first scholars to note the linguistic impact of the 1960s on whites was David Claerbaut. He became interested in Black Language as a result of his early experience as a white teacher in what he described as "a virtually all-Black urban school." In his *Black Jargon in White America*, published in 1972 (now unfortunately out of print), Claerbaut soundly critiques this absorption of "Black jargon" by white America:

A vast number of once uniquely black terms have in recent years been pirated by white society, especially by the white youth culture. Although imitation is often considered the highest form of compliment, and although a certain amount of cultural interchange is natural, such indiscriminate theft is deeply resented by many blacks. I am uncomfortable when I hear young whites glibly using originally black terms...as though they have been imported directly from white northern Europe along with the rest of the culture. This thievery is evident even in the media, as the use of black jargon by white entertainers is a common practice on radio and television...much of this represents a naive attempt to identify with black people and form some sort of meaningful bond. It requires little insight, however, to understand that such practices hardly bring about this idealistic objective. Stealing a man's culture is hardly a way of befriending him. Respecting it does.

As Claerbaut notes, not all Blacks are flattered by this imitation. Black writer Langston Hughes contended that ordinary Harlemites had never heard of the "Renaissance, and if they had, it hadn't raised their wages any." About this out-migration of Black Culture, Hughes bemoaned, "They done taken my blues and gone."

Senator Patrick Leahy, at a 1998 Senate Judiciary Committee hearing, during an exchange between Senator Orrin Hatch and Attorney General Janet Reno, says "CHILL, Orrin." An airline ad showing a white sunbather against white sands and blue water, features the caption CHILL OUT. A 1998 advertisement in *People* magazine touts a book on growing American plants "We may not know JACK about cows but we sure as heck know our beans." President Clinton promotes his antidrug ads that are designed to "knock America UPSIDE THE HEAD" and get the country's attention. A Kentucky Fried Chicken radio ad commends the fast-food diner on its "pretty, hot, and tasty" chicken, as a voice says that KFC should give out "PHAT degrees." A white female lawyer on a talk show in 1998 says, "The Monica [Lewinsky] evidence helped Republicans; they were on Clinton like WHITE ON RICE." Two white females, interviewed for a 1998 *New York Times Magazine* article about problems encountered by professional women, both speak about being HIT ON by men on the road: "If you're attractive, you're going to get hit on." Linguist Michael Adams, in a 1998 research article in *American Speech,* lists several Black Language words (e.g., THROW DOWN) in the "[restaurant] server's lexicon," concluding that "it should not surprise anyone that African-American Vernacular English has lent terms to restaurant jargon, as to most other registers of American English." A white male in his early sixties, in line at the local bank, jokingly responds to a comment made by a middle-aged white female teller with "Let's not start that. Don't even GO THERE." A high-ranking white female university administrator introduces the keynote luncheon speaker with accolades about her dedication: "She works TWENTY-FOUR-SEVEN." The list of crossovers is endless. Yeah, BROTHA Langston, yo blues is long gone.

One of the most startling examples of crossover I've seen is from a 1992 book for children (illustrated throughout with white faces and playful animals), entitled *Kids Shenanigans* (by the editors of Klutz Press). The book contains illustrations for various ways of "giving FIVE," including the old FIVE ON THE SLY. The illustrations, referred to as "Hand Jive," call to mind the African language pattern of "talking" with the hands, by way of slapping palms. It is a pattern that has survived in African America and is today practiced as the HIGH FIVE by millions of mainstream Americans who have no idea of its origin. An interesting twist to this bit of crossover is that Black linguist Benjamin G. Cooke had exactly this idea almost three decades ago, to publish a pamphlet based on his research on the various styles of what he called "giving and getting skin." He labeled these styles "emphatic, superlative, greeting, parting, complimentary, agreement, sly," and there were different combinations of styles. Cooke's idea was to round out his pamphlet with illustrations of actual Blacks performing the various styles of FIVE. Unable to interest a book publisher, he ended up incorporating his ideas into a research article, with photographs of the various "giving and getting skin" styles, which was published in a 1972 academic book, edited by Thomas Kochman, *Rappin' and Stylin' Out: Communication in Urban Black America* (University of Illinois Press).

What is it about the language and culture of U.S. slave descendants, these outcasts on the margins of American life, that makes

By permission of Doug Marlette and Creators Syndicate.

crossover so rampant, especially given the fact that the *people* who create the language and culture can't cross over? In his 1957 essay on the "language of Hip," Norman Mailer spoke on the phenomenon of what he called the "white Negro." He attributed the cultural and linguistic absorption to the dynamism in Black life, its stubborn rebelliousness against societal constraints, and Blacks' fierce determination to live life on their own terms. African American writer Nelson George, discussing the "topic of rap and white folks" in his 1998 book, *hip hop america,* speaks to one dimension of the absorption of Blackness in terms of the carefree, wild abandon it stirs up: "They [whites] don't feel the music like a black kid from Harlem might. No, they feel it like white people have always felt black pop. It speaks to them in some deep, joyous sense as a sweet memory of childhood fun." Writer Donnell Alexander, in his 1997 article in *Might,* "Are Black People Cooler Than White People?" contends that it's the tryin-to-make-a-dollar-outa-fifteen-cent outlook that explains the crossover: "Cool, the basic reason blacks remain in the American cultural mix is an industry of style that everyone in the world can use. It's making something out of nothing. It's the nigga metaphor. And nigga metaphor is the genius of America."

The absorption of African American Language into European American culture masks its true origin and reason for being cause the "nigga metaphor" is born from a culture of struggle. Yeah, it's gon be a party tonight, yall, but in the morning, the gas man gon shut off the heat cause the bill ain paid—and it's zero degrees outside! Then too, putting the Black imprint on the linguistics of America can represent distinct African American values at odds with Euro-standards. "Fat," spelled PHAT in HIP HOP, refers to a person or thing that is excellent and desirable, reflecting the traditional African value that human body weight is a good thing, and implicitly rejecting the Euro-American mainstream, where skinny, not fat, is valued, and everybody is always on a diet. Black senior citizens convey the same value with the expression "Don't nobody want no bone."

Whites get the "nigga metaphor" at bargain-basement prices. They don't have to PAY no DUES, but reap the psychological, social, and economic benefits of a language and culture born out of enslavement, neo-enslavement, Jim Crow, U.S. apartheid, and twentieth-century hard times. Lacking the depths of this experience, sometimes whites get it all wrong, and crossover goes awry, as when *Boston* magazine used the phrase "Head Negro in Charge" on its cover in a 1998 profile about Dr. Henry Louis Gates, Chair of Harvard University's Afro-American Studies Department. "Head Negro in Charge" is a sanitized version of the Ebonics phrase H.N.I.C., "Head Nigga in Charge." This usage ignited a national controversy and calls from prominent African Americans for the magazine to apologize. The irony is that the article itself heaped lavish, high praise on Gates, lauding his struggle against racism and poverty and celebrating his accomplishments over the years. The use of "Head Negro in Charge" was the magazine's attempt to be with it, trendy, or, in Ebonics, DOWN, to represent the Black Vernacular, the subject of much of Gates's research and scholarly work. However, native speakers of U.S. Ebonics know that the term references a historical tradition dating back to enslavement wherein whites selected Black leaders and authority figures and put them in charge to keep other Blacks in line. Thus the phrase is used in a SIGNIFYIN sense to suggest that the "head nigga" is not really in charge at all. While some H.N.I.C.s may call themselves that, such self-descriptions are understood as tongue-in-cheek and cause nothing more than a soulful chuckle among Black speakers of Ebonics. But it is quite another matter for those outside the Black Experience to use the phrase, regardless of whether they use "Nigga" or "Negro."

Another crossover gone awry which occurred in 1998 involved a white teacher using the book *Nappy Hair*, which was written by a SISTA, Carolivia Herron. In spite of African-Centeredness, the Black COMMUNITY has a lingering ambivalence about NAPPY hair, which comes from the history of racial domination wherein white Americans' hair (straight, or non-nappy) set the standard, and Black hair (non-straight, nappy) became just another one of those features of the "inferior" race. The SISTA's book intends to celebrate the value of this different kind of hair in the human family, and so by using the book, the white teacher sought to teach her Black students something about the value of and tolerance for differences. However, the African American parents knew that "nappy hair" is one of those double-edged phrases, like H.N.I.C., and that some Blacks, still insecure about our NAPS, use the phrase "nappy hair" as a name-calling word. Perhaps it is this lingering legacy of everything white as "superior," and everything nonwhite as "inferior," that made those Black parents protest loudly and vigorously, setting off a national controversy. HIP HOP journalist Upski, a European American writing from the "front lines of the White Struggle," speaks on the crossover business in this way in *The Source*, May 1993:

> Even lifetime rap fans...usually discount a crucial reason rap was invented: white America's economic and psychological terrorism against Black people—reduced in the white mind to "prejudice" and "stereotypes," concepts more within its cultural experience.

Whatever the motivation for crossover, one thing is certain: in these postmodern times, there is a multibillion-dollar industry based on Black Language and Culture, while at the same time, there is continued underdevelopment and deterioration among the people who produce this language and culture. So how come Black people don't have no culture? Ralph Wiley, author of *Why Black People Tend to Shout*, says, "Black people have no culture because most of it is out on loan to white people. With no interest."

## FROM HOME TO HOMEY

SIGNIFYIN, LYIN, TALKIN TRASH, SNAPPIN, and other forms of OLD SCHOOL language are all over the place today as the HIP

HOP generation reaches back to the 1960s and 1970s for a taste of Blackness. Coming correct, with all due respect...engaged in a conscious return to the Source...making their way toward an African identity for the twenty-first century...these HOMIEZ are in search of HOME.

They are not the first generation to look for home. Forcibly removed from their native land, homeless Africans in America have been on a continual quest for home since 1619. After Emancipation, they thought they could make home the rich, fertile land of the South. But with the end of Reconstruction and the institutionalization of Jim Crow, they became sharecroppers trapped in a new form of enslavement. When they left the South, during the Great Migration and after the world war years, in their quest for home in the PROMISED LAND of the North, they continued to call the South HOME and DOWN HOME. Of course, what they found in the PROMISED LAND was urban blight, poor housing, inadequate schools, police brutality, and other social problems of the "inner city."

On one level, anyone from the South was referred to as HOME, or HOMES. A person from your hometown in the South was referred to as your HOMEGIRL or HOMEBOY. But on a deeper level, HOME came to mean any Black person. Black soldiers during World Wars I and II used the term HOMES or HOME SLICE to greet new Black soldiers joining the ranks. The symbolic significance of HOME in the saga of Africans in America was powerfully captured in a collection of essays covering the years 1960 to 1965, published by LeRoi Jones (now Amiri Baraka) in 1966. He entitled his book, which he described as his "ideological autobiography," *Home*. In the opening title essay, Baraka writes:

> One truth anyone reading these pieces ought to get is the sense of movement — the struggle, in myself, to understand where and who I am, and to move with that understanding...these moves, most

• • • • • • • • • • • • • • • • • • • • • • • • • • • • • • • • • • • • • • • • • • • • •

times unconscious…seem to me to have been always toward the thing I had coming into the world, with no sweat: my Blackness.

It is not a great journey from DOWN HOME to HOMES to HOMEY. The language (as well as the music and other cultural forms) of HIP HOP is very much rooted in this twentieth-century tradition of HOME, particularly in the language of the generation who came of age during the Civil Rights–Black Power movements of the 1960s and 1970s. Words and phrases from those years are recycled and sometimes modified among HIP HOPpers—JAM, JOINT, FUNKY, FORTY ACRES AND A MULE (the name of filmmaker Spike Lee's production company), TLC (the name of the female HIP HOP group), GIT IT ON, IT'S ON, and on and on. Continuing throughout all the generations is the "nigga metaphor." And when B-BALL star "Sir Charles" Barkley and Spike Lee are proudly characterized as Nineties Niggers (a phrase Barkley himself coined), we are reaching way back to enslavement, when the BAD NIGGA was born. Bad niggaz dared to buck ole massa, they didn't take no shit from Blacks or whites, and in each generation down through the years, some of them done even live to tell about it.

Hip Hop is a potent force, not only because of the creative richness of its cultural and linguistic productions, but also because of its sheer numbers within the African American population. Nearly 53 percent of African Americans are under thirty, and nearly 40 percent are under twenty, according to Farai Chideya's data in *Emerge* magazine's October 1998 special youth issue. "Black America is a young America," *Emerge* quite rightly asserts in its "Special Report." The fact that there are generational clashes between the HIP HOP NATION and the forty-five-plus crowd just means that a whole buncha folk don't know what time it is. Hip Hop is thus expanding, rightfully so, to stamp its own linguistic imprint upon the game. P.E.'s Chuck D., the "Commissioner of Rap," as *Time* magazine called him in its special 1999 issue on Hip Hop, sums it up this way:

Rap music/hip-hop is...the child of soul, R. and B. and rock 'n' roll, the by-product of the strategic marketing of Big Business... This grass-roots transformation of culture has spread over the planet like a worldwide religion for those 25 and under...It's something to see videos connect white kids in Utah to black kids in South Chicago to Croats and Brazilians. This is the sound and style of our young world, the vernacular used in today's speak from scholastics to sports...It's difficult to stop a cultural revolution that bridges people together. Discussing differences through artistic communication and sharing interests in a common bond—rap music and hip-hop have achieved that in 20 years.

In the meantime, there remain deep and widening social contradictions in U.S. society and within the African American sector as well. Still very much in existence are the "two separate societies," one Black, the other white, which the National Advisory Commission on Civil Disorders (also known as the "Kerner Commission") warned the nation about in the wake of the REBELLIONS of the 1960s. As Andrew Hacker's 1992 study demonstrated, there is continuing racial injustice and economic inequality between Black and white Americans. According to Pem Davidson Buck's 1997 study, prison growth is "approaching the nearly complete racial homogeneity of concentration camps...Nationwide 6 percent of the population—African American men—provides nearly 50 percent of the prison population...and are incarcerated in jails and prisons at a far higher rate than are whites, 3,109 [Blacks] as compared to 426 [whites] per 100,000 population."

Compounding the Black condition, the African American community itself is subdividing into two separate societies, an expanding middle-class group of haves, enjoying unparalleled prosperity, and a very large and troubled group of have nots. In addition to being solidly middle-class, the haves tend to be older (forty-five-plus) and predisposed to the older and more mainstream culture, the have nots younger and celebrants of the newer HIP HOP Language and Culture. Additionally, there is a geographical separation due to the creation of Black suburbs and other economically segregated residential enclaves. Speaking about the haves, New York linguist Arthur Spears provides a lucid analysis:

> Such Blacks are victims of not realizing how fast cultural change has occurred in Black America since the 1960s...Under segregation, upper-status Blacks did have a clearer picture of the range of behaviors throughout the social continuum. Those who have reached the age and position to see their writing published in major outlets of hegemonic discourse such as the largest circulation newsweeklies and *The New York Times* are too old and too removed by class and cultural change to retain any authority they may once have had.

Language factors into this contradiction in African America: the haves generally are bilingual (at least to some degree), speaking both U.S. Ebonics and the language of commerce, business, and mainstream politics—i.e., "standard English," or the Language of Wider Communication/LWC. The have nots are generally monolingual, speaking primarily Black Language, and the LWC to a minimal degree only, or in some cases, not at all. Depending on their generational group, their gender, and their perception of what it means to be Black in white America, the have nots may dis the Language of Wider Communication spoken by their middle-class BROTHAS and SISTAS. The same holds true for the haves, who may dis the Black Talk of their have-not BROTHAS and SISTAS, depending on their age, gender, and their ideology about Blackness and whiteness.

Often lost in the swirling contradictions is the fat (and *phat*) price tag on U.S. Ebonics, which is used to sell everything from McDonald's, Coca-Cola, and Gatorade to snow blowers, sneakers, and shampoo for white hair. Rappin SISTAS Salt-N-Pepa bust rhymes about

Cover Girl cosmetics, the Trix cereal rabbit gives the HIGH FIVE, and, according to SounData, whites buy 71 percent of all Rap Music,[12] the language of which is U.S. Ebonics to the max. Up in this mix also are writers, artists, intellectuals, activists, and some just plain everyday Black folk—both in the older, middle-class, and in the younger, HIP HOP generation—who seek to chart a pathway through these contradictions, who continue to push the Black Language envelope, on a mission to work out the unfinished business of what it means to be and talk like home.

# NOTES

▲▲▲▲▲▲▲▲▲▲▲▲▲▲▲▲▲▲▲▲▲

1. "Dead presidents" is a reference to money, derived from the U.S. government's practice of printing pictures of U.S. presidents (dead ones only) on various denominations of paper currency. This phrase was popular from the 1930s through the 1960s. "Benjamins" is the 1990s Hip Hop term for money, from the picture of Benjamin Franklin on the $100 bill. Other Hip Hop terms are *Franklin faces* and *big faces* (a reference to the enlarged "Franklin" and presidential images on currency issued around the mid-1990s, particularly on the $20, $50, and $100 bills).

2. Throughout this "Introduction" and in the dictionary that follows, I use both the labels "African American" and "Black" to refer to Americans of African descent in the United States, just as I use the labels "European American" and "white" to refer to Americans of European descent in the United States. Readers will note that "Black" is capitalized, whereas "white" is not. First, *Black* as a racial designation replaced *Negro,* and *Negro* was capitalized (at least since 1930), whereas *white* was not. Second, for people of African descent in America, *Black* functions to designate race *and* ethnicity because the slave trade and U.S. enslavement practices made it impossible for Blacks to trace their ethnic origins in Africa. This has not been the case for Europeans in the United States, who typically have labeled themselves German, Italian, English, Irish, Polish, etc., according to their European ethnicity. In fact, it was not until the emergence

of *Black* that European Americans raised questions about the lowercasing of *white*.

3. The first cargo of enslaved Africans was brought to the colony of America in 1619; this exposure would have launched the Africanization of English if it had not begun earlier. According to linguist David Dalby, five Africans were taken to England in 1554 to learn English and serve as interpreters in the slave trade and in Britain's colonization campaigns in Africa. The "African use of English" began in 1557 when three of the five returned to the African Gold Coast. Obviously, after only three years of learning English, their language would not have been the same as that of the British; rather their English would have been Africanized.

4. Although the struggle for freedom has been ongoing since 1619, the term "Black Freedom Struggle" is generally used to characterize the organized mass movement for Black empowerment that began with Mrs. Rosa Parks's now famous refusal to surrender her bus seat to a white man in Montgomery, Alabama, on December 1, 1955. Southern custom required that Blacks sitting in the COLORED section give up their seats if the white section was filled. Her unwillingness to do so led to Mrs. Parks's arrest and set in motion the movement that would lead to the eradication of laws supporting racial segregation. The Black Freedom Struggle includes the Civil Rights Movement, led by Dr. Martin Luther King, Jr., and the Black Power Movement, spearheaded by Malcolm X. The terms "Black Liberation Movement" and "Black Movement" are also used to describe this era in the African American Experience.

5. From J. E. Blackwell. *Mainstreaming Outsiders: The Production of Black Professionals.* Bayside, N.Y.: General Hall, 1981.

6. The Harlem Renaissance is considered to be an era of great flowering of Black talent in literature, music, and the arts. In the "Negro Renaissance" and the era of "The New Negro," Harlem

was viewed as the cultural mecca of New York. Thus whites flocked uptown, seeing to soak up Black Culture. Many whites financially supported struggling Black artists during this period.

7. Reverend Jesse Jackson, quoted in Clarence Page, "African American or Black? It's Debatable," in the *Detroit Free Press*, January 1, 1989, and in Isabel Wilkerson, "Many Who Favor Black Favor New Term for Who They Are," in the *New York Times*, January 31, 1989.

8. The Traditional Black Church refers to the Protestant denominational sects, dating back to enslavement, which fused African styles of worship and beliefs with European American tenets of Christianity. The denominations are the African Methodist Episcopal Church (A.M.E.), the African Methodist Episcopal Zion Church (A.M.E.Z.), the Christian Methodist Episcopal Church (C.M.E.), the Church of God in Christ, the Pentecostal Church, the Holiness Church, the Sanctified Church, and the Baptists (of which there are three groups: the National Baptist Convention, U.S.A., Incorporated; the National Baptist Convention of America, Unincorporated; and the Progressive National Baptist Convention). The worship forms of the Traditional Black Church include a belief in spirit possession, that is, that a person's body can be taken over by a divine force (the Holy Spirit), expressed by talkin in tongue, holy dancin, shoutin, and moanin; the use of up-tempo, soulful music, songs, and musical instruments (drum, organ, guitar); and call-response interaction between preacher and congregation, as well as between members of the congregation during the Church service. Historically and down to the present day, the Church has been a critical institutional force in the liberation, survival, and day-to-day life of Black people. Many slave rebellions were planned in the Church, and there is a history of activist leadership among preachers dating from preacher Nat Turner, who, in 1831, led what has been deemed the greatest slave rebellion, to Civil

Rights leader Reverend Dr. Martin Luther King, Jr. Further, the Church has served as an important social unit where there is some kind of activity almost every day of the week and where everyday people have opportunities to develop and exercise their abilities in speaking, teaching, singing, organizing, and planning. It is not surprising that there is a return to the Church by many Black youth today. In *The Black Church in the African American Experience,* published in 1990, C. Eric Lincoln and Lawrence H. Mamiya sum it up this way:

> The Black Church has no challenger as the cultural womb of the black community. Not only did it give birth to new institutions such as schools, banks, insurance companies, and low-income housing, it also provided an academy and an arena for political activities, and it nurtured young talent for musical, dramatic, and artistic development...Multifarious levels of community involvement [are] found in the Black Church, in addition to the traditional concerns of worship, moral nurture, education, and social control. Much of black culture is heavily indebted to the black religious tradition, including most forms of black music, drama, literature, story-telling, and even humor.

9. The Traditional African World View refers to underlying thought patterns, belief sets, values, ways of looking at the world and the community of men and women which are shared by traditional Africans. Although there are differences in the many ethnic groups in terms of customs, spirits, languages, and deities, there are deep structure themes of life acknowledged by traditional Africans, for instance, a belief in the unity of the spiritual and the material aspects of existence, with the spiritual domain assuming priority.

10. "Forty acres" is symbolic of reparations for enslavement and has been a recurring phrase in the Black Experience since the Civil

War. In 1866, Congress proposed a bill to strengthen the Freedmen's Bureau and authorized it to make forty acres of land from confiscated Confederate property available to each household of ex-slaves. This legislation was designed to make the "freedmen" self-sufficient and to compensate them for 246 years of free labor. However, President Andrew Johnson vetoed the bill, and Congress was unwilling or unable to override the veto. The total value of the forty acres of land today is estimated to be around five hundred billion dollars. A national Black organization continues to push for reparations: N'COBRA, the National Coalition of Blacks for Reparations for African Americans, has headquarters in Washington, D.C. In 1989, Detroit congressman John Conyers introduced H.R. 40 to establish a commission to study the reparations issue and the impact of over one hundred years of racial segregation since 1877, the end of Reconstruction. Although the Commission to Study Reparation Proposals for African Americans Act has been reintroduced into every congressional session since 1989, President Clinton's Presidential Initiative on Race Commission, appointed in his second term (1996–2000) to study the issue of enslavement and race in American life, did not address the issue of reparations.

11. The statistics about Highway I-95 come from Melba Newsome, "Power: The Usual Suspects," in *Vibe* magazine, September 1998. The *Detroit News* reports a similar pattern on the Florida turnpike, where the Orange County Drug Squad conducted more than six times as many searches on Black motorists as on whites. According to Congressman John Conyers, this is a national problem: African Americans comprise 14 percent of the population, but account for 72 percent of all routine traffic stops (quoted in the *Michigan Chronicle*, July 1–7, 1998).

12. From "Black Cultural Images Prove Lucrative for Ad Agencies," by Tony Chapelle, *Detroit Free Press*, January 26, 1998.

# SELECTED
# REFERENCES

▶◆◆◆◆◆◆◆◆◆◆◆◆◆◆◆◀

Adger, Carolyn Temple, Donna Christian, and Orlando Taylor. *Making the Connection: Language and Academic Achievement Among African American Students.* Washington, D.C.: Center for Applied Linguistics and Delta Systems Co., Inc., 1999.

Alleyne, Mervyn. *Comparative Afro-American.* Ann Arbor, Mich.: Karoma Publishers, 1980.

Asante, Molefi Kete. "African Elements in African American English." In Joseph Holloway, ed., *Africanisms in American Culture.* Bloomington: Indiana University Press, 1990.

Baugh, John. *Black Street Speech: Its History, Structure, and Survival.* Austin: University of Texas Press, 1983.

———. *Out of the Mouths of Slaves: African American Language and Educational Malpractice.* Austin: University of Texas Press, 1999.

Bennett, Lerone, Jr. *Before the Mayflower: A History of Black America.* Chicago: Johnson Publishing Company, 1969.

*Black Scholar, Ebonics I; Ebonics II.* Special Issues, 1997.

Blassingame, John. *The Slave Community: Plantation Life in the Antebellum South.* New York: Oxford University Press, 1979.

Botkin, B.A., ed. *Lay My Burden Down: A Folk History of Slavery.* Chicago: University of Chicago Press, 1945.

Buck, Pem Davidson. "Prison Labor: Racism and Rhetoric." In Arthur Spears, ed., *Race and Ideology: Language, Symbolism, and Popular Culture.* Detroit: Wayne State University Press, 1999.

Calloway, Cab. *Hepster's Dictionary.* 1938.

Claerbaut, David. *Black Jargon in White America.* Grand Rapids, Mich.: William B. Eerdmans, 1972.

Dalby, David. *Black Through White: Patterns of Communication in Africa and the New World.* Bloomington: Indiana University Press, 1969.

Dawsey, Darrell. "Debating the N-Word." *Emerge,* June 1993, 35–36.

Dillard, J. L. *Black English.* New York: Random House, 1972.

Du Bois, W.E.B. *The Souls of Black Folk.* 2nd ed. New York: Vintage Books/Library of America, 1990. First published in 1903.

Franklin, John Hope. *From Slavery to Freedom: A History of Negro Americans.* 3d ed. New York: Random House (Vintage Books), 1969.

——. *Reconstruction After the Civil War.* Chicago: University of Chicago Press, 1961.

Gilyard, Keith. *Voices of the Self.* Detroit: Wayne State University Press, 1991.

Hacker, Andrew. *Two Nations.* New York: Maxwell Macmillan, 1992.

Herskovits, Melville. *The Myth of the Negro Past.* Boston: Beacon Press, 1941.

Holloway, Joseph E., ed. *Africanisms in American Culture.* Bloomington: Indiana University Press, 1990.

Hurston, Zora Neale. "Glossary of Harlem Slang." *The American Mercury,* 1942. [Also available in *Spunk,* New York: Marlowe and Company, 1985.]

*Journal of English Linguistics.* "Special Issue on Ebonics," June 1998.

Kochman, Thomas. *Black and White Styles in Conflict.* Chicago: University of Chicago Press, 1981.

——, ed. *Rappin and Stylin Out: Communication in Urban Black America.* Urbana: University of Illinois Press, 1972.

Labov, William. *Language in the Inner City: Studies in the Black English Vernacular.* Philadelphia: University of Pennsylvania Press, 1972.

Lincoln, C. Eric, and Lawrence H. Mamiya. *The Black Church in the*

*African American Experience.* Durham, N.C.: Duke University Press, 1990.

Major, Clarence. *Juba to Jive.* New York: Penguin, 1994.

McDavid, R. I., and V. G. McDavid. "The Relationship of the Speech of American Negroes to the Speech of Whites." *American Speech* 26 (February 1951): 3–17.

Morgan, Marcyliena. "The Africanness of Counterlanguage Among Afro-Americans," in Salikoko Mufwene, ed., *Africanisms in Afro-American Language Varieties.* Athens: University of Georgia Press, 1993.

Mufwene, Salikoko S., ed. *Africanisms in Afro-American Language Varieties.* Athens: University of Georgia Press, 1993.

——, John R. Rickford, Guy Bailey, and John Baugh, eds. *African American English: Structure, History and Use.* London and New York: Routledge, 1998.

Perry, Theresa, and Lisa Delpit, eds. *The Real Ebonics Debate: Power, Language, and the Education of African American Children.* Boston: Beacon Press, 1998.

Rickford, John R. *African American Vernacular English (Ebonics): Features and Use, Evolution and Educational Implications.* London: Blackwell, 1999.

Smitherman, Geneva. *Talkin and Testifyin: The Language of Black America.* Detroit: Wayne State University Press, 1986.

——. *Talkin That Talk: Language, Education, and Culture in African America.* London and New York: Routledge, 1999.

Spears, Arthur K. "African American Language Use: Ideology and So-called Obscenity," in Salikoko Mufwene, ed. *African American English.* London and New York: Routledge, 1998.

Stuckey, Sterling. "Identity and Ideology: The Names Controversy." In *Slave Culture: Nationalist Theory and the Foundations of Slavery.* New York: Oxford University Press, 1987.

Turner, Lorenzo. *Africanisms in the Gullah Dialect.* Chicago: University of Chicago Press, 1949.

Wiley, Ralph. *Why Black People Tend to Shout.* New York: Penguin, 1992.

Williams, Robert L., ed. *Ebonics: The True Language of Black Folks.* St. Louis: Institute of Black Studies/Robert Williams Associates, 1975.

Williams, Selase W. "Substantive Africanisms at the End of the African Linguistic Diaspora," in Salikoko Mufwene, ed., *Africanisms in Afro-American Language Varieties.* Athens: University of Georgia Press, 1993.

Wolfram, Walter, and Nona H. Clarke, eds. *Black-White Speech Relationships.* Washington, D.C.: Center for Applied Linguistics, 1971.

Woodson, Carter G. *The Miseducation of the Negro.* Washington, D.C.: Associated Publishers, 1933.

**A AND B**

Two musical selections by a Gospel singer or group during a Traditional Black Church service or on a musical program. "The mass choir is being asked to give an A and B on Sunday afternoon's program."

**A AND B CONVERSATION**

A discussion or conversation between two people. A third party interfering may be told, "This is an A and B conversation, so you can C yo way out of it." See also DIPPIN.

**ABOUT**

See BE BOUT.

**ACE**

Best friend. "D has been my ace since first grade." Also *ace kool* and *ace boon coon* (older term).

**ACE BOON COON**

See ACE.

**ACE KOOL**

See ACE.

**AFRAAMERICAN**

See AFRICAN AMERICAN.

**AFRIAMERICAN**

See AFRICAN AMERICAN.

**AFRICAN**

1) In the language of activist and AFRICAN-CENTERED

Blacks, any person of African descent in the DIASPORA —
Black American, Jamaican, Haitian, etc. — not limited to Continental Africans; when written, may be spelled *Afrikan*. 2) The
name used by enslaved Africans to refer to themselves and their
churches and organizations from 1619 until roughly 1800. 3) In
the language of working-class Blacks and the Black so-called
"masses," used primarily to refer to Continental Africans.

AFRICAN AMERICAN

A person of African descent, born in and a citizen of the United
States, whose U.S. ancestry dates back to the enslavement era —
i.e., a Black American, as distinguished from a Jamaican, Haitian, or other Diasporic African. The term has been in widespread usage since about 1988, but it was also used to some extent during the 1960s, as well as during the nineteenth century.
Writing it with a hyphen may trigger resentment among some
Blacks because other U.S. ethnic group names are now generally
represented without a hyphen, such as Asian American, Hispanic (or Latino/Latina) American, Italian American, Polish
American, etc. Also *AfriAmerican, AfraAmerican*.

AFRICAN-CENTERED

1) Refers to a person, event, or operation that is focused on
Africans and African Americans. 2) Refers to a perspective in
which Blackness and Africa are the center, focus, or subject,
rather than the object.

AFRICAN HOLOCAUST

Term used by Black activists, writers, Hip Hop artists, to refer to
the enslavement of African people in the United States and
throughout the DIASPORA. It captures the experience of the
wholesale destruction of a group of people and the consequences, yet to be assessed, of the *African holocaust* on present-
day Black communities. Estimates of the number of Africans
forcibly removed from their native lands during the European
slave trade range as high as one hundred million, not all of whom

reached the so-called "New World." Millions of Africans perished as a result of torture, disease, and the horrendous Middle Passage across the Atlantic Ocean. Thousands committed suicide.

AFRICAN PEOPLE'S TIME

A reference to the African American concept of time, being in tune with human events, nature, the seasons, and natural rhythms, as opposed to being a slave to the clock, which represents artificial, rather than natural, time. Those outside the culture often think of this as Blacks always being "late." However, the African American view is that being "in time," that is, in tune with emotions, feelings, the general flow of things, is more critical than being "on time." The challenge continues to be how to reconcile an "in time" way of life with the "on time" lifestyle of white America. Also *Colored People's Time, CPT, CP Time.*

AFRIKAN

See AFRICAN.

AFRO

A hairstyle that is NATURAL, that is, not straightened by chemicals or heat, trimmed along the hairline, and worn full and thick or thin and cropped close to the head. Highly popular among both females and males during the 1960s and 1970s; not as widespread in the 1990s, but still worn, particularly by females. Also *fro, natural.* See also NAPPY.

AFROAMERICAN

See AFRICAN AMERICAN. *AfroAmerican* is not as common today as *African American.* Used during the 1960s and 1970s, as well as during the nineteenth and early twentieth centuries.

AFRO-SAXON

See EUROPEAN NEGRO (newer term). *Afro-Saxon* is believed to have been coined by Continental Africans in the 1970s. However, the term also relates to the title of a 1965 book, *The Black Anglo-Saxons,* a widely discussed critique of the Black American middle and professional classes, by sociologist and clinical psychologist Dr. Nathan Hare, a former Howard University professor and founder of the first African American Studies department (at San Francisco State University in 1968).

AFTER-HOUR JOINT

A place where people party, as well as gamble, drink, or do drugs, after the official closing of bars and clubs. Operated illegally, with prices substantially above those of legitimate entertainment places.

AIN A THANG / IT AIN A THANG

Expression used to convey the idea that whatever "it" is, it's not a problem or obstacle, it can be dealt with. Title of Rapper Jay-Z's 1998 JAM (featuring Jermaine Dupri) "Money Ain't a Thang." Resurfacing HIP HOP version of the 1970s expression, "It ain no thang."

AIN STUDYIN YOU / HIM / HER / THAT

A dismissal of the person or matter at hand, no intention of dealing with the person, object, or situation. "I done tol you I ain studyin bout that ol car." Also *ain studyin bout you/him/her/that.*

AIRISH

Cool and breezy. "It seem a mite airish out here."

AK

An AK-47 assault rifle. "Today I didn't even have to use my AK / I gotta say it was a good day" (Rapper Ice Cube, on his 1992 album, *The Predator*). The AK has long been a weapon of choice among the criminal elite; it holds thirty rounds of ammunition and can be shot from the hip because of its pistol grip. Its bullets can pierce bulletproof vests and other body armor. The original AK was a Soviet-designed weapon; the Chinese version was exported to the United States. During George Bush's presidency, its import for civilian use was outlawed, but it could still be purchased legally in gun stores for $300–$500. In 1994, President Bill Clinton signed a ban on the import and manufacture of the AK and other semiautomatic assault rifles. However, it is estimated that there are still 100,000 AKs that are legally in the United States. It can also be purchased in the street, in both semiautomatic and automatic conversion forms, at prices ranging from $100–$1,000.

ALL IN
Strongly persuaded by a person or situation; to be really supportive of a person or thing.

ALL IN THE KOOL-AID AND DON'T EVEN KNOW THE FLAVA
Nosy; butting in on someone's else conversation or business.

ALL IS WELL
An expression used to indicate that a person has been in a bad or threatening situation, but that everything is now all right and under control.

ALL THAT
1) Excellent, fantastic, superb, highly accomplished in an area or endeavor. "The Sista is bad, she is definitely all that." 2) Used in the negative sense to refer to someone who is arrogant. "He always be acting like he all that." HIP HOP term crossing over.

ALL THAT AND THEN SOME
Even better than ALL THAT. Also *all that and a bag of chips*, crossover.

ALL THE WAY LIVE
An extremely lively, exciting, desirable event, person, or experience. "My boy was all the way live at that concert!" Also *live* (newer form).

ALL THE WAY THROUGH
Totally exasperated with someone or something; outdone, taken aback by a person, action, or statement. Also *too through*. See also THROUGH.

ALLEY BALL
The game of basketball played in urban neighborhoods. Derived from the practice of attaching the basketball net to the back of a building or to a garage in the alley, which is generally located in back of the building in older urban areas. The paved

concrete alley, used for storing garbage and trash, becomes the basketball "court."

ALTAR CALL

In the Traditional Black Church, a summons, issued usually from the pulpit, for the entire congregation to come forth for a special prayer; everyone is required to come forward or "march" to pray at the altar. Also *prayer march.*

AMEN CORNER

1) A section of the Traditional Black Church, where the congregation engages in continuous, dynamic responses and *amens.* Historically, the "corner," usually in a front pew, where the older members sat, especially older women, the Church "mothers," who were perceived as the "watchdogs of Christ" and who often led the congregation in responses. With the 1990s resurgence of participation in Traditional Black Churches, especially among younger Blacks, sometimes the entire church appears to be the "Amen Corner." 2) By extension, outside the Church world, a reference to any area where there are expressions of strong support and high feeling for a speaker or performer.

AMP

Stirred up; in a heightened emotional state. From the shortened way of referring to a stereo amplifier, which magnifies, heightens, "stirs up" the sound. From Public Enemy's "Fight the Power," on their 1990 album, *Fear of a Black Planet:* "I'm ready and...amp/Most of my heroes don't appear on no stamps." Also *geek, geek up* (older terms).

AND YOU KNOW THAT!

An expression of agreement; a reaffirmation of something that's been said.

ANGEL DUST

Phencyclidine (PCP), an animal tranquilizer, used as an illegal drug, has a hallucinogenic effect. Used as an "upper" in the 1960s and 1970s; perceived by Blacks as a "HONKY thang," i.e., a drug more commonly used by whites than Blacks. The term, which has now crossed over into general U.S. slang, probably derived from the African American way of describing the effect of the drug: "That shit *[angel dust]* dem honkies be usin put you up there with the angels." Also *PCP*. See also SHERM.

ANKH

A T-shaped cross with a loop on top, symbolizing fertility and life; a popular African artifact, worn as jewelry.

ANN

1) A derisive term for a white woman. 2) By extension, used to refer to any uppity-acting Black woman, especially one who "acts white." Also *Miss Ann*.

THE ANOINTED

Traditional Black Church term for those who have been SAVED and who bear witness to the wonders and power of God. See also WASHED IN THE BLOOD.

APPLAUSE

Gonorrhea. Derived from older term "the clap."

APPLE

A man's cap-style hat, with an exceptionally wide brim, stylish in the 1960s and 1970s; from THE APPLE, by association with the bigness of New York City.

THE APPLE

New York City. Also *the Big Apple*. Term originated with early African American jazz musicians. Crossover term.

A-RAB

An Arabic person. Pronounced AY-rab. Some Arab Americans think that *A-rab* is a different word from "Arab," and that it was coined by Blacks to CALL Arabs OUTA THEY NAME. This has become an especially sensitive point in places where there are large numbers of Arabs, such as Michigan, which has the largest concentration of Arab Americans in the United States. However, *A-rab* is not a unique Black *word* but a Black *pronunciation*. Nor is it a racial epithet. It merely reflects the way African Americans speak English, in this instance, probably modeled on such pronunciations as HO-tel, MO-tel, PO-leece, DE-troit.

ARE YOU RIGHT?

1) A Traditional Black Church phrase, raising a question about one's spiritual status, that is, "Are you saved? Are you right with God?" 2) By extension, used outside the Church (as are many Traditional Black Church terms and expressions) to refer to a person's moral status, that is, "Are you honest and principled? Do you have good intentions?" The Sista said, "I asked the nigga was he right? Cause if he ain't, he better git right befoe he come up in here!"

AROUND THE WAY

1) Describes somebody from the HOOD, presumed to be a person with a similar background and cultural reality. "I need an around the way girl in my life." 2) In the near vicinity. "I just saw her around the way."

AS GOD IS MY SECRET JUDGE

Expression used to affirm the truth of, or to prove one's assertion. "As God is my secret judge, I didn bus on the Brotha."

ASHY

Describes the whitish or grayish appearance of skin due to exposure to wind and cold, which shows up more on African Americans than European Americans due to Black people's darker skin pigmentation. The late Rapper Notorious B.I.G. said: "I went from ashy to classy," that is, from being an unsophisticated, rough, country-bumpkin type, who let his "ash" show, to an upscale, well-groomed, no-ash-showing BIG WILLIE PLAYA (from the album *Life After Death*, 1997).

ASS

1) Added to the end of a word or expression to give the description extra emphasis. The Brotha asked, "How come they call it the 'British Empire'? It ain nothin but a po-ass country!" That is,

England is a very poor nation, materially, thus hardly meriting the label "empire." 2) Used after YO, my, etc. to refer to punishment, retribution, or some negative consequence that is likely to result from an action or inaction. "If you mess up this time, it's yo ass." Crossover use.

ASS FROM A HOLE IN THE GROUND

Expression used to describe a person pretending to have knowledge, especially a "know-it-all" who doesn't have MOTHER WIT and lacks good judgment. "He up there runnin his mouth and don't know his ass from a hole in the ground." Crossover expression. Also *shit from Shinola*.

ASS ON ONE'S / HIS / HER SHOULDER

Expression used to refer to a person who is acting arrogant or who has a TUDE. "We was tryin to talk to her, but she had her ass on her shoulder."

ASS OUT

1) No funds, out of money, broke. "We couldn't go to the Method Man concert cause I was ass out." 2) By extension, used when something desirable is all gone. "I wanted some of dem chitlins but they was ass out."

A.T.L.

Atlanta. "What up wit all the Rappers moving to A.T.L.?"

ATTITUDE

See TUDE. *Attitude* has crossed over, but *tude* has not.

AUDI 5000

See OUTTIE 5000. Also *outa here* (newer term); *Later* (older term).

AUNT HAGAR'S CHILLUN

Older term for African Americans.

AUNT JANE

An African American woman who identifies more with the European American race than her own, does not support Black causes, and may even work against such causes. Also *Aunt Thomasina*.

AUNT THOMASINA

Female version of the label *Uncle Tom*. See AUNT JANE.

AW-IGHT

All right.

B

1) A form of address for a male or female, though more common for males; probably a shortened form of BLOOD. "Yo B, whassup?" Sometimes the initial of the person's first name is substituted for "B." 2) Euphemism for BITCH.

B-BALL

1) The game of basketball. Also *hoop.* 2) To play basketball. Also *hoop, shoot some hoop.*

B-BOY

A male follower of HIP HOP. Originally (in the Bronx and Harlem in the 1970s) *B-boys* referred to BROTHAS who would

By permission of the artist, Craig Rex Perry, and *Young Sisters and Brothers Magazine.*

regularly "break" out into a dance movement in response to the DJ's scratching of a record. The term *B-boy* is believed to have been coined by the entertainer Kool DJ Herc. "Break" dancing, a rhythmic, intense type of dancing, with twirls, turns, and intricate, fancy steps, is rooted in African and Caribbean dance movements.

B-MORE

Baltimore.

BABY

A form of address for a male or female. Among males, at one time, the term was perceived as demonstrating not only solidarity, but also security about masculinity. That is, the man who used it was secure enough about his manhood to address another man as *baby* and not worry about being perceived as a homosexual.

BABY DADDY

Baby's daddy, that is, a child's father, generally one not married to the child's mother and considered insignificant. The phrase gained currency from the popular 1997 jam "My Baby Daddy" (by B-Rock and the Bizz). Originally a DIS of the BROTHAS, the linguistic counterpart, *baby momma,* emerged as a label for irresponsible mothers who are thus also insignificant. Underlying both phrases is a sad SIGNIFYIN commentary on the deteriorating state of male-female relationships in the COMMUNITY and the negative impact of these relationships on Black children.

BABY FACTORY

Negative reference to a woman who has had a lot of children, generally outside of marriage. "What she got over there—a baby factory?"

BABY GIRL

A form of address for a female, usually one younger than the person speaking. Conveys solidarity and closeness. Used by diva Aretha Franklin throughout "A Rose Is Still a Rose" (1998), in

which she consoles and advises a younger Sista who has been
emotionally wounded by a man.

BABY MOMMA

See BABY DADDY.

BABY SIS

See BABY GIRL.

BACK

The buttocks, generally those of a female. If roundly ample in
proportion to a woman's body, viewed as sexy. "Baby got back."
Also *behind, boody* (older terms); *bumper kit* (newer term).

BACK SLIDIN

Traditional Black Church term referring to a retreat to the world
of sin; getting off the spiritual pathway.

BACKIN THE NUMBERS

See NUMBERS.

BAD

1) Good, excellent, great, fine. Loan translation from the
Mandinka language (spoken by the Mandingo people of West
Africa), *a ka nyi ko-jugu,* literally "It is good badly," meaning, "It
is very good," that is, it is so good that it is *bad.* Crossover use. 2)
Powerful, tough, aggressive, fearless. During the cold war,
Muhammad Ali nearly created an international diplomatic disaster when he said to the Tanzanian people, "There are two bad
white men in the world, the Russian white man and the American white man. They are the two baddest men in the history of
the world." In contrast to the white press and white mainstream
speakers, the Tanzanians and African Americans understood that
Ali was not hurling an insult; rather he was attesting to the om-
nipotence and superpower status of the two countries and their
respective heads of state. This use of *bad* has still not crossed over.

BAD HAIR

Hair that is naturally tightly curled (KINKY, NAPPY), not
straight. A negative expression; in this instance *bad* means "not
good." A number of Blacks, especially those who are AFRICAN-

CENTERED or political activists, reject this view. See also
GOOD HAIR.

**BAD MOUTH**

1) To DIS and/or gossip about a person. 2) To talk negatively
about a thing. From the Mandinka language spoken by the
Mandingo people of West Africa, *da jugu*, "slander, abuse," literally "bad mouth." Crossover expression.

**BAD NIGGA**

An African American, generally a male, who is rebellious, aggressive, and refuses to succumb to the oppression of the dominant Euro-American culture; one who "doan TAKE NO SHIT
from nobody, Black or white."

**BAG**

1) A person's activities, area of specialization, or preference. 2) A
person involved in the drug trade is said to have the *bag* or to be
the *bag* man/woman (older use). 3) A quantity of marijuana or
other drug, such as a DIME *bag*, NICKEL *bag*, etc. Crossover
meaning.

**BAIL**

To leave.

**BAILIN**

Posting bail to get out of jail; implies that it's a regular occur-
rence for the person.

**BALL**

1) The basketball used in B-BALL. 2) To play basketball. 3) To
dance, BALLROOM style.

**BALL OUT**

An expression used in PICK-UP GAMES, to stop play momen-
tarily; the ball is taken out of play. "Ball out, I got somethin in
my eye."

**BALLA**

1) A man who has a lot of female relationships, a "ladies' man."
See also PLAYA. 2) A large-scale, big-time crack dealer, in California gang language.

BALLIN

1) Playing basketball superbly. 2) Accumulating large sums of money by selling crack or other drugs.

BALLISTICS

Facts, data. "KICK the *ballistics*," meaning, inform us, enlighten us, present the factual information.

BALLROOM

1) An elaborate slow dance in which the couple glides all around the dance floor. 2) To dance in the ballroom style.

BAMMA

Unfavorable term used to describe a person from the South, who is perceived as "country," without social refinement, unsophisticated. "Steve from South Carolina is a true bamma." Probably derived from the shortened version of "Alabama."

BANANA

Name for an Asian who identifies with whites: yellow on the outside, white on the inside.

BANANAS

Unbelievable, incredible, awesome. "That new Chris Tucker flick is bananas."

BANGER

A member of a gang. Also *gangbanger*.

BANGIN

1) Participating in a gang and all its activities. Also *gangbangin*. 2) Having sex. 3) Fighting.

BANJY BOY

A gay male in HIP HOP Culture who dresses like the straight males in Hip Hop. Also *block boy* (older term).

BANK

1) A large sum of money. Someone who always has money is said to "keep plenty of *bank*." 2) To make money, in any amount that the person considers to be a lot.

BANKROLL

A large amount of money, or at least what appears to be a large

amount, carried by a person; however, see PHILLY/
PHILADELPHIA BANKROLL.

BAREFOOT AS A RIVER DUCK

An expression used to describe a person walking around without any shoes on.

BARS

Rims on a car, in flashy colors and designs, as in the HAMMER,
a car with gold and chrome rims. It could cost as much as seven
thousand dollars for four rims.

BASE

1) To criticize or talk harshly to someone. "Look, man, you don't
have to base like that. I'm just tryin to help you." 2) To use cocaine by heating it with other ingredients and smoking it in a
large pipe. Also *freebase.*

BASEHEAD

A person addicted to FREEBASIN cocaine (older term).

BE ABOUT

See BE BOUT.

BE BOUT

To do something or to be involved in doing something, especially something meaningful. "Them Sistas in the hood is bout
the people's business." See also BOUT IT.

BE SOMEBODY

To make something productive or positive out of one's
life. Probably from the Reverend Jesse Jackson's well-known
call-response ritual with Black audiences, "I am somebody."

BEAM ON

To gaze intently at a person; to stare. "The Brotha was beamin
on my girl, here, givin her plenty of play."

BEAM UP

To get high on drugs. Probably derived from the television program "Star Trek," where Kirk and company are "beamed up" to
distant places in the universe.

**BEAMER**

A BMW automobile. Also *Five Hundred.*

**BEAR**

An ugly, unattractive person. Also *booguh-bear.*

**BEAR WITNESS**

1) In the Traditional Black Church, to give testimony, vocally, or through shouting and praising, to the power of God, in particular, to some experience or deed. 2) By extension, outside the Church world, to attest to an experience, fact, or event.

**BEAST**

A derogatory term for a white person, especially a white male.

**BEASTLY**

Ugly.

**BEAT DOWN**

1) A beating. 2) To fight a person, to beat somebody up badly.

**BEAUCOUP**

See BOO-COOS.

**BEAUTICIAN**

A term commonly used by senior African American women to refer to their hairdresser.

**BEAUTY SHOP**

A place where women get their hair done; often a gathering place where women RAP, debate, discuss, network, and provide support for one another. Like *beautician,* term more common among senior Black women.

**BÉ-BÉ KID** (pronounced *bay-bay*)

An undisciplined, unruly child who "acts out." Originally associated with children of single, low-income African American women, often perceived as neglecting their kids and leaving them to raise themselves, as portrayed in the cartoon movie *Bé-Bé's Kids,* featuring the late comic genius Robin Harris, who coined the term. However, the term quickly expanded to refer to *any* disruptive child (including a white, middle-class kid) who acts outrageous, is disobedient, and does what he/she wants to do.

BE-BOP
   See BOP.

BEE-YOTCH!
   Elongated, spirited pronunciation of BITCH, usually heard in
   RAP songs.

BEEF
   1) Conflict, squabble, a problem. Older term resurfacing in HIP
   HOP. 2) Euphemism for DICK.

BEES
   That's how it is, that's the way it goes, that's life; an existential
   reference to the human condition. Also *bees dat way.* Also
   spelled *bes, be's, bee's.*

BEES DAT WAY
   See BEES.

BEFOE GOD GET THE NEWS
   Expression that conveys the speed with which something is said
   or done, happens in a split second, so fast that it occurs even before God knows about it—an impossibility—which thus magnifies or intensifies the description. "When she saw him coming,
   my girl got OUTA HERE befoe God got the news" (said about a
   Sista's fast getaway from a bill collector).

BEHIND
   See BACK.

BENJAMINS
   1) $100 bills, from the picture of Benjamin Franklin on the bill.
   2) Money in general. See also DEAD PRESIDENTS.

BENT
   1) Unattractive. 2) Drunk.

BENZ
   A Mercedes-Benz automobile. Also *Benzo.*

BENZO
   See BENZ.

BET
   An afirmative response, meaning, "All right," "Yes," "Okay."

## BETTA ASK SOMEBODY

Older expression, resurfacing in HIP HOP, used to indicate that people are acting as if they know what they are doing or talking about when they really don't, or that they are in control of a situation, when in actuality they are not. "Hip Hoppers think they invented 'yo momma' jokes, but they betta ask somebody" (because these jokes are part of the Black Oral Tradition and date back to the African past and enslavement in the United States). This phrase from the Oral Tradition appears in J. Mason Brewer's 1968 collection, *American Negro Folklore*, in an interesting variation, or perhaps a mispunctuation: "Needun be walkin' roun' heah wid yo' nose all snotty / If you don't know better, ast somebody."

## BETTA RECOGNIZE

1) To become aware of, to come to terms with — to recognize — the truth, reality, or power of something. "[Congresswoman] Maxine Waters is right. Did the white folk think they could bring them drugs over here and the white kids wouldn't get caught up in it too — they betta recognize!" 2) To take heed of, to take notice of somebody, with respect for and due recognition of what that person represents. "The Brotha betta recognize, don't he gon lose that woman."

## BID

1) A popular card game, played with partners, four people per game. A traditional social event with verbal rituals and social conventions; provides an opportunity for competitors to display skill in SIGNIFYIN, LYIN, and other aspects of the African American Verbal Tradition. Also *Bid Whis, Whis*. 2) To state the number of books over six that one expects to win in the game of *Bid*, "I bid five." 3) The *bid* itself, "What is yo *bid*?" 4) A prison sentence; the amount of time one has to do. For example, a "skid bid" is a light sentence. See also DO A BID.

## BID WHIS

See BID.

**BIDDY**

A teenage female. Also *bitty*.

**BIDNESS**

Any personal affair, event, experience, or activity one is involved in. "I got some bidness to take care of" might refer to anything from paying a utility bill to confronting somebody about a deal that's gone awry. *Bidness* is the AAL pronunciation of "business." See also PUT SOMEBODY'S BIDNESS IN THE STREET, TAKE CARE OF BIDNESS.

**BIG**

Pregnant.

**THE BIG APPLE**

See THE APPLE.

**BIG D**

See D.

**BIG FACES**

Reference to money, from the mid-1990s new style of currency, in particular, $20, $50, and $100 bills, with very large size faces of dead presidents.

**BIG FOE**

Hard-core, tough, usually big, urban police detectives given wide latitude and discretion to investigate organized crime, such as gambling, prostitution, NUMBERS, ROLLIN, etc. Resented—and feared—throughout the COMMUNITY because of their brutality, their arrogant policing style in the HOOD, and their assumption that all citizens in the hood are criminals. Older term, derived from the practice of assigning four detectives to an unmarked police car. *Foe* is the AAL pronunciation of "four."

**BIG FOUR**

See BIG FOE.

**BIG FUN**

An exceptionally good time, generally in reference to a party or social event.

BIG LIPS

A derogatory reference to a person's large, full mouth. Also *thick lips*. An older term reflecting rejection of African American physical features, a view out of step with 1990s fashion and beauty trends. The "big-lipped" look is now sought after, with women whose lips are Euro-thin applying heavy lipstick to create the illusion of thick lips.

BIG MOMMA

1) The grandmother in the Black family, typically the authority in the family, regardless of whether or not she is physically "big." Older use. 2) An affectionate form of address for a stout woman.

BIG PAPER

A lot of money. Also *tall paper*.

BIG-TIME

Added after a word to indicate "very much, extremely." "You busy big-time," that is, You are extremely busy.

BIG-TIMIN IT

See LIVIN HIGH OFF THE HOG.

BIG UPS

HIP HOP phrase used to pay homage, to compliment a person, group, locale, business. Often used in SHOUT OUTS. Also *props, propers* (older term).

BIG WILLIE / BIG WILLIE PLAYA

1) A person who is affluent, accomplished, powerful, a major player in any field or area of life. Generally, but not exclusively, used in reference to a male. 2) A man who has a lot of female relationships. See also PIMP, PLAYA.

BILL

A hundred dollars, either in several small bills or a single hundred-dollar bill. Crossover term.

BIP BAM, THANK YOU, MAM!

1) A SIGNIFYIN expression used especially by women to refer

to a man who completes the sex act in a matter of seconds, and it's all over for the woman. 2) By extension, any quick premature action or behavior. Older phrase resurfacing. Also *Wham bam, thank you, Mam!*

BIRD

Euphemism for PUSSY. "Have you heard? The bird, bird, bird—the bird's the word" (a common chant that plays on the disguised meaning of bird).

BITCH

1) A generic term for a female. Women of varying ages use the term among themselves in a generic, neutral way. Rapper Nikki D: "It ain't like we hate niggas [Black men]. We love 'em...but bitches gotta get down with one another just like men do... We've got to come together" (from *The Source*, June 1993). Men also use the term in this generic way: "[I'm] through bein a playa and a balla / Jes want me one bad bitch so I can spoil her" (Rapper MA$E, "Can't Nobody Hold Me Down," from Puff Daddy and the Family, *No Way Out*, 1997). However, use of the term by males may not be accepted by all women. 2) Used by males and females to refer to a weak or subservient male. A "bitch-ass nigga." 3) In basketball or other competitive games, players may use the term to unsettle their opponents so they'll lose their COOL—and the game. 4) May be used in reference to objects and things. "They towed the bitch before I could get back down there to pick it up" (said in reference to someone's stalled car that got towed while the person was looking for help). Also *B* (euphemism).

BITE

1) To give exaggerated praise to someone; to ingratiate oneself in order to receive something from someone. The person who does this is said to be *biting*. 2) To copy a style, a look, a behavior. "After seeing Mary J. Blige in concert, they ran out to the mall to bite the look." 3) To vigorously and intensely work vagi-

nal muscles during sexual intercourse, producing a pleasurable sensation men describe as *biting*. See also SNAPPER.

BITIN

See BITE.

BITTY

See BIDDY.

BK

1) Any Burger King restaurant, believed to have been popularized by the Rap group De La Soul: "She's a BK Mademoiselle, wrinkly uniform and bottom bell and some jelly stuff on her sleeve" (from their 1991 album, *De La Soul Is Dead*). 2) Black Killers, a Midwest gang, no longer in existence.

BLACK

1) Used interchangeably with AFRICAN AMERICAN. Still preferred by some Blacks. Likely to trigger resentment if not capitalized. Before the late 1960s, was considered a negative term. 2) A form of address, as in "Yo, Black," or "Whassup, Black?" 3) Refers to any person of African descent anywhere in the world.

BLACK AND TAN

Any bar or place of entertainment catering to African Americans. An older term derived from the color diversity of African Americans, ranging from dark ("black") to light ("tan") complexions.

BLACK BOTTOM

Area in Detroit where large numbers of Blacks, of all social classes, were concentrated from the 1920s through the end of World War II. In the early years, it was a thriving, bustling center of African American businesses, stable schools and neighborhoods, and upscale entertainment places where Ella Fitzgerald, Dinah Washington, Sarah Vaughan, and other greats appeared. With continued overcrowding, housing segregation, and the eventual flight of middle-class Blacks, *Black Bottom* came to be a "ghetto slum" by the 1950s. See also BOTTOM.

**BLACK THANG**

A reference to any cultural or social practice, behavior, or attitude unique to or stemming from the African American Experience.

**BLACKER THAN THOU**

A SIGNIFYIN expression used to describe an African American who thinks he/she sets the standard for Blackness and DISSes other African Americans for not acting or thinking "Black enough."

**THE BLACKER THE BERRY, THE SWEETER THE JUICE**

Long-standing proverb from the Oral Tradition, referring to the power and desirability of Black skin color; resurfacing in HIP HOP. A variation is used in a slogan to support historically Black colleges: "The Blacker the college, the sweeter the knowledge."

**BLAZE / BLAZE UP**

1) To light a marijuana cigarette. Also *fire it up.* 2) To get high on marijuana.

**BLAZIN**

Excellent, extraordinary.

**BLESSED**

Traditional Black Church term to describe a person who has confessed to and been rescued from his/her sins and is now a devout follower of Christ. Pronounced bles-SED. See also SAVED.

**BLOB**

See SLOB.

**BLOCK**

To interfere with a man who's trying to establish a relationship with—HITTIN ON—a woman. Euphemism for *cock block.* A man who does this is said to be a *cock blocker.*

**BLOCK BOY**

See BANJY BOY (newer term).

BLONDIE

A negative term for a white female.

BLOOD

A generic term for any person of African descent; a positive term, noting the genetic kinship and shared bloodlines of African people. Older term.

BLOODS

A gang in Los Angeles, whose name was derived from the (older) term for Blacks—BLOOD. By the end of the 1980s, the *Bloods* and the CRIPS, a rival L.A. gang, had spread and set up outposts in other cities, and received a good deal of media attention in the 1990s. The role of these two gangs in the 1992 Los Angeles RE-BELLION (triggered by the "not guilty" verdict for the police officers in the Rodney King beating) and their truce and participation in efforts to heal and rebuild Los Angeles made the *Bloods* and *Crips* almost household words in the COMMUNITY.

BLOW

1) To sing, play an instrument, or RAP exceptionally well; to achieve excellence in one's work. "Aretha, Quincy, P.E.— now them Bloods can blow!" 2) To lose something or someone because of one's unwise actions. "He got a gamblin jones, blew his ride, his woman, everythang." 3) A jazz performance. 4) Cocaine in a powdered form that is sniffed, SNORTed. Crossover meaning.

BLOW OUT

Natural hair with the tight, natural curls (NAPS) blown out with a hair dryer to make the hair look full, a popular style in the 1960s and 1970s.

BLOW THE GLASS

To smoke crack in a pipe.

BLOW UP

1) To suddenly reach the top, to achieve overnight success in any area or endeavor. "I got a new job, Momma. I'm bout to blow up!" 2) A NATURAL hairstyle, cut short.

**BLOW UP THE SPOT**

To make a certain club, concert, or social gathering a popular place, the place where everyone wants to be.

**BLOWED**

High on drugs or liquor.

**BLUE**

The police. Also *blue light special.*

**BLUE-EYED DEVIL**

A European American; less often, but also, a European. Also *devil.*

**BLUE-EYED SOUL**

A reference to the existence of deep feeling, high emotion, intense spirituality—SOUL—in European Americans and Europeans. Also *blue-eyed soul Sista/Brotha.*

**BLUE-EYED SOUL SISTA / BROTHA**

See BLUE-EYED SOUL.

**BLUE LIGHT SPECIAL**

1) A cheap, low-quality brand of clothing, furniture, or other item. 2) See BLUE.

**BLUES**

1) A feeling of depression, often resulting from a love relationship that's not going right. 2) Used to describe a person who is incarcerated; derived from the type of clothes that person is now wearing, the typical drab blue prison uniform. "He's wearing the blues these days."

**BLUNT**

Marijuana rolled in cigar paper, creating a large marijuana cigarette that has the look of a cigar. See also PHILLY BLUNT.

**BMT**

Black man talking; used to reinforce a statement. "Lissen up! This is a BMT." Stated in an authoritative tone from somebody who obviously knows what he's talking about, the statement may be accepted—even by women—as reflecting a healthy injection of ego. However, if an assertion of authority based strictly on maleness, rather than knowledge, women may perceive it as a chauvinistic statement.

BMW

1) Black man working. Expression that SIGNIFIES ON racism and economic discrimination that results in overwhelming numbers of African American men being unemployed; thus, one working is a luxury, like the BMW automobile, and a rarity because he has beaten the odds of a system arrayed against him. 2) Black man's wheels—the BMW automobile—emerging term to convey the developing preference for BMWs among prosperous Black men.

B.N.I.C.

Boss Nigga in Charge. See H.N.I.C.

BO-DICK

See BO-JACK.

BO-JACK

See BOZACK (newer term).

BOARDS

Rebounds in basketball, derived from the ball bouncing off the backboards. "Yall gon have to start hittin the boards if yall wanna win!"

BODACIOUS

Bold, superb, outrageously HIP. Crossover term.

BODY BAG

A condom.

BODY SHOP

A hospital; place for "fixing" the body.

BOGARD (pronounced *BO-god*)

To aggressively take over or take charge of something. From film star Humphrey *Bogart*, who played strong-arm tough guys. Older term that resurfaced in HIP HOP: "I don't ask, the Ice jes bogard" (from Rapper Ice-T's 1988 *Power* album).

**BOGUE**

Derogatory, negative, not good. From the Hausa language in West Africa, *boko,* literally "deceit" or "fake."

**DA BOMB**

The bomb; superb, excellent, the height or ultimate quality of something.

**BONE**

1) A marijuana cigarette. 2) The penis. 3) A dollar bill. 4) A skinny person, usually female; a negative term. "You betta start eatin, girl. Don't nobody want no bone." 5) To perform sex, from the male viewpoint. Probably a resurfacing of and variation on *love bone* (older term).

**BONE OUT**

To leave.

**BONED OUT**

1) Without money. 2) Describes a man who has just completed sex with a woman.

**BONES**

1) The game pieces in dominoes; a popular game, with individual opponents, played by matching rectangular-shaped pieces of ivory, each piece labeled with a series of black dots. 2) Dice (older meaning).

**BOO**

1) Term of endearment used to address a person's significant other. Also *my boo.* 2) Marijuana (older term). Crossover use.

**BOO-BOO**

Euphemism for *shit.*

**BOO-COOS**

A lot of something, many, very much. From AAL pronunciation of French *beaucoup.* Probably came into Black Talk from soldiers fighting in Europe during the two world wars. The French were reported to have been friendly and receptive to African American soldiers.

**BOODY**

1) See BACK. For emphasis and dramatic effect, may be pronounced "boo-tay." See also GIT SOME BOODY. 2) Weak. 3) Gullible.

**BOODY CALL**

A summons, by phone, pager, or other means, for sex, usually late at night. The "summons" may not always be explicitly stated, but both parties know that it's a "boody call."

**BOODY GREEN**

A dance performed by moving the hips suggestively while bending the knees; popular in the 1950s and 1960s. Also *Boody Queen.* The dance resurfaced in early HIP HOP, as *The Butt,* performed in Spike Lee's film *School Daze.*

**BOODY QUEEN**

See BOODY GREEN.

**BOOGIE**

1) Any kind of dance step or dance event; originally from *boogie-woogie,* a form of dancing popular in the 1930s. 2) To party, have a good time. Crossover term.

**BOOGIE DOWN**

To party.

**BOOGIE-WOOGIE**

See BOOGIE.

**BOOGUH-BEAR**

See BEAR.

**BOOJEE**

1) Describes an elitist, uppity-acting African American, generally with a higher educational and income level than the average Black, who identifies with European American culture and distances him/herself from other African Americans. Derived from "bourgeois/bourgeoisie." 2) Describes an event, style, or thing that is characteristic of elitist, uppity-acting Blacks. "It was one of dem ol boojee thangs."

**BOOK**

1) In BID, the four cards played each round. See also SET BOOK, TURN A BOOK. 2) To leave. 3) To study (older usage). Both meanings have crossed over.

**BOOM**

A filler expression, with no particular meaning. "First, I'm gon finish college, then, boom, Ima git a good job. Boom. Git a dope ride. Git that crib. Hook it up like I want. Boom. I'm gon be livin large."

**BOOM BOX**

A large portable stereo. Sometimes carried around on a routine basis, usually by males. Crossover term.

**BOOMIN**

1) Good-looking. 2) Playing loud and deep bass tones on one's stereo or BOOM BOX.

**BOONES**

Boone's Farm, a brand of cheap wine.

**BOOST**

To shoplift, generally with the intention of selling the stolen goods. Term dates to the 1950s according to Clarence Major (*Juba to Jive*, 1994). Crossover term.

**BOOSTER**

A person whose principal source of income is derived from shoplifting and then selling the stolen merchandise. Older term resurfacing in the 1990s. Dates to the 1930s, according to Clarence Major (*Juba to Jive*, 1994).

**BOOT**

An African American. The term is used neutrally (by Black seniors usually), but may come from a term with rather negative associations, bootblack.

**BOOT UP**

1) To get ready to fight. 2) To put on a condom.

**BOP**

1) A dance with a partner, executed with intricate steps, twirls,

and turns; dates from the 1950s, but still current in some circles. 2) A form of jazz combining African and European rhythms, associated with the music of Charlie Parker, Dizzy Gillespie, and Thelonious Monk; a variation of the term BE-BOP.

**BOPPIN**

Walking in a certain rhythmic, graceful, cool way. "He was just boppin down the street." Crossover meaning.

**BORN AGAIN**

Describes a person who has been rescued (SAVED) from the world of sin and transformed to a different level of existence.

**BOSS**

Older term that has crossed over. See DEF (newer term).

**BOSS LIKE HOT SAUCE**

SuperBOSS; excellent, superb, more boss than boss.

**BOSTON**

In the game of BID, to win every round of play, to turn all the books (see TURN A BOOK). Also *run a Boston.*

**BOTTOM**

Any area of any city or town where African Americans live. Also *bottoms.* Over time, this has come to refer to a run-down or slum area in the COMMUNITY. See also BLACK BOTTOM.

**BOTTOMS**

See BOTTOM.

**BOUNCE**

To leave.

**BOUT**

See BE BOUT.

**BOUT IT**

1) Agreeable with something. "Whatever my boo wonnuh do, I'm bout it." A variation of older term BE BOUT resurfacing in HIP HOP. Popularized by Rapper Master P's 1997 *I'm Bout It,* the double-length soundtrack to an underground film that he produced about his earlier life as a drug dealer and GANGSTA.

He financed and starred in the film, which mainstream distributors rejected. Nonetheless, in the first week of the film's release (on videotape), it sold more than 220,000 copies. Also DOWN FOR or DOWN WIT. 2) Describes a person or thing that is very good, excellent; up on contemporary culture, in the know. May also be expressed as *bout it, bout it.* "I always knew he was a bout it, bout it, Brotha." Also DOWN.

BOUT IT, BOUT IT

See BOUT IT.

BOX

1) See BRICK. 2) A stereo. Crossover meaning.

BOX ON THAT FOX

Expression used to convey aesthetic appreciation for a good-looking woman (FOX) who has a shapely body (BOX).

BOY

1) Used to refer to, but not to address, one's male friend or associate. "Me and my boys was chillin." *Boy* should never be used to address any Black male over eight or nine years old; considered insulting. 2) Any male that one identifies with, whether personally known to the person or not; used with *my, your, his,* etc. "Ice Cube gave Project 2000 nem some money for they program? All right! That's my boy." 3) Heroin, older meaning that has crossed over.

BOYFRIEND

A form of address for, or reference to, any male; used primarily by females.

BOZACK

Euphemism for DICK. Also *Bo-jack* (older term).

BRA STRAP

To be "on a woman's *bra strap*" is to impose oneself on her, to bother or hassle her, to intrude into her space. For the male version, see JOCK STRAP.

BRAIDS

Used to refer to a wide variety of styles, most involving the use of synthetic or human hair "extensions" braided into the natural hair. Worn mainly, but not exclusively, by women. In the 1990s a wide variety of *braids* were created: box braids, individuals, zillions, etc. The original braid style was *corn rows,* very small braids arranged in rows of identical size and very close to the scalp, often adorned with beads, colored rope, and other ornaments. Style dates back to ancient Africa.

BRANG ASS TO GIT ASS

Response to a threat to do bodily harm to a person; indicates that the person doing the threatening can also be harmed.

BRANG / BRING IT ON

1) Response to a challenge to a person's leadership, situation, position on an issue, or to a threat to do bodily harm; indicates that one is up to the challenge. 2) By extension, applied to lesser personal challenges. A Brotha at the dentist, initially complaining because he has to get a shot with "that big-ass needle" in preparation for a tooth extraction, finally gets ready for the challenge, and says: "Okay, brang it on!" See also COME WIT IT. Also *set it out.*

BREAD

Money.

BREAK

1) To run or get away. 2) In basketball (and occasionally also football), to FAKE OUT the defense and create scoring opportunities in such a way as to break the defender's spirit and embarrass him/her.

BREAK DOWN

To go low to the floor while dancing.

BREAK HIM / HER OFF

To provide sexual pleasure to someone.

BREAK HIM / HER / THEM OFF SOMETHING

To provide a satisfying performance, let someone know what you are capable of, in entertainment, or in conversation; give them your best.

**BREAK IT DOWN**

To explain something, usually something complex. Also *run it down.*

**BREAK IT OFF**

To give up money.

**BREAK ON SOMEBODY**

1) To talk negatively about somebody. 2) To embarrass a person in front of others.

**BREAK OUT**

1) To leave. 2) To bring something out of the place where it has been stored or kept. "In a couple of weeks, when I lose this weight, Ima break out the red dress."

**BREAK SOMEBODY'S FACE**

To hurt someone's feelings.

**BREAK WIDE**

To leave in a hurry.

**BREAKDOWN**

A shotgun.

**BREW**

Beer. Crossover term.

**BRICK**

1) A woman with a sexy, attractive shape, especially if she has BACK. "She's built like a brick"; "She's a brick." Also *brick house, box.* Older meaning. 2) In basketball, a hard shot that misses the basket and hits the backboard or rim with an ugly sound. See also THROW UP A BRICK. 3) Bone-chillingly cold. Newer, HIP HOP meaning.

**BRICK HOUSE**

See BRICK.

**BRIGHT**

Describes a light-complexioned Black person; used without the ambivalent meanings associated with YELLA and *high yella.*

## BRING / BRANG THE NOISE!

1) To drop knowledge, to state the truth about society loudly and clearly as everybody parties to the beat. 2) To turn on or turn up the music; git loud and LIVE; let's PAR-TAY. Also *Pump up the volume! Pump it up!* (older terms).

## BRO

See BROTHA.

## BROAD

A generic term for a woman, used by senior women as well as men. Generally not derogatory.

## BROCCOLI

Emerging HIP HOP term for marijuana.

## BROKE

Physically unattractive.

## BROKE-ASS J

In basketball, reference to lack of jumpshot skills. "He got a broke-ass J; ain made nothin all day."

## BROKE DOWN

Describes a stylish way of wearing a hat (usually by a male), such as cocked to one side or tilted forward.

## BROTHA

Any African American male. Derived from the Traditional Black Church pattern of referring to all male members of the Church "family" as *Brotha*. Also *Bro*.

## BROWN-SKIN

Refers to an African American whose skin color is between light- and dark-complexioned.

## BS

Crossover expression for *bullshit*.

## BUCK

1) A negative term for an African American man; dates back to enslavement. 2) To shoot at somebody. 3) To take somebody's money.

**BUCK WHYLIN**

Engaging in general conversational chit chat, in the LYIN and SIGNIFYIN of the Black Verbal Tradition. See also SHOOT THE SHIT, SHOOT THE GIFT.

**BUCK WILD**

Describes a person or persons acting very wild, crazy, out of control, usually at a party or other social event.

**BUCKET**

A beat-up car, usually an older model.

**BUCKET OF BLOOD**

A rowdy, rough place of entertainment—enter at your own risk.

**BUD**

Marijuana. Crossover term.

**BUDDHA / BUDDHA GRASS**

Marijuana.

**BUFFALO SOLDIERS**

Black soldiers in the nineteenth-century U.S. Cavalry; so named by Native Americans because of the soldiers' bravery, similar to the courage of the buffalo, which the Native Americans revered—hence *buffalo soldier* was a term of high respect. Many went on to become the nation's first Black cowboys. Mario Van Peebles's 1993 film, *Posse,* portrayed *buffalo soldiers* who fought in the Spanish-American War.

**BUFFALO STANCE**

The posture taken by the BUFFALO SOLDIERS before attack, positioning themselves for battle. By extension, today *buffalo stance* refers to an aggressive posture, standing in a position ready to fight.

**BUG**

To get on somebody's nerves; to irritate a person. From the Mandinka language of the Mandingo people, *baga,* and the Wolof language, *bugal,* "to annoy." Older term that has crossed over. Also *bug out* (newer term).

**BUG OUT**

1) To have fun, act CRAZY, engage in a fit of laughter about something. 2) To annoy, irritate. "No matter where I go, my man complains; he bugs me out." Also *bug* (older term).

**BUGGIN**

Acting crazy, behaving irrationally. See also TRIPPIN.

**BULLDAGGER**

Derogatory term for a lesbian.

**BULLET**

A one-year prison sentence.

**BUM RUSH**

To take over something.

**BUMP**

To have sex. A resurfacing and extension of the name of the 1970s dance, THE BUMP. Also *bump 'n' grind, bump titties*.

**THE BUMP**

A 1970s dance in which partners bumped in rhythm against each other's lower bodies.

**BUMP ONE'S GUMS**

To talk excessively.

**BUMP UP**

To play music louder.

**BUMPER KIT**

See BACK.

**BUMPIN**

1) High-energy, loud, especially in reference to music. 2) Describes a song with a lot of bass sound. 3) See DEF.

**BUN**

To have sex.

**BUPPIE**

Black urban professional. A middle-class, sophisticated African American; one who is into materialism and self-indulgence, rather than DOWN FOR Black causes.

**BURN**

1) To cook extremely well and produce food of superior quality and taste. 2) To give someone a sexually transmitted disease. 3) To deceive or manipulate someone into doing something not in that person's best interests, particularly in reference to deceiving someone financially. Meanings (2) and (3) have crossed over.

**BURNER**

A firearm of any kind—gun, rifle, etc.

**BUS**

To have fun, HANG OUT.

**BUS A CAP**

To shoot a gun. *Bus* is AAL pronunciation of "bust." Also *pop a cap, peel a cap.*

**BUS A RHYME**

To create RAP lyrics and rhymes.

**BUS ON SOMEBODY**

To inform on a person who has been doing something he/she shouldn't be doing.

**BUS ONE'S NUTS**

To have an orgasm, generally used in reference to males.

**BUS SOME CARDS**

Expression used to initiate a card game.

**BUS SOMEBODY**

To catch a person red-handed doing something he/she shouldn't be doing.

**BUS SOMEBODY OUT**

To have sex with someone, from the male viewpoint.

**THE BUS STOP**

See THE HUSTLE.

**BUSH**

1) Female pubic hair. Crossover meaning. 2) Marijuana.

**BUSINESS**

See BIDNESS.

BUST A CAP, BUST ON SOMEBODY, etc.

See BUS A CAP, BUS ON SOMEBODY, etc.

BUSTA

An unpopular person who is not with it, who consistently ruins the social atmosphere, either because he is not COOL and DOWN, or because he is a phony, a fake. Generally used for males.

BUSTED

Caught doing something one wasn't supposed to be doing, something wrong or against the rules; can involve either being caught directly or being informed on by someone. Sometimes used humorously for small infractions, as in the case of the SISTA who caught her allegedly dieting GIRLFRIEND at a Baskin Robbins ice cream store: "Girl, what you doin up here in '31'? Un-huh, girlfriend, you done got busted." See also BUS ON SOMEBODY, BUS SOMEBODY.

BUSTIN OUT

Describes someone who is looking good at the moment because the person is well dressed, has an attractive hairstyle, looks physically fit, or any of a variety of reasons.

BUSTIN RHYMES

HIP HOP term for the creation and/or use of rhyming song lyrics, generally applies to those who are doing the rhyming in a superb, creative style.

BUSTIN SUDS

Washing dishes.

THE BUTT

See BOODY GREEN.

BUTTA

Butter; describes something that is smooth, excellent, very nice. "Yo, baby, you butta with that jump shot."

(GOT DA) BUTTA FROM THE DUCK

Expression used to convey the total completion or exhaustiveness of a task, a job thoroughly and completely finished. The expression intensifies the thoroughness of the action that was performed, i.e., it was so complete that it accomplished the impossible (because ducks don't produce butter).

BUY A WOLF TICKET
See WOOF.

BUY A WOOF TICKET
See WOOF.

BUZZ
A high from liquor or drugs. Crossover term.

CAESAR
See QUO VADIS.

CAKES
1) Euphemism for PUSSY. 2) Cocaine, crack, or heroin.

CALI
California.

CALL MYSELF / YOURSELF / HERSELF
To consider yourself to be doing something; to intend to do a thing without actually achieving your objective. "Girl, what you call yourself doing?" That is, What do you think you're doing?; and "I call myself having this dinner ready on time," that is, I had every intention of accomplishing that goal, but I didn't.

CALL SOMEBODY OUT
1) To challenge somebody about a certain point or issue. 2) To challenge somebody to a fight.

CALL SOMEBODY OUTA THEY NAME
To insult someone; to talk about a person in a negative way, especially to call someone a name or to hurl an accusation at that

person. "She come talkin bout I stole her ring. I don't appreciate nobody callin me outa my name" (i.e., callin her a thief).

CAMEO CUT

See FADE.

CAN I RUN WIT YA?

Can I be on your team? Used in pick-up basketball.

CANDY CANE / CANE

Cocaine, in either powdered form or as crack.

CAN'T KILL NOTHIN AND WON'T NOTHIN DIE

Expression indicating that the person is having a hard time, that they are doing bad, especially economically. Often used as a response to WHASS HAPNIN? and WHAT UP?

CAP'N (CAPTAIN) SAVE A HO

A man who lavishes money and anything else on a woman in order to win her over and to keep her. HIP HOP version of the older term "sugar daddy."

CAP ON

1) To SIGNIFY ON somebody, to DIS a person; can be done seriously or in fun. 2) A bullet.

CARBON COPY

A phony, a fake, a WANNABE.

CASE

A person's business, situation, or personal state. See also GIT OFF MY CASE, ON SOMEBODY'S CASE, ON THE CASE.

CAT

1) Generic reference to any male, older term dating back at least to 1930s, very popular in the 1950s to the 1970s, resurfacing in the 1990s through HIP HOP. 2) Euphemism for PUSSY. 3) Synthetic drug that is potentially explosive, stronger than ICE.

CAT FACES

Wrinkles in clothes when ironing them, used today mainly by senior Blacks.

CAT WALK

See GANGSTA LIMP (newer term).

CATCH YOU LATER

Goodbye. Older expression that has crossed over. Also *Later* (another older term); *outa here, Outtie 5000* (newer terms).

CATTIN

See GANGSTA LIMP (newer term).

CAVE

A EUROPEAN AMERICAN, also sometimes a European; a derogatory term. Derived from the belief among some Blacks that whites led a barbaric existence in caves in Europe during the heyday of ancient African civilization.

CCM

Cold cash money.

CHANGES

1) Problems in one's personal life; unanticipated emotional experiences. Crossover meaning. 2) In jazz, a departure from the main melody, during which the musician improvises.

CHARLIE

Derogatory term for white male. Also *Mista Charlie, Charles, Chuck.*

CHECK

1) To criticize somebody's behavior to get them to stop doing what they're doing. Also *put somebody in check.* 2) In basketball, to stay close to (to guard) another player and attempt to prevent that player from shooting or passing the ball.

CHECK A TRAP

1) To monitor the status of a situation or plan; to check on one's business, especially in the underground economy. 2) To visit, spend time with, or check on a man or woman that one is having an affair with. "He went uptown to check his trap" (said in reference to a married man who went to visit his girlfriend).

CHECK IT IN

Used in street robberies and muggings as a demand for the person to surrender his/her coat, money, or whatever object the mugger demands.

CHECK HIM (OR HER, IT, THIS, ETC.) OUT

Pay attention to something or someone; observe this or analyze it. Crossover expression.

CHECK UP

1) In basketball, said to goad the person who is CHECKING you, daring them to play tighter defense. "You can't hold me. Check up, nigga." 2) Used to start play after a pause. "Yall ready? Awight, then check up."

CHECK YOSEF

Monitor your words, actions, behavior. "Yourself" pronounced *yosef* in AAL.

CHECK YOU / CHECK YOU OUT

See you; goodbye. Crossover expression.

CHEDDAR

Money.

CHEESE

1) See CHEDDAR. 2) Crack cocaine.

CHI-TOWN (pronounced *SHY-town*)

Chicago. Also *Windy City*.

CHICKEN EATER

Derogatory term for a Traditional Black Church preacher. Traditionally the preacher ate Sunday dinner at a church member's house and was given his pick of the chicken, with the children eating last, whatever was left. They expressed their resentment by calling the preacher a *chicken eater*.

CHICKEN HEAD

Lightheaded, dumb female.

CHICKEN SHIT

Small-time; petty; inadequate. Crossover expression.

CHIEF

Form of address for a male.

CHILL

1) To relax, hang out, either in the street or at home. Crossover term. Also *chill out, max* (newer terms); *cool, copasetic* (older terms). 2) To stop doing or saying something. 3) To calm down from a high emotional state. Also *chill out, take a chill pill* (newer terms); *cool it* (older term). Crossover term.

CHILL OUT

See CHILL.

CHILL PAD

See CRIB.

CHILLIN

Relaxing, taking it easy. Crossover term. Also *coolin it* (older term).

CHINA WHITE

Asian heroin.

CHITLIN CIRCUIT

Small bars, clubs, modest places of entertainment located in Black, poor areas of the South during segregation. Most Black entertainers, such as Bluesman B. B. King and comic genius Moms Mabley, performed on the *chitlin circuit,* generally doing one-nighters or making otherwise rather limited appearances before moving on, usually by bus or car, to the next stop on the *circuit.* The term *chitlins,* as well as the delicacy itself, is still in current use throughout the COMMUNITY; however, *chitlin circuit* is now used mainly by Black seniors. See also CHITLINS.

CHITLINS

The intestines of the hog; require extensive cleaning and long hours of cooking. Historically discarded by European Americans and eaten only by Blacks; now an expensive delicacy that many Blacks can't afford. See also CHITLIN CIRCUIT.

CHOCOLATE CITY

Any city with a predominantly African American population. From the JAM "Chocolate City" by popular 1970s FUNK group Parliament-Funkadelic, founded by musical guru George Clinton, who also coined the phrase "Vanilla Suburb" in the same recording. Clinton and P-Funk are enjoying a revival in HIP HOP; they are featured in Dr. Dre's "Let Me Ride" video.

CHOKE

To lose your nerve in the face of pressure; to fail to accomplish something in a high-stakes situation which you are capable of, or may even have done before, but not under pressure. Also *sell out*.

CHOOSE

To select a partner for love or sex. The person who gets selected is said to have been *chose*.

CHOSE

See CHOOSE.

CHRONIC

1) Marijuana. 2) "The Chronic," title of popular 1992 Rap album featuring Dr. Dre and Snoop Doggy Dogg (now Snoop Dogg).

CHUCK

See CHARLIE.

CHUMP

A person who is a pushover, one who lacks nerve.

CHUMP CHANGE

A small amount of money. Also *crumbs*.

CHURCH FAMILY

Traditional Black Church term to refer to all the people who belong to the same church.

CHURCH FOLK

Traditional Black Church term for people who are active in Church life anywhere, not necessarily members of the same church.

**CLAIM**

To indicate the gang you belong to.

**CLEAN**

1) Stylishly dressed. Also *laid*. 2) Dressed up, whether in the current style or not. 3) Free of drug use; older meaning that has crossed over. 4) Totally, completely; "I clean forgot the time"; "All the food was clean gone." Crossover meaning.

**CLIP**

A clip for an automatic or semiautomatic gun.

**CLIPPED**

See GIT CLIPPED.

**CLOCK**

1) To stare at, to watch. 2) To make a lot of money. 3) To hit someone. 4) To sell drugs.

**CLOW**

A game played with dice.

**CLOWN**

1) To ridicule, humiliate. Also *house*. 2) To talk or act inappropriately, especially in public; to act up. 3) A state of having fun; one's good-time, partying spirit. "I really got my clown off at that party."

**CLUCKHEAD**

A person addicted to crack (or other drugs).

**CO-SIGN**

To verify or affirm a statement or action of another person; to take sides with a person, to back him or her up. A 1960s term resurfacing in HIP HOP. Derived from the once all-too-frequent requirement of a racist system that African Americans have someone *co-sign* for them before they could obtain credit to buy a car, furniture, or even small items.

**COAL**

1) Added in front of a word to indicate that something is being done intensely or strenuously . "We just coal chillin," meaning,

We are really relaxing. 2) Describes a person who tells it like it is, dares to speak the unvarnished truth, is very critical, and cuts to the chase. Also *coal-blooded*. 3) Describes something that is superb, excellent. "The concert was coal." "Cold" is rendered as *coal* in AAL.

COAL-BLOODED
See COAL.

COAL CHILLIN
See COAL.

COAT
Court. To date someone; also to flirt with, or HIT ON, someone. Probably from the AAL pronunciation of "court." Used today mainly by Black seniors.

COCK
Vagina.

COCK BLOCK, COCK BLOCKER
See BLOCK.

COCK DIESEL
See DIESEL.

COCK STRONG
See DIESEL.

COCK SUCKA
A man who is weak, passive, emasculated. Derived from the notion that a man who performs oral sex on a woman is a weakling; the myth is that African American men don't GO DOWN ON women.

COCKTAIL
A marijuana cigarette butt smoked by putting it in the end of a regular cigarette that has had some of its tobacco emptied out. Crossover term.

COCONUT
A Latino/Latina who identifies white, is brown on the outside but white on the inside. See also BANANA, OREO.

COLD

    See COAL.

COLD-BLOODED

    See COAL-BLOODED.

COLOM

    Marijuana imported from Colombia. Also *commercial.*

COLOR SCALE

    The gradation of skin color values, from very light-complexioned to very dark-complexioned.

COLOR STRUCK

    Describes an African American obsessed with, and preferring, light-complexioned Blacks and/or whites; a negative term because it stems from a denigration of Blackness.

COLORED

    Term for people of African descent in the United States; preferred racial label from the nineteenth century until about the 1930s and 1940s. Still heard among senior Blacks today. See also COLORED PEOPLE, PEOPLE OF COLOR.

COLORED PEOPLE

    People of African descent; today used primarily by Black seniors. Also *Colored.* The founders of the NAACP, the oldest Civil Rights organization in the United States, used this racial designation when they organized the NAACP in 1909. It has remained the National Association for the Advancement of *Colored People* ever since, despite the shifts from NEGRO to BLACK to AFRICAN AMERICAN. With the burgeoning population of "Colored" groups (Latinos/Hispanics, Asians, etc.), this designation may be revived as a generic term for PEOPLE OF COLOR. In fact, in the 1990s when the Reverend Dr. Benjamin F. Chavis, Jr., was director of the NAACP, he proposed to extend the NAACP agenda to include Hispanics, Asians, and Native Americans/American Indians, who, like African Americans, face discrimination as *Colored People.* See also COLORED, PEOPLE OF COLOR.

## COLORED PEOPLE'S TIME

Also CPT, CP TIME. See AFRICAN PEOPLE'S TIME.

### COLORS

Symbolic colors that show one's group affiliation. Although associated with gangs, other groups, such as motorcycle clubs, use the term also.

### COME

Expresses indignation at or disapproval of someone's actions or words. In a conversation between a man and a woman, the SISTA said, "Don't come tellin me bout no late buses and all that; you just late and you messed up."

### COME AGAIN

Used to express disapproval. Diva Lauryn Hill uses this phrase to chide do-wrong BROTHAS in "Doo Wop (That Thing)" from her 1998 multiplatinum CD, *The Miseducation of Lauryn Hill.*

### COME BACKED UP

Used by women to describe a state of unfulfilled sexual need, lack of orgasm, due either to a period of extended celibacy or to a male partner who is inadequate.

### COME CORRECT

To speak or make an assertion that is in accordance with appropriate, ethical standards; to behave in a morally, socially, or politically appropriate way.

### COME OUT

To lose one's hair. "The PERM was too strong and my hair come out." Also *fall out.*

### COME OUT OF A BAG

To act contrary to expectations; to behave illogically for the situation. "You can try talkin to him, it might help, but ain no tellin, he might come out of a bag."

### COME WIT IT

Response to a challenge, telling the person to produce whatever he/she has that is a potential threat. Suggests that the person being challenged is able to withstand whatever comes his/her way. Often used in sports, card playing, verbal dueling, and other forms of competition; also used in physical confrontations. See also BRANG/BRING IT ON. Also *set it out.*

COMIN UP

Moving into a higher income bracket rapidly, whether through legitimate or illegitimate means.

COMMERCIAL

See COLOM.

COMMUNITY

African Americans as a group, either local or nationwide.

COMPANY

Visitors at one's home. "Momma said yall can't have no company while she at work."

CONEY ONEY

A Detroit gang; no longer in existence.

CONK

A male hairstyle, popular before the 1970s, in which the hair is STRAIGHTENed using a mixture of lye, white potatoes, and eggs. Also *do, process.* Malcolm X wrote about the experience in his *Autobiography:* "I got a can of Red Devil lye... 'It's going to burn when I comb it in—it burns *bad.* But the longer you can stand it, the straighter the hair.'...I couldn't stand it any longer; I bolted to the washbasin." Later Malcolm writes: "This was the trip to Michigan in the wintertime when I put congolene on my head, then discovered that the bathroom sink's pipes were frozen. To keep the lye from burning up my scalp, I had to stick my head into the stool and flush and flush to rinse out the stuff." This scene was poignantly reproduced in Spike Lee's film *Malcolm X.*

CONSTANT

A person who is a perennial or habitual part of a scene or situation, usually hanging around to run a scam, as, for example, an ex-student on a university campus who plies drugs to current students.

CONVERSATE

To carry on a conversation, usually a lively, colorful one.

CONVERSATION

One's RAP (in the romantic sense); the style of talk one uses to HIT ON a man or woman.

COOCHIE

Euphemism for PUSSY.

COOKIE

Crack in a rock or solid form.

COOKIN

1) Doing something energetically and with skill. Crossover meaning. 2) Playing jazz with intense enthusiasm, fervor, and excellence.

COOKIN WITH GAS

Used as a response of encouragement to a speaker or performer, meaning, "That's right, Go 'head, you ON THE CASE."

COOL

1) Relaxed, calm. Also *chillin* (newer term); *copasetic* (older term). 2) Okay, that's fine with me. Also *copasetic.* 3) Excellent, great. Also *def.* 4) Composure, calmness, a state of not displaying one's feelings or reactions. All are crossover meanings.

COOL IT

See CHILL (newer term).

COOL OUT

See CHILL (newer term).

COOLIN IT

See CHILLIN (newer term).

COOLNESS

Composure, calmness. Also COOL.

COP

To obtain something. "I copped a new ride, and she didn't like it, so I copped a tude."

COP A PLEA

To surrender, to give in. Crossover meaning.

COPASETIC

1) Relaxed, calm. Also *cool* (newer term); *chillin* (latest term).
2) Okay, fine with me. Also *cool*. Although used primarily by Black seniors, *copasetic* may be resurfacing in HIP HOP. Used in "Shu-Be" by the group Guess: "Everything is copasetic."

CORN ROWS

See BRAIDS.

CORNY

Stale, not with-it. Also *wack*.

COTTON

In basketball, refers to the type of basket that is made when the ball goes through the net without hitting the rim, smoothly, soft as cotton.

COULDN'T HIT HIM / HER IN THE BEHIND WITH A RED APPLE

Used to refer to a person who is arrogant or conceited.

THE COUNT

The population. Taken from jail life, where it refers to the counting of the inmates periodically performed by guards in order to ascertain if any prisoners are missing. Anybody who gets killed or is otherwise missing is said to have been "taken off *the count.*"

COUNTERFEIT

In the game of BID, the BOOK of cards that the player who has the BID discards before the first round of play.

COVER

A blanket or quilt.

CP TIME

Colored People's Time. See AFRICAN PEOPLE'S TIME.

CPT

1) Colored People's Time. See AFRICAN PEOPLE'S TIME.
2) Compton, California.

CRABS

An insulting name used by the Los Angeles gang the BLOODS for their former rivals, the CRIPS.

CRACK ON

To level a verbal discount, or DIS, on a person, either seriously or in fun.

CRACKED OUT

Thoroughly and completely addicted to crack.

CRACKER

A derogatory term for a white person. Possibly derived from the sound of the master's whip during enslavement; by extension, any white person.

CRACKHEAD

Person addicted to crack. Crossover term. Also *smoker, puffer, rock star.*

CRACKIN BUT FACKIN

Making humorous or joking statements that also contain facts.

CRAPPED OUT

1) To have lost out in any major competition or struggle. 2) To have hit rock bottom.

CRAZY

1) A lot of; very much; a great deal. "He got crazy digits at the party," meaning, He collected a lot of phone numbers and addresses. Also *mad.* 2) Going against conventional behavior for African Americans, particularly against European Americans' conventions and expectations for Blacks; a long-standing meaning. Lonne Elder's play *Ceremonies in Dark Old Men* contains the line: "Don't nobody pay no attention to no nigga that ain crazy," meaning, In order to draw attention to your cause or situation, you must go against the norms that the system has set for Blacks. 3) Describes any action that is unconventional or nonconformist, whether political action or not. 4) Describes a

person who is having fun, telling jokes, making everybody laugh with his/her behavior or comments. Also *sick*.

CREEP

1) To sneak out with somebody other than your spouse/partner.

2) To stalk somebody maliciously.

CREW

See POSSE.

CRIB

A house; one's home. Also *den, joint, pad* (older terms); *chill pad* (newer term).

CRIMEY

A person's close associate, coworker, or friend, particularly one with whom you have worked in a situation of struggle.

CRIPS

A gang in Los Angeles. The name is derived from the founder of the *Crips*, who was a member of the Chicago gang Blackstone Rangers. After being shot and crippled in Chicago, he moved to Los Angeles and established his own gang, naming it the *Crips*. The *Crips* and their former rivals, the Bloods, received widespread public attention in the 1990s. See the discussion at BLOODS.

CRONZ

A gun.

CROSS OUT

Gang term for defacing or crossing out the graffiti of a rival gang.

CROSS OVAH

See GO OVAH.

CROSS THE BURNING SANDS

The initiation ritual of African American fraternities and sororities. See also GO OVAH.

CRUMB SNATCHERS

Children. Also *rug rats, table pimps*.

CRUMBS

    1) People in street life who are larcenous and treacherous, LOW-LIFE. 2) Unimportant people, not necessarily low-life. 3) See CHUMP CHANGE.

CRYSTAL

    Cocaine that hasn't been diluted (CUT) with baking powder, quinine, or other fillers; "pure" cocaine.

CUFFED

    Arrested.

CURB

    Ugly; undesirable.

A/THE CURL

    Originally referred to the JHERI-CURL; now also used to refer to any of the several spinoff imitations of the JHERI-CURL.

CUT

    1) To put a person in his/her place; to verbally set someone straight; tell someone off. "If she say one more thang to me, Ima cut her every which way but loose." 2) To dilute the strength or purity of anything (not just drugs). "When you makin this kind of pie, you got to cut the lemon with a lot of sugar." 3) To injure a person by using a razor or knife. "My partners got cut bad in that fight." 4) The latest hit record.

CUT SOMEBODY SOME SLACK

    To ease up the pressure on someone; to give somebody a break from being criticized. Also *give somebody some slack, slack.* Crossing over.

CUTTIN UP

    1) Acting crazy or irrational. 2) Acting in a very humorous way to entertain.

CUZ

    A form of address (and reference) to your HOMEY.

**D**

    Detroit. Also *Big D*, which has not crossed over. Also *Motor City, Motown,* which have crossed over.

**D**

    1) Defense in basketball. 2) By extension, defensive posture and moves in general. 3) Euphemism for penis.

**D-UP**

    1) To tighten up the defense in basketball. 2) By extension, to intensify your defensive mode in any area of your life where you are vulnerable.

**D-WHUPPED**

    See DICK-WHUPPED.

**DAISY DUKES**

    See DAZZEY DUKS.

**DAMN SKIPPY / YOU DAMN SKIPPY**

    Expression used to emphasize an assertion or statement. "Yeah, they refunded my money. You damn skippy."

**DANK**

    Marijuana.

**DAP**

    1) Respect. When used as a gesture, as in "Give me some dap," one person's fist taps the other person's fist in a vertical position. 2) Stylishly dressed.

**THE DAP**

    A style of handshake executed with elaborate movements; very popular among Blacks during the Vietnam War and today among Vietnam veterans.

**DARK-SKIN**

Used to describe a dark-complexioned African American.

**A DAY LATE AND A DOLLAR SHORT**

Expression used to describe someone who is unprepared, disorganized, unready, or who has failed to live up to his/her promises or duties.

**DAY ONE**

The first day something started, the beginning. "I been doin it this way since Day One [the first day of the person's employment], and now he come tellin me I ain doin it right."

**DAZZEY DUKS**

Very tight, scanty female shorts that reveal the flesh of the lower buttocks. Derived from the name of the female character Daisy Duke, who wore such shorts in the early 1980s television sitcom "The Dukes of Hazzard." Resurfacing in HIP HOP; used as the title of the 1993 jam "Dazzey Duks" by Rapper Duice.

**DBI SYNDROME**

Declaration of Black Inferiority; used in reference to Blacks with low self-esteem who have absorbed society's racism and feel that African Americans are inferior to European Americans.

**D.C.**

Washington, D.C. Mainly used by outsiders. See THE DISTRICT.

**DEAD**

Traditional Black Church term to refer to the absence of spirit, emotion, enthusiasm. In the Church, the motto is "If you got religion, you oughta show some sign." 2) By extension, used in the world outside the Church to describe an absence of spirit or feeling in any situation. 3) Describes a situation, person, or event that has been put to rest or forgotten; out of style.

**DEAD CAT ON THE LINE**

Something suspicious.

**DEAD IT**

Leave something alone; kill it.

**DEAD PRESIDENTS**

Money; derived from the U.S. government's practice of print-ing pictures of U.S. presidents (dead ones only) on various de-nominations of paper currency. See also BENJAMINS, BIG FACES.

**DEAD RAG**

A dead gang member. From the style of wearing a scarf or hand-kerchief around the head to identify one's gang affiliation.

**THE DEAL**

The actual situation or state of things; how things stand at a particular point in time. Older crossover term resurfacing in HIP HOP.

**DEALIN**

See ROLLIN (newer term).

**DEATH EATING A SODA CRACKER / LOOKS LIKE DEATH EATING A SODA CRACKER**

Description of someone whose appearance has undergone a drastic change, often someone who has lost so much weight that he or she looks sick.

**DECOY**

A fake drug; a mixture sold as crack or cocaine that is nothing but a mishmash of baby powder, quinine, baking soda, and other fillers. Also GANKER.

**DEEP**

1) Expression of how large a group is. "Them BROTHAS was in that RIDE ten deep." 2) Serious; describes a person, thing, or event that has a powerful or profound meaning or impact.

**DEF**

Great, superb, excellent. Derived from an older expression, DO IT TO DEF, using the AAL pronunciation of "death." *Doin it to def* means doing something excellently, superbly—DOIN IT TO THE MAX. Also *boss, bumpin, cool, dope, dynamite, fresh, hip, humpin, hype, jammin, kickin, mean, monsta, outa sight, phat, pumpin, slammin, stoopid/stupid, terrible, vicious.* Older terms but still in use in some circles. *Down, on, raw, straight, sweet* (newer terms).

DELIVER

To perform something to the maximum. "The concert was hype; my girls, Boss [RAP group], shonuff delivered."

DEN

See CRIB.

DEUCE

Two; frequently used in HIP HOP, whereas "two" is very infrequently used.

DEUCE-AND-A-QUARTER

A Buick automobile, the Electra 225 model; once a very popular status symbol (older term).

DEUCE-DEUCE

1) 22-oz. malt liquor. 2) .22-caliber handgun.

DEUCE-FIVE

A .25-caliber handgun.

DEVIL

1) Any white person, equating whites with the sinister, immoral, and corrupt character of Satan. From the Nation of Islam's (see THE NATION) founding tenet about the introduction of evil into the ancient Black paradise through the unwise creation of YACUB, a scientist whose inventive curiosity went too far and produced a monstrous *devil*, the white man. In recent years, under the leadership of Minister Louis Farrakhan, The Nation has moderated its position in this regard. 2) In the vocabulary of the FIVE PERCENT NATION, which was established by former members of the Nation of Islam in 1964, *devil* was extended to include any person who, like the "Caucasian white man," is perceived as immoral, corrupt, sinister, and evil.

DIASPORA

A generic reference to the various geographical areas outside of

Africa where Africans were enslaved, principally North, South, and Central America and the Caribbean, i.e., the so-called New World.

**DICHTY**

Uppity-acting, putting on airs; haughty, arrogant. Also *saddidy* (newer term).

**DICK**

Penis.

**DICK-WHIPPED**

See DICK-WHUPPED.

**DICK-WHUPPED**

Describes a woman who is so in love that she lets her MAN rule her and boss her around; a woman victimized by sexual desire. Also *d-whupped, whupped.* Males in a similar situation are said to be PUSSY-WHUPPED.

**DIE**

See SHOOT THE DIE.

**DIESEL**

Used to describe a male who has a muscular, large-sized build. Also *cock diesel, cock strong; thick* (older term).

**DIG**

1) To understand, comprehend. Crossover meaning. 2) To like or love a person, event, or idea. This meaning has not crossed over. "I don't dig nobody messin wit my feelings." From the Wolof language, *dega,* "to understand."

**DIG ON**

To observe or pay attention to something.

**DIGITS**

1) A phone number, pager number, and/or address. 2) The amount of a check, usually a paycheck. A resurfacing and extension of the term *digit,* meaning a set of numbers, used in the heyday of the NUMBER GAME to refer to a number that fell (see FALL) or was played.

DIME

1) A woman who is beautiful, considered a "ten." Also *dime piece.*
2) Ten dollars. 3) Ten years; often used in reference to a prison
sentence. 4) A quantity of marijuana selling for ten dollars (a
*dime* BAG). Crossover meaning.

DIME PIECE

See DIME.

DIP

To leave.

DIPPED

All dressed up; dressed very well.

DIPPIN

Being nosy; sticking your nose into or getting involved in another person's business or conversation. Also *dippin and dabbin.*
See also A AND B CONVERSATION.

DIPPIN AND DABBIN

See DIPPIN.

DIS

1) To discount or show disrespect for a person; to put someone
or something down. *Time* magazine described a measure of
stock performance that was not widely accepted as having been
"dissed by the Dow." 2) In BID, the cards that are discarded by
the bidder before play begins. 3) An expression of disrespect; an
instance of "dissin." Crossover term.

THE DISTRICT

Washington, D.C., term used by longtime residents. Also *D.C.,*
term used by outsiders.

DIVA

1) A stately, grand woman, a "trophy," who may or may not be a
beauty. 2) A female RAPper or other musical entertainer who is
superbly talented. 3) By extension, any accomplished woman in
any walk of life.

DIVIDENDS

Money.

**DJ**

1) A technician who accompanies the Rapper in RAP Music. 2) A disc jockey in the traditional sense, who selects and plays music for an audience, either live or on the radio.

**DL**

Down low; refers to something kept very quiet and secretive; also something done on the sly. Also *down low, low-low.*

**DO**

1) To have sexual intercourse with someone. 2) To perform oral sex on someone. 3) To beat up or kill someone. 4) See CONK.

**DO A BID**

To serve time in prison. See also BID.

**DO A BIG**

To commit a robbery.

**DO A FACE**

To meet with someone face-to-face.

**DO A GHOST**

To leave.

**DO-DO** (pronounced *due-due*)

Nothing; something unimportant. "What he was talkin bout didn mean do-do to me."

**DO-IT-FLUID**

Liquor, usually gin, believed to increase a man's sexual stamina and potency.

**DO IT TO DEF**

See DEF.

**DO IT TO THE MAX**

1) To do something intensely, vigorously, strenuously. 2) To do something to the height of excellence.

**(HE/SHE) DO NOT PLAY**

Expression used to describe someone who is serious, determined, decisive, authoritative, no-nonsense. "Don't be late for work cause my girl do not play": advice to be on time for work because the female supervisor—"my girl"—is very serious about the job.

DO-RAG

1) A scarf, handkerchief, or STOCKING CAP worn by a male to keep his hair in place and preserve his DO. The term originated in the era when do's, PROCESSes, and CONKS were stylish. See also HEAD RAG. 2) Among gangs, a scarf or handkerchief worn around the head to identify gang affiliation.

DO YO / HIS / HER THANG

To behave, perform, or do something in a unique way, according to one's individual style; used in reference to an activity, wearing a certain hairstyle or style of clothes, playing a certain role in a group, a unique contribution to something, your creation or idea. From the Mandinka language, *ka a fen ke,* literally "to do one's thing." Also simply *yo Thang.* "Las Vegas? Not the KID; that's yo Thang" (said by a SISTA to her husband, indicating that she does not wish to go to Las Vegas because gambling is not her style but his). Also DO YO OWN THANG.

DR. THOMAS

See TOM.

DR. WATTS

A hymn in the Traditional Black Church, characterized by a call-response style in which the song is "lined out." A leader calls out each line, which is followed in turn by the congregation's slow, plaintive tones, elongating each syllable. The *Dr. Watts* hymns were created and published by a white Englishman, Isaac Watts (1674–1748), a pastor and composer of hundreds of hymns, whose language and style reflect the plain speech of everyday people. Watts becomes *Dr.* Watts by virtue of the Traditional Black Church practice of designating preachers as "doctors" who administer to the spirit. The hymns were passed on to enslaved Blacks along with the Protestant form of Christianity after the American Revolutionary War; the "lining-out" style of singing reflects the antiphonal nature of African songs and the

Black interactive style of communicating. Explicating how these
hymns got the name *Dr. Watts*, the Smithsonian scholar, musi-
cologist, and founder of Sweet Honey in the Rock, Bernice
Johnson Reagon, writes: "Another example of this kind of naming [of an entire genre of songs and singing style after one of its
major composers] occurred as the eighteenth- and nineteenth-
century African American Christians developed their own distinct style of lining the new Protestant hymns. They sang the
hymns of Charles Wesley and John Newton, but it was the lyrics
of Isaac Watts that resonated so deeply within the collective psyche of the congregation that even today, in some communities
that still practice the lining-out tradition, all lining hymns are
called 'Dr. Watts'" (*We'll Understand It Better By and By: Pio-
neering African American Gospel Composers*, Washington, D.C.:
Smithsonian Institution Press, 1992).

DODGERS

Cockroaches.

DOG

1) A form of address and greeting used mainly, but no longer exclusively, by and for males. Also one's close friend or associate. A
symbol of bonding, most likely derived from the African American fraternity tradition of referring to pledges as *dogs*, as in
"Alpha dogs," pledges of Alpha Phi Alpha fraternity. Although a
symbol of male bonding, "Yo, dog!" was misunderstood by a European American male psychiatrist treating an incarcerated
African American male. The psychiatrist thought the BROTHA
was insulting him by calling him a "dog" and ordered the Brotha
confined. 2) A sexually promiscuous man, who, like the dog,
might copulate with any female. 3) An ugly female (older meaning that has crossed over). 4) To mistreat someone. 5) To insult
someone; to criticize or talk about a person negatively. Also
DOG SOMEBODY OUT.

DOG SOMEBODY OUT

To criticize, insult.

**DOGS**

1) Gym shoes. 2) Feet (older meaning that has crossed over).

**DOME**

Head.

**DOME PIECE**

A hat.

**DON'T DEAL IN COAL**

Expression used to convey the idea that a person does not date or engage in romance with any dark-complexioned African American.

**DON'T GO THERE**

Do not probe any further in that area; reference to a negative area of discussion. Crossover expression.

**DON'T MAKE ME NONE**

It makes no difference to me; it's irrelevant to me.

**DOO-WAH-DIDDY**

See DOODLEY-SQUAT, crossover term. *Doo-wah-diddy,* however, has not crossed over.

**DOO-WOP**

A style of blended, harmonious singing done by a backup group rendering a refrain or background sound that roughly approximates "doo-wop" (or "doo-wah"); popular in the 1950s and during the MOTOWN era of Black Music in the 1960s and 1970s. Resurfacing in some 1990s groups, such as Boyz II Men. DIVA Lauryn Hill gives a brief historical rendition of the *doo-wop* sound in her "Doo Wop (That Thing)" JAM from *The Miseducation of Lauryn Hill* (1998).

**DOOBIE**

A marijuana cigarette, or marijuana itself. Term in process of crossing over.

**DOODLEY-SQUAT**

Nothing, or if something, something unimportant. Longstanding term in the Tradition. In *Mules & Men* (1935), Zora Neale Hurston (as participant anthropologist) counters Mr. Pitts's as-

sertion "Dey say youse rich" with the statement: "Oh, Ah ain't got
doodley squat." In the 1990s, phrase is often shortened to "squat":
"That don't mean squat to me, I ain wit that." Crossover term.

DOOFUS

Describes a person, event, or thing that is inadequate, sloppy,
disorganized, unHIP.

DOPE

1) See DEF. 2) Marijuana, crack, or any other illegal drug.

DOPE FIEND MOVE

A wild or bizarre action; an unexpected move of desperation to
accomplish a goal.

DOT DAT EYE

Basketball term, to make a basket in spite of being checked by an
opposing player, thus giving the defender a "black eye."

DOUBLE DEUCE

See DEUCE-DEUCE.

DOUBLE DUTCH

A game of jump rope, played by females, in which players have
to jump over two ropes instead of one, as the ropes are turned
around and over each other in an "eggbeater motion," alternat-
ing between slow and super-fast speeds, depending on the incli-
nation of the players turning the ropes for the jumpers. The
double rope style is believed to have been brought by the Dutch
when they settled in "New Amsterdam" (now New York City).
The game reflects the Africanized character of other Black children's games, for instance, using rhymed chants to accompany
the jumping of the ropes. *Double Dutch* became popular in
urban HOODS because it could be played anywhere and did not
require expensive equipment. It began as a male tradition, but
the SISTAS took it over in the twentieth century, and it has become a training ground for developing rhythm, coordination,
and style. According to the American Double Dutch League
(founded in New York City in 1974), the game requires "sharp
reflexes, precise motor skills, and an analytic acumen that en-

ables space-time coordination among players. Its styles, themes, and group practices embody cultural symbols useful in exploring and negotiating adolescent identity." In 1993, the Annual Double Dutch Tournament was held at Columbia University in New York, taking the Sistas' game right on outside the hood. The American Double Dutch League seeks to make the game a part of the Olympics. A highly competitive game testing dexterity, concentration, and the ability to maintain one's COOL, *Double Dutch* is the Sistas' B-BALL.

DOUBLE R

A Rolls-Royce.

DOUBLE-UPS

The act of purchasing crack on the basis of two quantities, usually small, for the price of one.

DOWN

1) Agreeable to something, ready to do something; WIT THE PROGRAM, whatever it is. "We gittin ready to make this move. You down?" 2) See DEF. "The concert was down." 3) Added to the end of a word or expression for emphasis. A BROTHA wearing impressive diamonds was described as "iced down." A SISTA on a one-week fruit fast said she was "fruited down."

DOWN BY LAW

1) Describes an expert or experienced professional in his/her work, occupation, or GAME, whatever it is. 2) By extension, describes somebody with high status, or anything that's superb.

DOWN FOR

1) Loyal to someone. 2) In favor of or agreeable to a plan or program. "The Sistas was down for the boycott."

DOWN FOR MINE

Able to protect oneself.

DOWN HOME

See HOME.

DOWN LOW

"Nobody has to know/Let's just keep it on the down low" (said in reference to a love affair between two people who were each involved with someone else). Also *DL, low-low.*

DOWN PAT

To have mastered or learned something perfectly, as a routine, a game, a system, or a technique of doing something. Crossover expression.

DOWN SOUTH

Any place south of the Mason-Dixon Line, once considered the most racist part of the United States. However, Malcolm X coined the expression *up South,* to SIGNIFY ON the mythical notion, held by Blacks for over a hundred years after Emancipation, that the U.S. North was free of segregation and racism.

DOWN WIT

1) Part of a group. 2) Supporting or endorsing a group or a program.

DOWN WIT THE NATION

1) Used to describe a member of the Nation of Islam, led by Minister Louis Farrakhan. See THE NATION. 2) Describes anybody who supports or endorses the Nation of Islam.

DOWNTOWN J

In basketball, a jump shot attempted a long distance from the basket.

THE DOZENS / PLAY THE DOZENS

A verbal game of talking negatively about someone's mother (or sometimes other relatives, but in the classic game, the target is the mother) by coming up with outlandish, highly exaggerated, sometimes sexually loaded, humorous ritual "insults"; played among friends, intimates, close associates, and/or those HIP to the rules of the game. The objective is to outtalk one's competitor, get the most laughs from onlookers, and not lose emotional control. A fundamental rule is that the "slander" must not be literally true because truth takes the game out of the realm of play into reality. *The Dozens* tests not only your verbal skills, but also the capacity to maintain your COOL. A 1990s example is: "Yo momma so dumb she thought a quarterback was a refund." The term, though not the social ritual itself, is believed to have originated during enslavement, in a sales practice whereby auctioneers would mix defective "merchandise"—sick or older slaves—with other slaves and sell the whole lot in groups of a dozen at a bargain price. Thus a slave who was part of a dozens group might turn out to be "inferior." The game itself can be found in several cultures in Africa. For example, the Efik in what is now Nigeria used playful "slander" such as "child of mixed sperm" (that is, you have more than one father, in other words, yo momma a ho). *The Dozens* has been around in the African American Oral Tradition for centuries. The first known written documentation was in 1891, in a folk song from Texas, which contained the lines: "Talk about one thing, talk about another/But ef you talk about me, I'm gwain to talk about your mother." Langston Hughes published a collection of poetry entitled *Ask Your Mama* (1961), in which he uses *the Dozens* to SIGNIFY ON white racism, in lines such as: "They rung my bell to ask me/Could I recommend a maid/I said yes, your mama...And they asked me right at Christmas/If my blackness, would it rub off? I said, ask your mama." Among the "ceremonial insults" in scholar and folklorist J. Mason Brewer's 1968 collection are several "Dirty Dozens" lyrics that date back more than a century, such as: "Yo' mama's in de kitchen; yo' papa's in jail/Yo' sister's round de corner, hollerin' 'Hot stuff for sale.'" Although women play the game, it is more often played by men; women tend to SIGNIFY more so than *play the Dozens*. See also SNAPS (1990s term).

**DP**

Dom Perignon. Very expensive French champagne, touted as the oldest champagne on the market. Prices in 1999 ranged from $110 for a bottle of 1990 vintage to $375 for 1966 vintage. The drink of choice for many BIG WILLIE PLAYAS as well as the WANNABES.

DRAG

1) To deceive someone with a scheme of some kind, to con a person. Also *run a drag on.* 2) A person who puts a damper on the fun, a party, or other activity.

DRAMA

A situation of emotional distress, turmoil, or conflict; may be used in reference to any state of affairs or event. *Hustler* magazine publisher Larry Flynt's exposé of the marital infidelity of congressional officials during the Clinton impeachment trial was referred to as the "Flynt drama down in D.C." A snowstorm that tied up traffic, caused accidents, forced drivers to abandon their cars (unnecessarily, due to city officials' negligence) was referred to as the "snow drama." The *drama* may be perceived as affected, overindulgent, and exaggerated for effect, to arouse a response or to manipulate a person. Speaking of her retired and bored parents, a SISTA said, "I don't visit them too often, I can't handle it, too much drama."

DRAPED

Describes a person wearing a lot of gold jewelry.

DRAWS

Underpants (panties, undershorts). From "drawers."

DREADLOCKS

A natural hairstyle created by growing one's hair without combing it for several weeks or months; instead, the hair is twisted, and beeswax, coconut oil, and peanut oil are applied; the hair naturally develops into *locks,* loose, thick braids. Popularized by RASTAFARIAN musicians from the Caribbean, perhaps the most well-known being the late Bob Marley, *dreadlocks* epitomized Black rejection of Western society and what journalist Kenneth M. Jones called "a different kind of cool...the walk of Black spirits reaching back to Africa"

(*Essence,* October 1985). Worn by Rappers and other Blacks (both in and outside of HIP HOP Culture), *dreadlocks* have gained popularity beyond the RASTAS. Also *dreads.* See also RASTAFARIA.

DREADS

See DREADLOCKS.

DREAM BOOK

A book listing common dreams, names, events, and the numbers symbolizing these things; consulted by those who PLAY THE NUMBERS and/or the lottery in the belief that a dream represents good fortune if one can only interpet it accurately in order to get the lucky number that will be the winner. One very popular dream book during the heyday of the NUMBERS, and one still in use today by those who play the new state-controlled lotteries, is *The Three Wise Men.*

DRIVE-BY

A shooting done from a vehicle whose occupants shoot at someone on the street, often in disregard of innocent bystanders, and then drive on. "They call me 'Lucky' cause I been in five drive-bys and still here" (from the 1992 film *Trespass*). Crossing over into mainstream use in reference to nonviolent random or casual actions or behavior.

DRIVING WHILE BLACK

See DWB.

DROP

1) To enlighten; to inform; to explain. "Let me drop some science," that is, I'll explain the facts to you. 2) To release a CD or song.

DROP A DIME

To tell on somebody who is doing something wrong or illegal by reporting that person's activities to somebody who has power over the person committing the wrong. "We use to go over there all the time—fuck school—until one day somebody dropped a dime on us, and the counselor [the school counselor, to whom the informant had talked] tol my momma, and the shit hit the fan." A *dime* can be *dropped* to any authority figure—the police, a government agency (such as the IRS), a welfare office, a parent, or a school official. From the time when local public telephone calls cost a dime.

**DROP A LINE**

1) To initiate a conversation or otherwise indicate interest in developing a relationship with someone. 2) To call someone on the telephone.

**DROP A LUG**

To put someone down, either seriously or in fun (older term). Also *cap on, signify on, dis* (newer terms).

**DROP IT**

A verbal signal to begin, to start something.

**DROP SCIENCE**

To enlighten, to convey knowledge, information, facts, wisdom. Also *drop jewels, drop knowledge.*

**DROP TOP**

A car with a fabric top that can be lowered; a convertible. Older term resurfacing in HIP HOP: "I gotta go cause I got me a drop top / and if I hit the switch, I can make the ass drop" (that is, activate the LIFTS switch, thus raising the front end of the car and lowering the rear end), from Ice Cube's "It Was a Good Day" on his 1992 album, *The Predator.*

**DROPPIN BABIES**

Having a lot of children.

**DUCKETTES**

Money.

**DUDE**

A generic reference to any male. Used in reference to a male, but not as a form of direct address. Thus: "Ain't none of these dudes bad enough to beat me," but *not* "Hey, dude, how you doin?"

**DUES**

See PAY DUES.

**DUKE**

To fight.

**DUKIE**

Euphemism for SHIT.

**DUKIE BRAIDS**

Very large braids, usually worn by women. See BRAIDS.

**DUKIE CHAIN**

Very large gold rope-type chain, worn around the neck.

**DUKS**

See DAZZEY DUKS.

**DUMMY UP**

To become immobile, to freeze up, to become scared or tense in a situation. "When that big dog came rushing out, she just dummied up."

**DUNK**

1) In basketball, to drop the ball into the basket from a position above the rim. 2) By extension, to outdo or beat opponents or rivals by not playing by the usual rules, allowing them the chance to "block" your "shots," but instead pulling an aggressive surprise move "over their heads." A businessman lost a deal to a competitor, who used an unexpected, unusual business tactic to win the deal: "What can I say? Johnson beat me out, just dunked on me." See also SLAM-DUNK.

**DUST**

To add the drug PCP to marijuana.

**DUSTED**

1) High on the drug PCP. See also ANGEL DUST. 2) Outlandish or outrageous.

**DUTCHMASTER**

A cigar used to roll a BLUNT by removing the tobacco and replacing it with marijuana.

## DWB

Driving while Black (or Brown if used in reference to Latinos). Refers to local and state police traffic stops of African American motorists, particularly males, for no apparent reason. The motorist is generally not given an explanation for the traffic stop, and often no ticket is issued, leading to the conclusion that the person's "offense" was simply "driving while Black." A September 1998 *Vibe* magazine article ("Power: The Usual Suspects," by Melba Newsome) reported that in the Maryland area, Blacks account for 17 percent of the 111 million travelers on Highway I-95 each year, yet they make up 70 percent of the traffic stops. In Orange County, Florida, the drug squad that patrols the Florida Turnpike conducted more than six times as many searches on Black motorists who had been pulled over in traffic as on white motorists (*Detroit News*, April 26, 1998). And in Boston, in early December 1998, in a case believed to be the first of its kind, federal judge Nancy Gertner of the U.S. district court reduced the sentence of a Black man charged with gun possession because the large number of minor traffic offenses on his record raised "deep concerns about racial disparity" (reported in the *New York Times*, December 17, 1998). And it isn't just Maryland or Florida or Boston, but a growing, pervasive problem across the United States. This national crisis was a cover story in *Emerge* magazine (June 1999). According to African American congressman John Conyers, African Americans represent only 14 percent of the U.S. population, but they account for 72 percent of all routine traffic stops (Conyers, in the *Michigan Chronicle*, July 1–7, 1998). For that reason, Conyers introduced the Traffic Stops Statistics Act in 1998 and 1999 (not approved as of this writing in June 1999). The American Civil Liberties Union has set up a national DWB hot line [1-877-6-PROFILE].

## DYNAMITE

Excellent, great. Crossover term. See DEF, for newer HIP HOP terms.

# E

**EAGLE FLIES**

1) Statement used to refer to one's payday. From the symbol of the eagle on some U.S. currency. A recurring refrain in many traditional Blues songs: "The eagle flies on Friday, and Saturday I go out to play." 2) By extension, a reference to getting money from any source. See also GIT PAID.

**EAGLE-FLYIN DAY**

The day you get paid, either from a regular paycheck or from some other source. See also EAGLE FLIES.

**EARTH**

A woman, in the language of the FIVE PERCENT NATION.

**EARTHLY THINGS**

Traditional Black Church term referring to things you can see or feel.

**EASY**

Goodbye, see you later (older term). Also *I'm out, outa here, Outtie 5000*.

**EAT CHEESE**

To perform oral sex on a woman.

**EBONICS**

The Africanized language of U.S. Blacks and other Africans throughout the DIASPORA (such as the English Creole spoken by Jamaicans, the French Creole spoken by Haitians). A mixture of African and European languages. The term remains controversial in some mainstream groups; however, HIP HOP Culture seems not to share this perception. Some see the term as simply a neutral or generic label for a certain Black style of speaking; for instance, Brett Johnson refers to a "nonexistent trend toward corporate Ebonics" (in "Media Watch," *The Source,* November 1998). Some view the Ebonics issue that emerged from Oakland, California, onto the national scene as yet another example of the generational divide in African America. Bill Stephney, of Stepsun Records, says that the forty-five-plus crowd "are the same ones who have been dismissive of Hip-Hop ...There is a segment of the older Black generation, the middle class, the civil rights leadership, that is anti-youth. Most of them have no idea if Ebonics works as a method of reaching Black students" (quoted in David Kelly's article on Ebonics in *The Source,* April 1997). Some members of the Hip Hop generation loudly celebrate both the term "Ebonics" and the language. The late Hip Hop artist Big L., in his 1998 JAM "Ebonics," gives a lesson in Ebonics, using a kind of Ebonics glossary with interlocking rhymes, flaunting his vocabulary SKILLZ and his ability to FLOW. There is at least a segment of the older generation that is in concert with Hip Hop. Despite the national controversy unleashed when the Oakland School Board passed its resolution on Ebonics and the education of the district's African American youth in December 1996, the term has been used without controversy or incident by some Black scholars since 1973, when it was coined. Clinical psychologist Dr. Robert L. Williams, now professor emeritus at Washington University in St. Louis, coined the term at a 1973 conference on language and the urban Black child, which he convened under the auspices of what was then the Institute of Black Studies. In 1975, Williams published the book of conference papers and proceedings *Ebonics: The True Language of Black Folks.* In the Preface and Introduction, Williams writes: "A significant incident occurred at the conference. The black conferees were so critical of the work on the subject done by white researchers, many of whom also happened to be present, that they decided to caucus among themselves and define black language from a black perspective. It was in this caucus that the term Ebonics was created...[It] may be defined as 'the linguistic and paralinguistic features which on a concentric continuum represent the communicative competence of the West African, Caribbean, and United States slave descendant of African origin. It includes the various idioms, patois, argots, ideolects, and social dialects of black people,' especially those who have been forced to adapt to colonial circumstances. **Ebonics** derives its form from ebony (black) and phonics (sound, the study of sound) and refers to the study of the language of black people in all its cultural uniqueness."

EDGES

The hairline, the first part to GO BACK after hair has been STRAIGHTENed.

EDUCATED FOOL

A person with formal, "book" education, but no common sense, no MOTHER WIT.

EIGHT BALL

1) Olde English 800 malt liquor. Also *O.E.* (newer term). 2) Cocaine and speed mixed together. 3) One-eighth of an ounce of cocaine.

EIGHT ROCK

A very dark-complexioned African American.

EIGHT-SIX

To stop a planned activity or kill a course of action.

EIGHT TRACK

Two and a half grams of cocaine.

E-LIGHT

1) An uppity-acting, elitist African American, usually well educated and materially well-off, who looks down on less fortunate African Americans. 2) A European American–thinking Black who doesn't identify with the race or Black causes. Probably a play on the word "elite."

EL PEE
>An El Producto brand cigar, used to roll a BLUNT.

ELDERS
>1) Older men, usually leaders, in the Traditional Black Church.
>2) By extension, politically and spiritually developed, older wise men and women, whether in the Church or not.

THE ELECTRIC SLIDE
>See THE HUSTLE.

ENDS
>See N's.

THE ENEMY
>Traditional Black Church term for the devil, the forces of evil; can also refer to a person or thing that the devil is using to wreak havoc and negativity in a person's life. "See when that happened, and he came on me like that, I knew it wasn't nothin but the enemy."

ESSEYS
>HOMEYS of Hispanic/Latino descent. Derived from the popular greeting in Chicano Spanish, "Ese," loosely meaning, "Hey, man."

EUROPEAN AMERICAN
>An emerging term to replace "white American"; more precise in indicating the land of origin of the "white race," just as AFRICAN AMERICAN indicates the land of origin of U.S. Blacks. It brings the term for whites in line with racial labels for other groups in the United States, and is viewed as a healthy move away from the connotations of racial supremacy associated with the designation "white."

EUROPEAN NEGRO
>An African American who thinks like and identifies with European Americans, and who rejects Black causes and the Black community. Also *Afro-Saxon* (older term).

**EVERYTHANG IS EVERYTHANG**

Suggests the connectedness or oneness of people, places, events. Conveys the notion that things are as they should be, that everything is OKAY.

**EVIL**

Negative in disposition, disagreeable; mean-spirited (but not sinful). Describes a person with a bad—meaning "not good"—TUDE. "Can't nobody say nothin to him; he is one evil ol man."

**EVIL EYE**

A certain kind of look at a person that exhibits disapproval or anger. Stems from the belief that a person's eye has the power to bring bad luck or destruction upon somebody.

**EXTENSIONS**

Synthetic or human hair braided into one's own hair to create intricate styles.

**EYE BUSTED**

In pick-up B-BALL, used by an opposing player to taunt or belittle a defender when the opposing team makes a basket even though the defender was playing tight defense. "Yo, nigga, yall can't check us, you got that eye busted!" (That is, your eye was

By permission of the artist, Craig Rex Perry, and *Young Sisters and Brothers Magazine*.

not keen enough to discern and block the move, and so we were able to score.)

F
> Euphemism for FUCK.

F-IN
> Euphemism for FUCKin.

FADE¹
> A male hairstyle, high on top and very short or completely shaved on the sides and back; the top can be NATURAL or dreaded (see DREADLOCKS). Also *cameo cut, high top fade.*

FADE²
> To cause problems for somebody; generally used in the negative. "Don't fade me."

FADED
> 1) Out of style. 2) Old. 3) Overused. 4) Drunk.

FAG
> Short for "faggot." Derogatory term for a gay male. Though still in use, this is an older term that probably dates to the early 1900s, according to Clarence Major (*Juba to Jive,* 1994).

FAIR
> Used to describe an African American with a light skin color. Also *fair-skin, bright, yella, high yella, light-skin.*

FAIR-SKIN
> See FAIR.

FAKE OUT
> In basketball, to throw one's opponent off by pretending to make one move while actually making another.

**FALL**

Used in reference to the number that wins for the day (see NUMBERS). Also *fall out.*

**FALL OUT**

1) Used not only in reference to disagreement with a person, but also to dissatisfaction or severance of a relationship. "I'm gon fall all the way out with High-Tech Appliance if they don't stop raising they prices every other month." 2) To faint. 3) Used in reference to losing one's hair, not only from the natural process of getting bald, but also from a PERM or other unnatural event or condition, such as mental stress. Also *come out.* 4) Used in reference to the number that wins for the day. (See NUMBERS.) "Girl, don't you know I should be whupped, my name fell out today." That is, the set of numbers that symbolizes the speaker's name was the winning number for the day, but she didn't play it. (See DREAM BOOK.) Also *fall.* 5) To laugh hysterically and hard, such that one might "fall out" or collapse. "That fool Chris Rock [a comic] had me laughing so hard I liketa fell out."

**FAM**

Abbreviated form of "family." Refers not to one's blood kin, but to a group with which one strongly identifies, sometimes closer than blood kin. "Them Jersey cats hangin on the corner is my fam" (*The Source,* January 1998).

**FAMILIAR**

Acting outside acceptable social boundaries so as to suggest that you are on personal, intimate terms with somebody when, in fact, you are not. Often used to criticize inappropriate behavior toward the opposite sex. "One thang I don't like bout him, he act too familiar for me."

**FASS**

Describes a female who is acting grown-up (WOMNISH), especially in a sexual manner. The AAL pronunciation of "fast."

**FAT**

See *phat.*

FAT MAN AGAINST THE HOLE IN A DOUGHNUT

Used to express certainty about one's prediction or argument; indicates a willingness to risk everything against nothing due to a belief in the accuracy of one's prediction. "I bet you a fat man against the hole in a doughnut that Iron Mike [prizefighter Mike Tyson] can't make no comeback."

FAT MOUTH

1) To talk too much, especially about something one can't back up with facts. 2) To make wild, outlandish threats that one doesn't have the power or guts to execute. "Dat nigga don't want no action. He just fat mouthin." The term MURDER MOUTH also has this meaning. From the Mandinka language spoken by the Mandingo people, *da-ba*, "excessive talking," literally "big, fat mouth." *Fat mouth* has crossed over, but *murder mouth* has not.

FAY

See OFAY.

FEDERATED

Wearing excessive red, the color of the Los Angeles gang the BLOODS; used by their former rivals, the CRIPS, as a DIS.

FEDERELLIS

Federal law enforcement agents, in particular the F.B.I. (Federal Bureau of Investigation).

FEED SOMEBODY THE PILL

In basketball, to pass the ball to somebody.

FEEL YA

I feel you. That is, I understand you and empathize with your point.

FELL OFF

1) To have lost a lot of weight. 2) By extension, to have lost status, standing, and stature in a field. "Yall thought I had fell off, didn't you," says the Rapper YoYo in her duet with Rapper Ice Cube in their JAM "Bonnie and Clyde Theme."

FESS

1) To fake something; to pretend to be something you're not. 2) To promise to do something that you aren't really going to do.

FIELD NIGGA

An African American in the working class, or *un*-working class, i.e., Blacks laid off, unable to find work, or otherwise unemployed. Historically, an enslaved African who worked in the fields, as opposed to the HOUSE NIGGA, an enslaved African who worked in Ole Massa's household. The *field nigga* was believed to be more predisposed toward rebellion against enslavement than the HOUSE NIGGA, who was viewed as loyal to Massa. The historical roles were updated in the 1960s by Malcolm X, who asserted that those Blacks who were working-class, unemployed, and outside the system—*field niggas*—were likely to reject and rise up against racism and the system, since they were in it but not of it, whereas the African American middle and professional classes—HOUSE NIGGAS—were more likely to deny the existence of racism or make excuses for it, to identify with whites and the system, and thus unlikely to engage in protest or REBELLION.

FIEND

A person with a drug problem.

FIENDIN

Wanting something very badly, so much so that one is feeling and/or acting like a person addicted to drugs, a "dope fiend."

FIFTY-ONE

A cigarette that is part marijuana and part crack cocaine. Also *primo, roulie, sleef, spleefer.*

FIGURE

The winning number for the day in the NUMBER GAME or the lottery.

FINE

Good-looking; used for males or females.

**FINESSE**[1]

To smooth over something that has the potential for conflict or trouble; to use diplomacy in a SLICK way.

**FINESSE**[2]

Diplomacy; a type of SLICKness.

**FIRE IT UP**

To light a marijuana cigarette. Also *blaze up*.

**THE FIRST**

An expression tacked onto a statement to indicate that something has not been started even though it should have been. "Uhm spozed to be studyin, ain cracked book the first." That is, even though I am supposed to be studying, I have not even opened a book.

**FIRST MIND**

The initial idea or thought that a person has about something, believed to be the best course of action because *first mind* ideas come from intuition and natural instinct, untainted by the conscious mind. "If I had followed my first mind and played the dead role, I'd be rich now," meaning, If the speaker had played the number that symbolizes death, she would have HIT THE NUMBER for a large sum of money.

**FISH**

Euphemism for PUSSY.

**FIVE**

A slapping of palms to show affirmation, strong agreement, celebration of victory; also used as a greeting. Derived from a West African communication style, as in the Mandinka language, spoken by the Mandingo people, *i golo don m bolo,* literally "put your skin in my hand," a phrase used to accompany another phrase or statement requesting the listener's show of affirmation. African American women's five involves sliding one's forefinger across the forefinger of the other SISTA, and for the HIGH FIVE, touch forefingers with the hands held high. See

also FIVE ON THE BLACK-HAND SIDE, FIVE ON THE
SLY, HIGH FIVE, LOW FIVE, GIVE SOMEBODY FIVE,
GIVE SOMEBODY SOME SKIN.

FIVE AND DIME

Poorly dressed; showing bad taste in clothes.

FIVE HUNDRED

See BEAMER. A luxury Mercedes-Benz, 500-S class.

FIVE-O (pronounced *five-OH*)

The police; probably derived from the television show "Hawaii
Five-O." Also *The Man,* older term that has crossed over.

FIVE ON THE BLACK-HAND SIDE

A FIVE on the outer side of the hand rather than the palm side,
that is, on the darker, "Black-hand" side.

FIVE ON THE SLY

A FIVE with the hands held behind the back, down low, done
surreptitiously to assert camaraderie without the awareness of
onlookers.

FIVE PERCENT NATION

A group established by former members of the Nation of Islam
(see THE NATION) in 1964 under the leadership of Clarence
"Pudding" 13X. The name derives from the belief that only five
percent of humanity live a proper life, in accord with the "true
divine nature of the Black man who is God or Allah," and that
only those five percent will one day reign supreme. Also known
now as "The Nation of Gods and Earths," the *Five Percenters*
have had a significant impact on youth. According to Professor
Yusuf Nuruddin, of Medgar Evers College in New York: "The influence of the Five Percent Nation...has grown enormously....
[They have produced] offshoot or cognate groups that espouse
a similar ideology; one such group is the Zulu Nation in the
South Bronx....Many of the lyrics in contemporary Rap Music
make direct reference or strong allusion to Five Percenter ideology" (from "The Five Percenters: A Teenage Nation of Gods and

Earths," in *Muslim Communities in North America,* edited by Yvonne Yazbeck Haddad and Jane Idleman Smith, State University of New York Press at Albany, 1994).

FLAKY

Unreliable, shaky.

FLAT TOP

A hairstyle that is high, square, and flat on top; generally, but not exclusively, male. Similar to a FADE, but a fade can also be dreaded (see DREADLOCKS) on top.

FLAVA

1) Attractiveness. 2) Style.

FLEX

To try to impress people by showing off; used especially of males who try to impress by acting macho.

FLIP THE SCRIPT

To reverse the meaning of unfavorable words and statements by recasting the "script" from your perspective; to change the outcome of a debate or a judgment about an issue by reversing the terms of the argument. A kind of semantic inversion wherein "bad" becomes "good," and the tables are turned—in your favor.

FLOSSIN

Pretending, faking something; putting on a front; trying to appear calm and cool.

FLOW

To RAP very well.

FLY

A dance popular in the 1970s.

FLY¹

1) Exciting, dazzling, upscale, in the know. 2) Attractive. See also ON THE FLY, SUPERFLY.

FLY²

See JET (newer term). See also TRUCKIN.

By permission of the artist, Craig Rex Perry.

FOE-BY

A four-wheel-drive vehicle, such as a jeep. "Foe" is the AAL rendering of "four."

FOE DAY

Before daybreak. AAL rendering of "before day."

FOE-ONE-ONE (4-1-1)

The facts, the information on something, THE DEAL. From the telephone number 4-1-1, which was once commonly used to dial the operator to get telephone numbers—"Information," now "Directory Assistance." As Black Talk, the term dates from the 1960s; resurfaced in HIP HOP, as in Mary J. Blige's 1992 album and title song *What's the 4-1-1?* First used in African American music by Aretha Franklin: "Now, Kitty, you know when we talk, we have a lot of fun, don't we, girl? Dishing out the dirt on everybody and giving each other the 4-1-1 on who drop-kicked who this week" (from "Jump to It," the title JAM on her 1982 album, written and produced by Luther Vandross). AAL rendering of "four-one-one."

FOLK / FOLKS

1) African Americans. 2) A generic term for gang members, used particularly by those in prison to conceal their identity as gang members from prison authorities.

FOLKS

The name of a gang in southeastern Michigan.

FOR DAYS

1) For a very long time, so long that you've lost track of the time. "I couldn't get nothin done cause she stayed here for days." 2) A lot of. "At this club, there was cowboys for days."

FOR THE DURATION

For the remaining life or existence of something. "I thought she was going to be out of the country for the duration," said in reference to a Black expatriate, meaning, for the rest of her life. Crossover expression.

FORE DAY

See FOE DAY.

FORGET IT / YOU / THAT / etc.

See FUHGIT IT / YOU / THAT / HIM

FORTY

A forty-ounce bottle of malt liquor, which has higher alcohol content than beer; mostly sold in urban, inner-city HOODS. Also *forty dog, forty ounce.*

FORTY ACRES

See FORTY ACRES AND A MULE.

FORTY ACRES AND A MULE

Symbolic of reparations for enslavement; a recurring phrase in Black Culture and throughout the African American Experience since the Civil War. Filmmaker Spike Lee uses this phrase as the name of his production company. In 1865, Black preachers and other local leaders in Savannah, Georgia, met with Union General William T. Sherman and indicated that freedom meant having their own land. Sherman issued an order for each ex-enslaved family to receive forty acres of land in coastal South Carolina and Georgia, and for the army to loan them mules. In 1866, Congress attempted to make Sherman's Special Field Order No. 15 official goverment policy by the passage of a bill strengthening the Freedmen's Bureau and authorizing it to make forty acres of land from confiscated Confederate property available to each household of ex-slaves. This legislation was designed to make them self-sufficient and to compensate for 246 years of free labor. At the time of President Lincoln's Emancipation Proclamation, the four million "freedmen" had nothing, not even homes. However, this opportunity to establish a base of self-sufficiency for themselves and for future generations was not to be realized. President Andrew Johnson vetoed the bill, and Congress was unwilling, or unable, to override the veto. The total value of the *forty acres* today is estimated to be between three hundred and five hundred billion dollars. The Reparations Movement was reactivated with the establishment of N'COBRA (National Coalition of Blacks for Reparations for African Americans), headquartered in D.C., and the introduction of Congressional Bill H.R. 40 (House Resolution 40) by Congressman John Conyers. The more formal title of H.R. 40 is the Commission to Study Reparation Proposals for African Americans Act. Conyers introduced it in 1989, and it has been reintroduced in every congressional session since that time, most recently in the 106th Congress on January 6, 1999. The bill calls for the establishment of a commission to study the reparations issue, enslavement from 1619 to 1865, and the impact of over one hundred years of racial segregation since 1877 (the end of Reconstruction). Curiously, the report issued by Bill Clinton's Presidential Initiative on Race Commission, after fifteen months of study, did not address the issue of reparations. Although "and a mule" does not appear in the 1866 bill, the phrase results from Sherman's actions, combined with the wording in Congress's bill about "provisions and supplies" to be issued to the suffering freedmen. Also *forty acres, fifty dollars, and a mule.*

FORTY ACRES, FIFTY DOLLARS, AND A MULE
   See FORTY ACRES AND A MULE.

**FORTY DOG**

See FORTY.

**FORTY OUNCE**

See FORTY.

**FOUL**

1) Wrong; describes something that is not done properly. 2) Unprincipled. 3) Self-destructive.

**FOUR-BY**

See FOE-BY.

**FOUR-ONE-ONE**

See FOE-ONE-ONE.

**FOX**

A good-looking female. Also *stallion, star.*

**FOXY**

Good-looking, attractive; used for females. Crossover term.

**FRANKLIN FACES**

$100 bills, from Benjamin Franklin's picture on those bills. See also BENJAMINS, BIG FACES, DEAD PRESIDENTS.

**FREAK**

1) A person, male or female, whose sexual practices have no limitations, who will do anything sexually. 2) A generic term for any female; resented by most women when used by men. 3) To dance in a sexually provocative style.

**FREEBASE**

See BASE.

**FREESTYLE**

1) To perform spontaneous, unrehearsed RAP. 2) To DO YO OWN THANG, wear your own unique style of clothes or haircut, etc.

**FRESH**

See DEF.

**FRIED, DYED, AND LAID TO THE SIDE**

Describes hair that has been artificially STRAIGHTENed (*fried*) using a HOT COMB, creating a style with the hair pressed close to the head; the hair may also be dyed a loud, flashy color, such as flaming red, blond, etc.

FRO

See AFRO.

FROG

A promiscuous person; one who hops and jumps—like a frog—into anybody's bed.

FROGGY

See IF YOU FEEL FROGGY, LEAP!

FROM AMAZING GRACE TO FLOATING OPPORTUNITY

Expression used to emphasize a person's intention not to go along with a particular course of action; demonstrating intense disagreement with someone's viewpoint or actions. "You can talk from amazing grace to floating opportunity, I still ain gon do it." Also *from appetite to asshole.*

FROM APPETITE TO ASSHOLE

See FROM AMAZING GRACE TO FLOATING OPPORTUNITY.

FROM GIDDYUP / GIDDAYUP

See FROM JUMPSTREET.

FROM JUMPSTREET

From the beginning point of something; from the start. Also *from Giddyup/Giddayup, from the Git-Go, from the Jump/from Jump, from the Rip.*

FROM THE GIT-GO

Crossover expression. See FROM JUMPSTREET.

FROM THE JUMP / FROM JUMP

See FROM JUMPSTREET.

FROM THE RIP

See FROM JUMPSTREET.

FRONT[1]

1) A fraudulent person; someone who's not for real. 2) Gold caps on the front teeth. Also *gold front, mouthpiece.*

**FRONT**[2]

1) To pretend. 2) To confront someone about something they supposedly are doing or should have done (older usage). Also *front somebody off, put somebody on front street.*

**FRONT AND CENTER**

Right this minute.

**FRONT ON SOMEBODY**

To deceive someone.

**FRONT SOMEBODY OFF**

See FRONT[2].

**FRONT STREET**

The state of being on public display, vulnerable to attack or accusation, including physical attack; a position of accountability for one's words and/or deeds. See also PUT SOMEBODY ON FRONT STREET.

**FRUIT**

The Fruit of Islam, the security force of the Nation of Islam (see THE NATION).

**FRY**

To STRAIGHTEN the hair using a HOT COMB. Older term still in current use, especially among Black seniors; dates to the 1930s, appeared in Cab Calloway's *Hepster's Dictionary* (1938).

**FUCK**[1]

Used in reference to various nonsexual events to show emphasis or indicate disapproval. "I don't give a fuck," meaning, I do not care, it is irrelevant to me; "What in the fuck did you think you was doin?" meaning, What you did was extraordinarily wrong.

**FUCK**[2]

Used to dismiss something or someone as irrelevant or unimportant, in the sense of "forget that." See also FUHGIT IT / YOU / THAT / HIM.

**FUCKED UP**

1) Drunk on liquor or high on drugs. 2) Confused, disorganized,

distraught because of something that has occurred. 3) Beaten up.

FUHGIT IT / YOU / THAT / HIM

Euphemism for *fuck it/you/that/him/* etc. This expression uses the word "forget," rendered according to the pronunciation system of AAL.

FULL FACE

A complete application of makeup to the face, including the eyes and mouth.

FULL OF SHIT

Describes a person who is empty, full of nothing, who talks a good game but doesn't produce or follow through.

FUNDS

Money.

FUNK

1) The musical sound of jazz, the blues, work songs, Rhythm 'n' Blues, and African American music generally. 2) The quality of being soulful, FUNKY. 3) A bad smell; an unpleasant odor. 4) Euphemism for *fuck,* in its sexual meaning.

FUNKY

1) Very soulful; by extension, down-to-earth, the real nitty-gritty or essence of life. 2) In touch with the fundamental essence of life; in touch with one's body and spirit. 3) Describes the sound of FUNK, used as early as 1900 in the New Orleans jazz scene. 4) Having a bad smell; an unpleasant odor. 5) Acting unpleasant, disagreeable.

FUNKY FRESH

Older HIP HOP phrase to describe something that is super, exceptional, superior to FRESH. See also DEF.

**G**

A form of address for a male, usually one who is HIP or DOWN. From the FIVE PERCENT NATION's terminology. "G" is the seventh letter of the alphabet and represents "God"; in Five Percent ideology, the Black man is considered God.

**G**

To have sex.

**G-RIDE**

A stolen car.

**G THANG**

1) A reference to an experience, feeling, way of thinking, event, etc., that pertains to males, usually those who are DOWN. 2) A GANGSTA Thang.

**GAFFLE**

1) To rob, steal. 2) To cheat; run a con or scam on somebody. Also *gank*.

**GAME**

1) A series of activities and maneuvers to achieve a goal. 2) A story or RAP for obtaining what you want, used for manipulative and deceptive purposes. 3) A style of carrying and expressing oneself that enables one to achieve a desired end; to lack this style is referred to as "not having any *game*." 4) Criminal activities.

**GANGBANGER**

See BANGER.

**GANGBANGIN**

Belonging to a gang and participating in its activities. Also *bangin*.

**GANGSTA**

1) Used to refer to any event, activity, behavior, person, or object that represents a rejection of mainstream society's standards. 2) A rebellious, nonconformist person, a social "outlaw" who refuses to buckle under to white authority and white norms and is thus revered. Both meanings reflect a resurfacing and extension of the 1960s/70s concept of *gangsta,* referring to street life and street culture. 3) Marijuana. Also *ganja* (newer term, showing Caribbean influence).

**GANGSTA CLASS**

Characteristic of GANGSTAS; COOL; DOWN.

**GANGSTA LEAN**

A posture of leaning to the right side and slouching down while driving a car.

**GANGSTA LIMP**

A male style of walking or strutting with a slight dip in the stride; projecting a COOL, FLY, HIP image by the style of walking. Also *gangsta walk; pimp walk, pimp strut, cat walk, catting* (older terms).

**GANGSTA ROLL**

A large wad of paper money; a lot of money carried by a person.

**GANGSTA WALK**

See GANGSTA LIMP.

**GANGSTA WALLS**

White sidewall car tires; considered flamboyant and FLY; very popular in the 1960s and 1970s.

**GANJA**

Marijuana. Also *ganja weed; gangsta* (older term).

**GANJA WEED**

See GANJA.

**GANK**

See GAFFLE.

GANKER

See DECOY.

GAP MOUTH[1]

Describes a person who has a space (gap) between the upper middle two front teeth; perceived as sensual and sexy. Also *gap tooth*.

GAP MOUTH[2]

1) A person who tells your business; a "big mouth." 2) A person who has a reputation for performing oral sex.

GAP TOOTH

See GAP MOUTH[1].

GAS UP

1) To mess up. 2) To fill a person with flattery, "hot air."

GAT

A gun. Older term resurfacing in HIP HOP. Also *gauge*.

GATAS

Shoes made from alligator skins; very expensive, and popular as a symbol of success, especially among males.

GAUGE

See GAT.

G'D UP

Dressed up, according to whatever one's standards are. Probably a resurfacing and modification of GEARED UP (older term).

GEAR

Clothes. Probably a resurfacing and variation of GEARED UP (older term).

GEARED UP

See G'D UP (newer term).

GEE MO NITTY!

An expression of exasperation or bewilderment. "How many times I gotta explain it? Gee mo nitty!"

GEEK[1]

An unHIP person; a SQUARE.

By permission of the artist, Craig Rex Perry, and *Young Sisters and Brothers Magazine.*

GEEK[2] / GEEK UP

In a general state of exuberance, enthusiasm, excitement about something. AAL pronunciation of "geeked." Also *amp* (newer term).

GELEE (pronounced *gay-lay*)

A turban-style African headwrap worn by women.

GET A NUT, GET BUSY, etc.

See GIT A NUT, GIT BUSY, etc.

GHETTO

Refers to the African American community that is generally located in the core area of a city ("inner city"). Originally used to refer to a section of a European city that Jews were forced to live in. The "Black Ghetto" did not always contain dilapidated houses and deteriorating projects, nor were all of its residents poverty-stricken. The ghetto was HOME, the site and origin of SOUL. Until the era of the 1960s and 1970s, Black Ghetto communities were sites of thriving, bustling Black businesses, stable Black institutions, and neat, well-kept homes. Black professionals lived in these areas, alongside the Black poor. The social and cultural patterns reflected the Black Experience and the Black Tradition (e.g., extended family networks; RACE MEN and WOMEN active throughout the COMMUNITY). Because of this history, and in spite of the poverty, crime, joblessness, deteriorated housing, rampant drug activity, and shattered families that are now a part of the 1990s ghetto, there is a lingering sense of the ghetto as the symbolic site of African American cultural authenticity and "real" Blackness. In the late 1990s, a number of popular HIP HOP artists created songs exploring various dimensions of ghetto life: "Ghetto Love" (Da Brat, *ANU-THATANTRUM*, 1996); "Ghetto D" (Master P, *Ghetto D,* 1997); "Ghetto Fabulous" (Ras Kass, with Dr. Dre and Mack 10, *Rasassination,* 1998); "Ghetto Supastar" (Pras, *Ghetto Supastar,* 1998); "Ghetto Fabulous" (Mystikal, *Ghetto Fabulous,* 1998).

GHETTO BIRD

A helicopter, often used by police in ghetto communities.

GHETTO FABULOUS

Describes a person or thing that is fantastic, the height of something, according to the authentic, natural, "keepin-it-real" standards of Blackness that are believed to exist in ghetto communities. Also *ghetto fab.*

GHOST

See DO A GHOST, GIT GHOST.

GIDDYUP / GIDDAYUP

See JUMPSTREET.

GIFT

See SHOOT THE GIFT.

GIG

1) A dance or party. 2) In the lingo of jazz musicians, a job; a booking. 3) Any job. This meaning has crossed over.

GIG ON

1) To play with; to make a fool of. 2) To deceive a person.

GIRL

1) A way of addressing a female; used mostly between women, although it can be used by men with women friends. "Boy," by contrast, cannot be used as a form of address for males over eight or nine years old. 2) A generic reference to any female.

3) One's close friend. 4) Any female, not necessarily personally known, with whom one shares solidarity or whom one admires; a role model; used with *my, your, her,* etc. 5) Cocaine.

GIRLFRIEND

A form of address for, or reference to, any female.

GIT A NUT

To have an orgasm; used in reference to either a male or female. See also BUS ONE'S NUTS.

GIT BUSY

To start to do something—to party, talk, work, etc.; to begin to take care of business.

GIT CLIPPED

To be deceived or cheated, usually out of money. Crossover expression.

GIT DOWN

To do something enthusiastically and vigorously, such as dance, sing, work, or talk.

GIT GHOST

To keep a low profile.

GIT-GO

See JUMPSTREET. "When you settin up your own business, it's the Git-Go that kills you."

GIT GOOD TO SOMEBODY

To get carried away while doing something that starts out in a routine fashion. "He [the hairdresser] was jes suppose to be cuttin off a lil bit of hair so we could get this hairstyle, and it got good to him; next thang I know, I'm bald-headed!"

GIT HAPPY

To be overcome with religious ecstasy; to be possessed by the Holy Spirit. Expressed by shouting, crying with joy, religious/ holy dancing, TALKIN IN TONGUE. Also *git the Spirit.*

GIT IT ON

To start something enthusiastically, especially sex, a party, or a fight.

**GIT IT TOGETHA**

To compose oneself; to pull things together to achieve a purpose; to do things the way they should be done. Crossover expression. See also TOGETHA, which has not crossed over.

**GIT MINE / YOURS / HIS / HERS**

To obtain one's share of something; to get or take what is due you. Also *go for self/yours/his/hers*

**GIT OFF MY CASE**

Stop nagging me; stop pestering me about some situation. Crossover expression. See also CASE, ON SOMEBODY'S CASE.

**GIT ON THE GOOD FOOT**

To correct whatever needs improving; to put your best foot forward; to straighten out things. Popularized by James Brown's 1972 JAM.

**GIT OUT MY FACE**

Stop confronting me; remove yourself from my presence; I don't want to hear it. Crossover expression. See also GIT UP IN SOMEBODY'S FACE.

**GIT OUTA HERE!**

A response of enthusiasm or surprise.

**GIT OVAH**

1) A Traditional Black Church term referring to making it over to the spiritual side of life, having struggled and overcome sin. "My soul look back and wonder how I got ovah." 2) By extension, to overcome racism, oppression, or any obstacle in the way of your goal.

**GIT OVAH IT**

Forget about it, dismiss it from your mind; the state of affairs you are concerned about is not going to change, so accept reality. Often used by people who are challenging you to accept their actions, behaviors, or beliefs.

**GIT OVAH ON**

To deceive somebody; to fool a person.

GIT PAID

1) To obtain money, regardless of the means. 2) To have a steady income.

GIT REAL

To get serious; to stop fantasizing and dealing in illusions. Crossover expression.

GIT SKINS

To have sex. Also *hit the skins*. See also IN THE SKINS.

GIT SOME AIR

To go outside; to leave a place.

GIT SOME BOODY

1) To have sex with a woman. 2) To have anal sex, especially male-to-male.

GIT SOME LEG

To have sex with a woman.

GIT THE ASS

To get angry.

GIT THE SPIRIT

To be overcome with religious ecstasy; to be possessed by the Holy Spirit. Also *git happy*.

GIT UP

To leap and jump high, especially in B-BALL. See also HOPS.

GIT UP IN SOMEBODY'S FACE

To confront or argue with somebody face-to-face; to show disapproval of someone's actions while positioning oneself in close proximity to that person. See also GIT OUT MY FACE.

GIT UP ON THIS

Pay attention to this; listen carefully to what I'm about to say.

GIT UP ON YO MAN

In basketball, said when an offensive player is eluding the defensive player and getting positioned to score, thus a command to play tighter defense, to more closely and carefully "check" the offensive player you are guarding.

GIT WASTED
To get drunk on liquor; sometimes, to get extremely high on marijuana. See also FUCKED UP.

GIT WIT
1) To establish a relationship with someone. 2) To desire or try to have sex with someone. 3) To participate in or go along with something. "You can git wit this or you can git wit that."

GIT YO / MY / HIS BES HOLT
Get your/my/his best hold; a challenge to figure out and adhere ("hold") to the best plan or course of action (or best argument in a debate). "You want the job? Git yo bes holt and go for it."

GIT YO / MY / HIS GROOVE / FREAK / CLOWN / EAT / HUSTLE ON
To indulge in an activity. Help yourself; go on and do it.

GIVE A CARE
Euphemism for *give a shit*.

GIVE IT UP
1) To surrender a position or territory in competitive play. 2) To have sex. This meaning is also expressed as *give up the ass*.

GIVE IT YO / MY / HIS BES SHOT
To apply the very best one has to offer to a situation or a cause; to do everything one can to achieve success in a certain area.

GIVE SOME HEAD
To perform oral sex on a man.

GIVE SOMEBODY FIVE
To slap someone's hand in greeting, to show strong agreement, etc. Also *give somebody skin/some skin*. See also FIVE.

GIVE SOMEBODY SKIN / SOME SKIN
See GIVE SOMEBODY FIVE.

GIVE SOMEBODY SOME PLAY
To flirt; to show romantic interest in somebody.

GIVE SOMEBODY SOME SLACK
See CUT SOMEBODY SOME SLACK.

GIVE SOMEBODY SOME SUGAR
To kiss.

GIVE SOMETHING SOME PLAY
To show interest in and give one's attention to something.

GIVE UP THE ASS
See GIVE IT UP.

GLASS DICK
The pipe used to smoke crack.

GLASS HOUSE
A house where crack is sold; a drug house.

GLOCK
A powerful handgun, the regular clip of which is fifteen rounds, but which can be extended to eighteen to nineteen rounds; the bottom half is plastic, top half steel, to make it lighter than its predecessor, the NINE.

GLORY
Traditional Black Church term to refer to the wonders of God; His honor.

GO BACK
Used in reference to the return of STRAIGHTENed hair to its natural, curly (KINKY, NAPPY) state, due to exposure to water, sweat, or other types of dampness or moisture.

GO DOWN
To happen, occur, take place. "What went down was…"; "Now this is what's gon go down."

GO DOWN ON
To perform oral sex on someone.

GO FOR
1) To believe or accept something. "I'll go for that." 2) To succumb to verbal persuasion. "Since they went for my story, everythang turned out okay."

GO FOR BAD
1) Refers to a person who projects an image of toughness and

fighting ability. 2) By extension, refers to a person who projects an image of badness or toughness in any area.

GO FOR SELF / YOURS / HIS / HERS
   See GIT MINE / YOURS / HIS / HERS

GO FOR WHAT YOU KNOW
   To execute a move, play, or action that you have expertise in, particularly in a conflict or a threatening or tense situation.

GO OFF
   1) To lose control, react violently and/or irrationally, sometimes beyond what the situation calls for. 2) To perform anything outstandingly, taking it to another level.

GO OUT
   1) To die or be killed. 2) To be defeated. 3) To take a situation to the extreme. Also *go off*.

GO OUT LIKE A SUCKER
   To die as the result of a drug overdose or gang violence.

GO OVAH
   To endure the secret ritual that initiates one into a fraternity or sorority. The ritual itself is called CROSS THE BURNING SANDS. Also *cross ovah*.

GO TO BLOWS
   To fight vigorously or viciously.

GOAL TENDIN
   To interfere with someone who is trying to obtain sexual favors from someone. Also *cock block, block*.

GOD DON'T LIKE UGLY
   A popular saying from the Oral Tradition, meaning that some negative action, behavior, or attitude is displeasing to the Creator, and you will be punished.

GODDESS
   A braided hairstyle with very large braids twisted and piled atop the head.

**GOIN THROUGH CHANGES**

See CHANGES.

**GOLD DIGGER**

A woman who runs after men for their money; emerging also as a term for a man who pursues women for money. An older general slang term that has resurfaced in HIP HOP Culture. Also *sack chaser* (newer term, originated in Hip Hop).

**GOLD FRONT**

See FRONT[1].

**GONE**

Euphemism for *dead.* "My daddy been gone a year now."

**GONE HOME**

See HOME.

**GOOD**

Said with emphasis, refers to someone or something that is excellent or superb, not simply "good."

**GOOD HAIR**

Hair that is not naturally tightly curled, but naturally straight or slightly wavy; hair akin to that of whites. According to Black woman writer and anthropologist Zora Neale Hurston (author of the 1937 novel *Their Eyes Were Watching God*), *good hair* was also once referred to as *nearer, my God, to thee.* AFRICAN-CENTERED and activist FOLK reject this concept. See also BAD HAIR.

**GOOD LOOKIN OUT**

It is good that you were looking out for [someone or something]. A compliment and/or expression of gratitude to a person for taking care of someone.

**GOOD TO GO**

Ready to participate in an activity or event; predisposed to do or agree with something.

**GOT GAME**

1) Used to describe a person who plays basketball very well.

2) By extension, describes people who are expert at something, top-notch in their field.

GOT HIS / HER NOSE

A person who has another person vulnerable, helplessly and hopelessly in love with him or her, is said to have *got* that person's *nose*. See also NOSE JOB / NOSE OPEN.

GOT IT GOIN ON

Superbly or effectively doing something; refers to a successful or competent person or thing. "That new beautician, she got it goin on"; "Mickey D up there got it goin on this week."

(SHE / HE / THEY) GOT IT HONEST

Describes a person who has a certain personality attribute that is highly similar to a trait in one of that person's parents or relatives.

GOT YOUR BACK

An expression of support for a friend or comrade in any situation, event, plan, or scheme. From the idea of protecting the person against surprise "attack" by adversaries coming unexpectedly from the "rear."

GRANDSTAND

1) To talk BAD in a loud, aggressive, flashy manner. 2) To dress and act in a flamboyant manner so as to attract attention. 3) To show off. Also *showboat*.

GRAPEVINE

A source of information or news through the informal verbal networks of the COMMUNITY. Crossover term.

GRAY

A fairly neutral term for a white person; however, possibly from the gray color of Confederate army uniforms, and if so, originally must have referred to white racial supremacists.

GREASE

1) To eat. Older meaning. 2) Oil, vaseline, hairdressing, pomade

for the hair and/or skin to deal with the dry appearance of Black skin and scalp.

GREAT WHITE HOPE

A white person on whom European Americans are depending to excel in a field—usually a sport—where African Americans dominate. The first GREAT WHITE HOPE was probably the heavyweight fighter Jim Jeffries, who responded to a mass campaign to come out of retirement and reclaim the heavyweight title from the first Black champion, Jack Johnson. It proved to be a futile effort. On July 4, 1910, in Reno, Nevada, Johnson knocked Jeffries out in round fourteen.

THE GREATEST

Heavyweight boxing champion Muhammad Ali. Born Cassius Marcellus Clay on January 17, 1942, in Louisville, Kentucky, the grandson of a slave. He started boxing at age twelve, and by age eighteen, he had fought 108 amateur bouts. In 1960, he won an Olympic Gold Medal. At age twenty-two, entering the ring as a 7-to-1 underdog, he defeated the reigning champion, Black boxer Sonny Liston; shortly thereafter converted to the Nation of Islam, then more commonly referred to as the Black Muslims, under the Honorable Elijah Muhammad, and changed his name to Muhammad Ali. Before he dubbed himself "the Greatest," and got others to follow suit, he was called the "Louisville Lip," noted for his loud braggadocio about himself in general and his good looks, but most of all for his raps and rhymes about his ability to "float like a butterfly, sting like a bee." His Black Language power was not only daunting and unsettling to opponents, but it made boxing come alive for millions of Americans without any previous interest in the sport. Given to predicting the round in which his opponent would lose the fight, Ali's motto was "They all must fall in the round I call." He had predicted that Liston would fall in eight, but later told reporters, "If he gives me any jive, he goes in five." At the height of the

Vietnam War, Ali received an indefinite deferment on the grounds that he had scored too low on the army's test. Shortly after he joined the Nation of Islam, the army dropped the score required to pass its test to one point lower than Ali's score, thus making him eligible for the draft. At the time, the word in Black America was that Ali had come to be perceived as a threat to white America, with his membership in the Black Muslims and his vocal opposition to the war, and, according to what has now become legend in the COMMUNITY, the lowering of the army's score was directly aimed at him. In any event, within two years of his original 1-Y classification, Ali was swiftly reclassified and drafted. However, he refused induction and spoke out against the war: "Man, I ain got no quarrel with them Vietcong. No Vietcong ever called me nigger." The U.S. government retaliated, overruling the judge who had granted Ali status as a conscientious objector (on religious grounds), fined him $10,000 (a tremendous sum in 1960s dollars), sentenced him to five years in prison, and stripped him of his title and his boxing license. He was exiled from boxing from 1967 to 1970, as his case wound its way to the U.S. Supreme Court, which overturned his conviction. He returned to boxing and regained his title twice. Influenced by Malcolm X, he promoted AFRICAN-CENTEREDness long before it was fashionable. He identified with PEOPLE OF COLOR, such as the people he referred to as his "Asian brothers" in Vietnam. Economically, he broke with boxing tradition to make it possible for underdeveloped countries to reap the tremendous profits from his major championship bouts, scheduling the "Rumble in the Jungle," as he dubbed his 1974 fight in Zaire (now the Democratic Republic of the Congo), and his 1975 fight, which he dubbed the "Thrilla in Manila," in the Philippines. He won the 1974 "Rumble" against George Foreman, using what he called his "Rope-a-Dope" strategy (staying close to and using the ropes, making

Foreman exhaust himself trying to land punches, finally punching himself out, defeated by Ali's offense masquerading as defense). He won the 1975 "Thrilla" against Joe Frazier with a technical knockout; it was his third fight with Frazier and is still considered by many boxing experts to be one of the greatest fights of all time. Long a hero to Black Americans and to millions outside of the United States, Ali was for decades at the center of controversy in white America. Over the years since his retirement from boxing, Ali has become, ironically, a cultural icon to white Americans. Slowed by Parkinsonism, he was the subject of the 1997 Academy Award–winning documentary, *When We Were Kings.*

GRILL

1) The face. 2) The mouth.

GRIP

A lot of money; also a lot of anything valuable.

GRITS

1) Food of any kind. 2) Money. 3) One's business.

GROWN

Used to describe a young male or female who is acting and/or looking like an adult; generally used in a negative sense. "She is too grown for me" (said in reference to a ten-year-old girl conducting herself like an adult woman).

GROWN FOLK

Older people; adults. "Mobb Deep wonder why nigga blowed -'em out/Next time grown folks talkin, nigga, close yo mouth" (Tupac Shakur SIGNIFYIN ON a Rapper in "Against All Odds" from his 1996 *Makavelli* album).

GROWN FOLK BIDNESS

Adult matters; phrase used to make it clear that children are to be excluded from the conversation. "You kids go somewhere and play. This is grown folk bidness."

GRUB

To eat. "It's time to grub!"

**GSP**

> Golden shower people, that is, people who pee on you; wrong-doers, obviously not serving your best interests.

**GUMBY**

> 1) Awkward, silly-looking. 2) Hairstyle worn to one side. Derived from the cartoon character "Gumby," who has been wearing his hair that way for decades.

**GUT BUCKET**

> A "low-class" bar, club, or other place of entertainment. Blues music is sometimes described as *gut bucket* music.

# H

**HA-STEP**

> To do something halfway, not putting your all into it. From the AAL pronunciation of "half-step."

**HAIM**

> A job. Also *slave*.

**HAINCTY**

> Unpleasant, contentious; picky and petty; commonly used in reference to females who act this way.

**HAINTS**

> Ghosts. Older term used by seniors.

**HAIR DRESSED**

> Used in reference to getting one's hair done or styled. Older term used by seniors.

**HALF-ASS**

> Describes something inadequate, incomplete, sloppily done, halfway completed. See also HA-STEP.

**HALF-STEP**

See HA-STEP.

**HALF TRACK**

A quantity of crack purchased by the SMOKER, approximately $125 worth.

**HAMMER**

1) A good-looking woman; emerging as a term for a good-looking man also. 2) See BARS.

**HAND**

In BID, a round of play. See also SETTIN HAND.

**HANDKERCHIEF HEAD**

An UNCLE TOM–type person who defers to European Americans and their authority; may also act against the interests of Black people. Older term. Also *Tom, Uncle Tom, Uncle Thomas; Aunt Thomasina, Aunt Jane.*

**HANDLE THE BALL**

In B-BALL, refers to dribbling and passing moves, skill and confidence in moving the ball around toward the basket.

**HANDLE YOUR / MY / HIS BIDNESS**

To be on top of things, to take care of business; to be in charge of one's game or whatever it is a person is doing at the time.

**HANDS DOWN**

Of course, naturally. Older term resurfacing.

**HANG**

1) To party. Also *hang out.* 2) To endure or tolerate something. "I can't hang with that." 3) To stay put, remain somewhere. "Why don't you hang a while?"

**HANG OUT**

See HANG.

**HAPPY**

See GIT HAPPY.

**HARD**

Describes a person who is tough, hardened by life and experience.

**HARD LEG**

A male.

**HARD ROCK**

A generic term for any hardened, strong, tough person.

**HARD-HEADED**

Describes a person who refuses to listen to reason or obey a command, as in the proverb "A hard head make a soft behind."

**HARLEM WORLD**

The COMMUNITY of Harlem in New York City. Like the various BOTTOMS in other U.S. cities, Harlem historically had its own institutions, businesses, well-maintained housing, and a rich, thriving community culture. Also, like the other GHETTOS and BOTTOMS around the nation, Harlem is not a separate city. However, its community life is/was so distinct from that of the white area of New York City that it's like another "world."

**HARVEST**

Traditional Black Church term to symbolize the period during the year when God rewards the faithful, heaps blessings upon them, and replenishes or restores what was lost.

**HAT UP**

To leave. Probably derived from the act of putting on one's hat when leaving to go outside.

**HATA**

A person who verbally demonstrates resentment or opposition to the personal success or gain of someone else. Also *playa hata*. See also HATE ON SOMEBODY / SOMETHING.

**HATE ON SOMEBODY / SOMETHING**

To display, usually through words, envy, resentment, or opposition to someone else's success in any area or endeavor. The individual exhibiting the envy doesn't *hate* the person; they *hate on* the person by speaking against, or downplaying, that person's accomplishments. "All you old rappers trying to advance... Niggaz looking like Larry Holmes, flabby and shit, Trying to playa hate on my shit" (Tupac Shakur, "Against All Odds," from

. . . . . . . . . . . . . . . . . . . . . . . . . . . . . . . . . . . . . . . . .

*Makavelli*, 1996). Also can be used in the sense of a person who just "hates" in general, who is generally envious and resentful of others' accomplishments or possessions. "John always be hatin and shit." By extension, used in any situation when a person disagrees with a plan or course of proposed action, or the general sentiment. "Ain no point in hatin on my man, cause yo boy gon git his butt kicked" (in reference to opposing centers in a basketball game). Also *playa hate*. See also HATA.

HAVE CHURCH

An admonition to "make a joyful noise unto the Lord," to sing, shout, clap hands, play instruments, to worship with loud praise and joy. "Oh yeah, we havin church up in here." See also LET'S HAVE CHURCH!

HAWK

Extremely cold weather, made more so by the wind-chill factor. Also *Mista Wind, Joe Chilly*.

HAWKING

Staring at someone.

HE-SAY-SHE-SAY

1) Gossip. 2) Any statement that can't be verified; word-of-mouth, loose talk; hearsay in general.

HEAD

The end of the penis.

HEAD HUNTER

A woman who performs sex with men for drugs, or for money to buy drugs. Probably derived from the use of HEAD in referring to the penis. Also *strawberry*.

HEAD NIGGA IN CHARGE

See H.N.I.C.

HEAD RAG

1) A scarf or handkerchief worn around the head to indicate gang affiliation. 2) A scarf, handkerchief, or STOCKING CAP tied around the hair to keep it in place and preserve one's hair-

style. *Head rag* refers to such a head covering worn by a male or female; DO-RAG, however, refers only to a head covering worn by males.

**HEAD-UP**

Refers to a competition or confrontation of any kind—e.g., cards, basketball, a fight—involving just two opponents, ONE-ON-ONE. "Me and old Mose just sat there all night playin stud poker, head-up."

**HEADS**

1) One's children. 2) A generic reference to African Americans; possibly derived from a reference to hair, generally of major importance to Blacks.

**HEART**

Courage, boldness, no fear of confrontation. "My boy got a lot of heart, that's one thang he got goin for him."

**HEAT**

A gun. An older general slang term resurfacing in the usage of gang members.

**HEAVY**

1) Describes a person who is a profound thinker, or one with highly developed leadership skills. 2) Describes a person who has a high-status position at a job or in an organization. This meaning has crossed over.

**HEIFER**

A reference to any female; used by males or females; a fairly neutral term.

**HELLA**

1) A lot of, plenty. In "Ghetto Love," from the 1996 album *ANUTHATANTRUM*, female Rapper Da Brat declared her loyalty as she spoke about the "hella muthafuckas" desirous of her man's "occupation." 2) Very. "Steve's Soul Food is hella good."

**HELLIFIED**

Describes an unusual style or manner of doing something, unconventional but highly admirable. "You sho got a hellified way of explaining things."

HELLO!

Used to show strong agreement with or approval of something someone has said or done. When John's friend told him that he had purchased a new car, and a BENZ at that, John responded with "Hello!" Older term used mainly by Black seniors.

HELLO?

A call for an affirmative response, that is, Do you agree with me? Do you hear what I'm saying?

HEN DOG

Hennessy V.S. ("Very Special" cognac, drink of choice for many a PLAYA).

HERB

Marijuana. Crossover term.

HIGH

A state of excitement or exuberance, usually, but not necessarily, induced by liquor or drugs. Crossover term. See also NATURAL HIGH, which has not crossed over.

HIGH FIVE

A FIVE with the hands held high. Crossover expression and ritual.

HIGH ROLLER

1) A big-time drug dealer. 2) Anyone engaged in any big illegal moneymaking scheme.

HIGH TOP FADE

See FADE[1].

HIGH YELLA

See YELLA.

HIP[1]

1) Knowledgeable, aware of something; with-it. From Wolof *hipi*, literally "to open one's eyes." Crossover meaning. 2) See HYPE[1], DEF.

HIP²

To inform someone or make someone aware of something. "They hipped me to what was goin down."

HIP HOP

Urban youth culture, associated with RAP Music, break dancing, graffiti; probably derived from the partying style of DJs playing hype ("hip") music at a dance ("hop"). Three different New York entertainers have been credited with coining the term in the 1970s: Busy Bee Starski, DJ Hollywood, and DJ Afrika Bambaataa. However, according to Kool DJ Herc, the acknowledged father of Hip Hop, "only these three could argue it."

HIT

1) A verbal approach to a person for the purpose of establishing a relationship, to make the person your MAN or WOMAN. In its original use, a "hit" was primarily aimed at getting sex from a person. See also HIT ON. 2) A win in the lottery or NUMBER GAME. See also HIT THE NUMBER / LOTTERY. 3) An ingestion of drugs, usually heroin; older meaning that has crossed over. 4) Ugly. "He is truly hit." 5) In a card game, to request that the dealer give you a card from the deck. "Hit me." 6) Prediction of someone's being killed. "You hit," that is, you are as good as dead now because the "hit" will be coming. Variation of older use of *hit*.

HIT IT

1) To smoke, usually in reference to marijuana or crack. 2) To have sex.

HIT ME UP

To make contact, either by telephone or pager.

HIT ON

1) To make a verbal approach toward someone for the purpose of establishing a relationship. Done by males or females; when done with creativity, subtlety, and class, may be considered flat-

tering. In its original meaning, which Clarence Major (*Juba to Jive*, 1994) dates to the 1940s, the phrase referred primarily to approaching someone for the purpose of obtaining sex. This older meaning has crossed over. 2) To make a verbal request to a person for any purpose. "Brotha hit on me for a job, but we had done already hired somebody." This meaning has not crossed over.

HIT THE NUMBER / LOTTERY

To win in the NUMBER GAME or lottery.

HIT THE SKINS

See GIT SKINS.

## H.N.I.C.

Head Nigga in Charge; a Black person in charge, in a position of authority and/or leadership. A pejorative term that references a historical tradition dating back to enslavement, whereby whites selected Black leaders and authority figures and put them in charge of other Blacks to keep them in line. An ironic, SIGNIFYIN phrase suggesting that the "head nigga" is not really in charge of anything meaningful, or that he/she lacks power to do anything, even though, ostensibly, he/she is in charge. Blacks in charge of something may refer to themselves as "the *H.N.I.C.*," as does the actor Morgan Freeman in the role of dedicated educator Joe Clark, in the 1989 film *Lean on Me*; the former editor in chief of the new HIP HOP magazine *Blaze* listed himself as the "H.N.I.C." in the premier issue (Fall 1998). Such uses of the term, self-descriptions with a conscious touch of irony, may cause nothing more than a soulful chuckle in intimate circles or in communication within the COMMUNITY. However, like the word NIGGA itself, when used by non-Blacks, *H.N.I.C.* is perceived as insulting and triggers a profoundly negative reaction. This is what happened when a version of the phrase was used on the cover of *Boston* magazine (April 1998) in a profile about Dr. Henry Louis Gates, Chair of Har-

vard University's AfroAmerican Studies Department, a prolific
writer, and leading Black intellectual, whose honors include
a National Book Award and a MacArthur Foundation ("genius") Award. The magazine's cover read: "Head Negro in
Charge. Why Harvard's Skip Gates May Be the Most Important Black Man in America." The title of Cheryl Bentsen's
lengthy story on Gates also read: "Head Negro in Charge." The
article was the longest that had been done on Gates to date
(twelve thousand words), and it heaped high praise on him,
detailing his earlier life and struggles against racism and
poverty, and lauding his accomplishments over the years. However, its use of the "Head Negro in Charge" label revealed a
lack of understanding about the history and use of the term and
set off a local and national controversy and much media coverage: Boston's Mayor Thomas Menino asked the magazine to
apologize; African American minister, the Reverend Charles
Stith, backed by the Massachusetts Urban League and the
NAACP, launched a protest against the magazine and demanded
an apology for the use of this "historically offensive phrase";
the issue was covered on the *Today* show; *Newsweek* covered
the story, describing the conflict as "a tempest over a headline."
Not issuing any response at first, after a few days into the
controversy, Gates bemoaned the furor that had been generated
and lamented the possibility that this incident might "ex-
acerbate racial tension" in Boston. Also B.N.I.C. (Boss Nigga
in Charge).

HO

*Ho* remains a controversial word, although it is used even among
some women. This is generally in intimate, informal conversations, almost as *girl* is used as a form of linguistic bonding.
(Sista says to her homegirl, "Un-huh, I saw you out there flirting,
you ol' ho; girl, you a mess!") It seems to be a flipping of the
script, as in the case of the use of BITCH among women: taking

## WHERE I'M COMING FROM                                      BY BARBARA BRANDON

the negative, turning it on its head, and stripping the word of its power to define and delimit women. While some male RAP artists have been soundly chastised for the "bitches and ho's" in their lyrics, if women continue to flip the script, using the words *bitch* and *ho* in what New York linguist Arthur Spears would call this "evaluatively neutral" way, there may well come a time when both words will lose their negative punch. At that point, we may also see a decline in the use of these words by RAP artists.

**HO CAKE**

Euphemism for PUSSY.

**Ho! Ho!**

An expression used at a party, dance, or other lively social event, suggesting a call to all present to PAR-TAY.

**HOE**

See HO.

**HOG**

A Cadillac car. Older term.

**HOG MAWS**

The stomach of a pig, eaten as a delicacy; not as expensive as CHITLINS, but pretty costly nonetheless.

**HOLDING DOWN**

Controlling turf or an area, according to gang talk.

**HOLE**

In basketball, the basket.

**HOLLA**

1) To contact, talk to. "Holla at me when you get back in town."

2) To shout, holler.

**HOLLER**

See HOLLA.

**HOLY GHOS**

Holy Ghost of the Christian Trinity (Father, Son, Holy Ghost). From the Traditional Black Church.

**HOME**

1) A generic reference to any area south of the Mason-Dixon Line, the original U.S. "home" to the African enslaved population and the birthplace of virtually the entire Black population from Emancipation until the Great Migration out of the South after World Wars I and II. Thus, "My momma nem went home last month" does not refer to the current home of the speaker, but to a place in the South where the speaker and her family are from. Also *down home.* 2) A generic reference to a person of

African descent. 3) By extension, any place or thing associated with NITTY-GRITTY Blackness. 4) A Traditional Black Church reference to a spiritual Home in Heaven. "I got a Home not built by worldly hands." Funeral services are referred to as *Homegoing* celebrations. The SAVED person who dies is said to have *gone Home*. Also *Home on High*. 5) See HOMEY.

HOME ON HIGH

See HOME.

HOME SLICE

1) A Black person; Black people. 2) See HOMEY.

HOMEFOLKS

1) Black people; a Black person. 2) See HOMEY.

HOMEGIRL / HOMEBOY

1) A fellow gang member. 2) A Black person. 3) See HOMEY.

HOMEGOING

See HOME.

HOMES

1) A Black person; Black people. 2) See HOMEY.

HOMEY

1) A person from one's neighborhood. Also *homegirl/homeboy*. Crossover terms and meaning. Also *homes, home, home slice*, and *homefolks*, terms which have not crossed over. 2) A Black person. Also *homegirl/homeboy, homes, home, home slice, homefolks*. This use of these words has not crossed over.

HOMO

A derogatory term for a gay male.

HONEY[1]

A generic, positive reference to a female. The young BROTHA said, "The spot was live, and it was lots of honeys there!"

(YO / HIS / HER) HONEY[2]

Your lover, significant other. Used by males or females.

HONKY

A negative term for a white person. Probably derived and borrowed from the name-calling and expression of resentment by settled European Americans against central and Eastern European immigrants, who were negatively referred to as "hunkies" (from *Hungarians*). Blacks, in competition with these immigrants in the first half of the twentieth century, generalized the term to all whites. Also *hunky*.

HOO-RAH

A lot of noise; loud talk. "Yall cut out all that hoo-rah."

HOOCHIE

A sexually promiscuous female. Also *hoochie momma*.

HOOD

1) Neighborhood, especially the neighborhood where you live or have grown up; your roots and a place where you feel welcome and at home. 2) Short for *hoodlum*, a rowdy, aggressive, hard-nosed, street-fighting type of man or woman.

HOOD RAT

A sexually promiscuous female who is from the HOOD. In some circles, the phrase is jokingly attributed to made-up Latin, from the so-called "Latin root word *hood ratis*."

HOODOO

The negative component of the VOODOO religion.

HOODOO MAN

A male supposedly skilled in the art and practice of the magical system of the VOODOO religion, which was transplanted to the United States (also the Caribbean and Latin America) from West Africa during enslavement. A distortion of the role of the Voodoo priest and a mockery of the extensive knowledge, training, and experience of the Voodoo healer/doctor. The *hoodoo man* claims to be able to cure any sickness, put on and/or remove hexes from people, increase one's sexual prowess, predict the number (see NUMBERS), etc.—all for a fee, of course. The number of *hoodoo men* is not as great as it once was, but they are still to be found in the COMMUNITY. Although there were and are *hoodoo* women, the practice of HOODOO has been largely dominated by males.

HOOK

1) A phony; an imitation. 2) The police. 3) In HIP HOP Music, the refrain, the repeated line that gets the attention of the listener and by which the song comes to be known.

HOOK SOMETHING UP

To create, design, or arrange something; to fix something up according to one's own style or TIP, as in decorating, or *hooking up*, an apartment or house, selecting and coordinating a wardrobe or an outfit, restyling an old car, setting up a special pleasure trip, etc.

HOOK-UP

1) A deal or arrangement gained through a friend who has contacts and connections. 2) Anything attractive, artistic, or great that a person puts together that reflects his/her uniqueness — a stylish outfit, a beautifully decorated CRIB, a creative answering machine message or business card, etc. 3) To make a deal or arrangement, to make something happen, make a connection. "Hey, I finally saw yo Brotha. Why don't you hook a Sista up?" that is, introduce me to your Brother.

HOOKED

Describes something or someone that is attractive, tastefully put together, upscale.

HOOP

1) See B-BALL. See also TAKE IT TO THE HOOP. 2) To play basketball. Also *shoot some hoop*. 3) To laugh loud and heartily. "They was jes hoopin and hollin when I got to the party."

HOOPTY

An old, broken-down car.

HOPS

Ability to leap and jump high, especially in B-BALL. "That Brotha got good hops." Also *ups, springs* (newer terms); *rise, sky* (older terms). See also GIT UP.

**HOT**

1) Refers to music, usually jazz, that is very fast-tempoed and played with fervor and high energy, the speed generating "heat." Probably from the Mandinka language spoken by the Mandingo people, *goni*, literally "hot," also "fast." 2) By extension, refers to high energy generated in any activity. "The Lakers done got hot now," suggesting that they're starting to play great basketball. 3) Stolen goods.

**HOT-BLOODED**

Describes a person, often female, with high sexual energy, a person whose libido is stronger than average. Also *hot-natured*. See also A LOT OF NATURE.

**HOT COMB**

A metal comb, heated, used to STRAIGHTEN hair. Also *hot iron*.

**HOT CURLERS**

Iron curlers, heated, used in curling the hair.

**HOT IRON**

See HOT COMB.

**HOT LADY**

A woman, usually someone in the COMMUNITY, who sells stolen goods at bargain prices.

**HOT-NATURED**

See HOT-BLOODED.

**HOT SAUCE**

A peppery sauce, very hot and spicy. Believed to be from a recipe dating to enslavement that was possibly brought over from Africa. Marketed commercially today; distinct in taste from the popular European American version of *hot sauce* (Tabasco sauce).

**HOUND**

A promiscuous man; derived from many women's perception of men as "dogs who will fuck anythang," a view depicted in the "Women's War Council" scene in Spike Lee's 1991 film *Jungle Fever*.

**HOUSE**

> 1) To take something from somebody; to take over, exert one's power. 2) See CLOWN.

**HOUSE NIGGA**

> See FIELD NIGGA.

**HUMP**

> To have sex. Crossover term. A male in the act of lovemaking is said to have a HUMP IN HIS BACK, an expression that has not crossed over.

**HUMP IN HIS BACK**

> See HUMP.

**HUMPIN**

> 1) Very attractive; good-looking. 2) See DEF.

**HUNG**

> Used to describe a male whose penis is large. Crossover term. Also *hung low*, which has not crossed over.

**HUNG LOW**

> See HUNG.

**HUNKY**

> See HONKY.

**HUSH YO MOUF!**

> A response of surprise; a reaction to startling or incredible information.

**HUSTLE**

> A scheme or work, either legal or illegal, for obtaining money.

**THE HUSTLE**

> 1) A popular group dance, done in a line formation. Also *the Electric Slide, the Bus Stop, the Madison* (older terms, same dance). 2) An older dance done by couples (New York).

**HUSTLER**

> One who survives and makes money by deviousness and schemes, usually illegal but nonviolent, such as by various gambling games involving the NUMBERS, shooting pool, PICK-UP basketball GAMES, etc.

HYPE[1]

See DEF. Probably a resurfacing of and variation on *hip* (older term).

HYPE[2]

Deceptive, propagandistic statements or stories, particularly European American propaganda.

/

IBWC

Intelligent Black Women's Coalition, a group founded by the Rapper Yo-Yo. The *IBWC* term and concept, without reference to the group, is used by female Rappers and HIP HOP feminists as a symbol of solidarity and WOMANIST assertion.

ICE

1) Diamonds. Older term resurfacing. 2) A synthetic drug that is potentially explosive; not as strong as CAT. 3) Label for a person who is bold, daring, calculating, in control, superCOOL. 4) By extension, reference to a person who speaks the plain, unvarnished, cold, hard truth. "Did you hear what she said? Ice, baby, ice." Rappers' names and lyrics symbolize this quality—"Ice Cube," "Ice-T," "Vanilla Ice." 5) To kill.

ICE DOWN

Wearing a lot of diamonds. "Did yall see Keisha at that concert? My girl was ice down." Also *icey.*

ICE PEOPLE

White people, from a perception of whites as cold and ruthless. According to some Black Nationalist ideologies, Caucasians lived in cold climes in Europe and thus developed a cold, inhumane system of thought.

IF YOU FEEL FROGGY, LEAP!
    Used as a challenge to fight.

IG

    To ignore someone by refusing to speak or otherwise acknowl-
    edge their presence. Older term still in use that dates at least to
    the 1930s, listed in Cab Calloway's *Hepster's Dictionary* (1938).

ILL

    See SICK.

ILLIN

    See TRIPPIN.

I'M OUT

    See UHM OUT.

IN DA ZONE

    Describes people performing at the maximum, as if they are in a
    magical place, or zone, where everything they do comes out
    right. "He could shoot from Mars and it would fall. He in da
    zone now," referring to a B-BALL player making all the baskets,
    not missing any shots.

IN EFFECT

    Describes somebody or something that is present and operative
    in all his/her/its glory, a force to be reckoned with. "My crew is
    in effect."

IN FULL EFFECT

    Present and operating at a high level of intensity, at maximum,
    greater than just being IN EFFECT.

IN LIKE FLIN

    Describes someone who is accepted by a person or group; well
    received. From the James Bond–type character in the 1965
    movie *Our Man Flint,* who GITS OVAH in the film. AAL pro-
    nunciation of "Flint." Older term.

IN THE DAY / BACK IN THE DAY

    1) Refers to a past era that was the heyday of someone or some-
    thing. 2) By extension, any past era, whether it was the heyday or
    not.

IN THE HOUSE

Indicates the significant presence of someone — that he or she is now here in our midst. "Yo! MC Too Smooth is in the house." And, "Yo, who's in the house?" the DJ asked. "Mickey Mouse is in the house, and Donald Duck don't give a fuck," the party people answered.

IN THE MIX

1) Refers to a DJ's synthesizing or mixing together sounds from various records to create a new sound. 2) Interfering with a plan; involved in somebody's business. "Everythang was all right until she got in the mix." 3) Involved in gang activity.

IN THE SKINS

Having sex. See also GIT SKINS, HIT THE SKINS.

IN THE STREET

1) Not at home. See also STAY IN THE STREET. 2) HANGing OUT, partying. See also RUN THE STREET. 3) Describes a lifestyle that is an alternative to the working-class style of the COMMUNITY.

IN THERE

Attractive, looking good.

IN YO FACE

1) In basketball, refers to a defensive player closely guarding, that is, "up in the face of," an offensive player. 2) Expression used when a player has made a basket in spite of all vigorous attempts by an opposing player to prevent it, scoring right in the defensive player's face, so to speak. 3) By extension, describes any issue, problem, or confrontation that has become personalized, or a crisis that has hit home. This use has crossed over.

INDO

Marijuana.

INK TOWN

Inkster, Michigan, a small city (by 1990 Census, population of 28,800), located outside Detroit, predominantly African American. In the 1920s, large numbers of Blacks from the South moved there to work at the nearby Ford Rouge Automobile plant. In the oral history of Michigan's Black COMMUNITY, *Ink Town* is known as the little town that the late industrialist Henry Ford built for his Black workers, to keep them separate from his white workers, for whom he built the small town of Dearborn, bordering Detroit. (Of course, official historical records provide no documentation for this claim.) With the decline of blue-collar work and the deindustrialization of the U.S. economy, *Ink Town* deteriorated considerably. According to the 1990 Census, the average Black income there is $9,656 per person; there is only a 66 percent high school graduation rate.

IRON MIKE

The heavyweight prizefighter Mike Tyson, so named because of his strong body and his powerful knockout punch, which makes one feel as if he were being hit with iron. Tyson rose from oppressive childhood circumstances to become, at age twenty, the youngest world heavyweight champion in history. Despite his heroic stature in the eyes of many, he remains controversial. In 1992, he was sentenced to six years in prison for rape. After his release, and his return to boxing, he fought Evander Holyfield in 1997 but was subsequently barred from boxing for biting Holy-field's ear during their fight. As of 1999, he was making a comeback, having adopted the Islamic faith, with his license restored and a knockout victory in his first fight since his suspension.

ISH

Euphemism for SHIT. Emerging in HIP HOP as a way of maintaining authentic Black Talk and at the same time warding off negative reactions to the language, especially from middle-aged Blacks. Used both in print and in song. The "Ill Nation's Guide to Hip Hop" on the Internet has a rating scale that uses the terms "Wack Ish" and "Dope Ish." In Pistol's review of Jay-Z's 1998 video film "Streets Is Watching," he writes, "The best ish had to be the Imaginary Player... When that ish came on, I fell out." On

*The Boulevard Connection ("Sut Min Pik")* 1998 album, Tame 1 and El Da Sensai, in "Haagen-Daz," rap about "the most clever ish you ever heard." And KRS ONE, Hip Hop's political conscience, on his 1995 album, *KRS ONE,* in the JAM "Build Ya Skillz," admonishes Rappers who lack lyrical talent and "talk too much ish."

ISSUE

May be applied to ordinary, everyday events, to signal a problem or potential source of conflict. "Now, if Girlfriend don't get this style right, we gon have a hair issue."

IT AIN HAPNIN

Statement to indicate that something is not going to occur, whatever the "it" is. "They want me to transfer to the St. Louis office, but it ain't hapnin."

IT'S ON

1) Statement indicating that something is about to be set in motion. "We just heard from my girl; let's git busy; it's on" (in reference to planning a wedding shower). 2) Indicating that a confrontation is about to occur.

JACK

A form of address for any male. "Hey, Jack, what's goin on?" (said to a man whose name is Harry). Also *G, B* (newer terms); *Bo-jack* (older term).

JACK

1) Short for JACK-SHIT, meaning "nothing." "They been workin all that time and ain got jack." 2) To take something from someone.

JACK D
Jack Daniels liquor.

JACK MOVE
A wild action; a bizarre move or behavior.

JACK-SHIT
See JACK.

JACK UP
To beat up, assault somebody.

JACKLEG
1) An unprofessional or phony preacher. Because of the significance of the Church and preachers, who are believed to be
"sent" or "called" by God, being a *jackleg* is a grievous offense in
and to the COMMUNITY. 2) By extension, *any* person who is an
amateur, or who pretends to be something that they're not, such
as a *jackleg plumber, jackleg mechanic, jackleg carpenter,* etc. Also
*shade tree.*

JAKE
Police.

JAM
1) A song or recording. 2) A party. 3) To confront someone. 4)
To party; to dance. 5) What musicians do when they play with
high energy and excitement. 6) To have sex. 7) To DUNK the ball
in B-BALL.

JAM SESSION
A gathering of musicians playing HOTly, THROWing DOWN.

JAMMIN
See DEF.

JAMMY
A gun.

JAW JACKIN
Talking excessively; literally "jackin off" at the mouth, or verbal
masturbation. Used, for instance, by the NBA great Sam Perkins
during the 1993 NBA playoff series. NBC commentators made

special mention of Perkins's use of the term, thinking it was new, but it dates back at least to the 1970s; "jawin," in fact, dates to the nineteenth century, according to Clarence Major in *Juba to Jive*. Also *runnin off at the mouth*.

JAWS TIGHT

Describes somebody who is angry. "You messed up, Bro. Her jaws is tight now!"

JAZZ

Not only refers to the music, but is used as a verb meaning "to speed up, to excite, to act uninhibited." Possibly from the Mandinka language, spoken by the Mandingo people, *jasi*, literally "to act out of the ordinary." Originally *jazz* referred to sexual activity.

JAZZY

1) Exciting, upscale, DOWN WITH the latest trends or fashions. 2) High, in good spirits.

JB

James Brown. A 1950s singer, entertainer, pioneer in funk, soul, and GITTIN THE SPIRIT in musical performances. The most sampled of OLD SCHOOL musicians by today's HIP HOP artists.

JEEP MUSIC

Good music, the kind that's good for PUMPIN UP THE VOLUME and listening to while CHILLIN in your jeep.

JERK SOMEBODY AROUND

To run a scam or deception on somebody. Crossover expression.

JET

1) To run fast. Also *motor, fly* (older terms). See also TRUCKIN. 2) To leave.

JHERI-CURL

Also referred to as a *Jheri*, this is a style or look created by using a chemical relaxer that replaces the natural, tight curl of Black hair with a straighter curl that has a shiny, wet look. Thus treated, the hair is generally worn loose, either long or short, but with little variation in terms of style. From the name of the person, Jheri Redding, who invented the process and introduced it to African American hairdressers in the 1970s. The fact that the *Jheri* caught on so among Blacks was a surprise to many *beauticians,* and to the Redding family as well. Since that time, there have been many adaptations by other manufacturers, but the terms *Jheri* and *Jheri-Curl* continue to be used to refer to all such processes since all result in the *Jheri-Curl* look. Because of its heavy, oily texture, the *Jheri* (as well as its imitations) often leaves greasy spots on clothing and furniture, which became the source of humor and SIGNIFYIN in the 1988 film *Coming to America,* starring comic genius Eddie Murphy.

JIGGA

The Rapper Jay-Z; probably from the combination Jay-Z + NIGGA. *Jigga* is used to replace "nigga" in several situations in which "nigga" would be disapproved of, for instance, in a group of middle-aged, middle-class Blacks.

JIGGY

Describes someone or something that is superb, excellent, DA BOMB. "She was looking jiggy at the spot last night." Also *butta, dope, fresh.*

JIM / JIMMY

Penis. Also *Jim Browski, Jimmy joint.*

JIM BROWSKI

See JIM.

JIM / JIMMY HAT

A condom.

JIM JONES

1) To poison someone. 2) A cigarette containing cocaine and marijuana dipped in PCP. Derived from the name of the African American cult leader Jim Jones. In 1977 he fled the United States with about a thousand followers, ending up in Jonestown,

Guyana, where they later committed mass suicide by drinking Kool-Aid spiked with potassium cyanide.

**JIMMY JOINT**

See JIM.

**JINGLIN**

Attractive, sexy; usually used in reference to women.

**JITTERBUG**

A superHIP, streetified person; the term is often used with a hint of scorn. From a fast popular dance done in the 1930s, suggesting a person who is fast and wild.

**JIVE**

1) Lacking in seriousness, not committed. 2) Deceptive, putting somebody on. Crossover term. See also SHUCKIN AND JIVIN.

**JOCK**

1) To ingratiate oneself with somebody by being overly involved in his world or by imitating her actions and behavior, often in an exaggerated way. 2) To approach somebody aggressively to establish a relationship.

**JOCK STRAP**

To be "on a man's *jock strap*" is to impose oneself on him, to be bothering or hassling him, to intrude into his space. For the female version, see BRA STRAP.

**JODY**

Any man having an affair with another man's wife or WOMAN. Probably derived from the name given to men rejected or deferred by the draft during major wars in the twentieth century. Such men were believed to prey on the wives and girlfriends left behind by the men who went off to war.

**JOE CHILLY**

See HAWK.

**JOHNSON**

Euphemism for DICK. Probably derived from association with the punching power of the first Black heavyweight champion,

Jack Johnson (1878–1946; held title 1908–1915), as well as from the racial controversy that arose after Johnson won the title crown. Whites campaigned for the former white champion Jim Jeffries (perhaps the first GREAT WHITE HOPE) to come out of retirement and win the crown back from Johnson. However, that was not to be: on July 4, 1910, in Reno, Nevada, Johnson beat Jeffries with a knockout in the fourteenth round. The penis as *Johnson* thus symbolizes the Black man's only source of power because the "white man took everything else," as one BROTHA put it. However, from another viewpoint, *Johnson* is considered pathologically overworked. Writer Audrey Edwards discusses the "sexual compulsion" of Brothas (prominent and everyday) who "have all been brought low and even taken out by that old slickster, the Johnson" ("The Trouble with Johnson," *Essence*, November 1998).

JOINT

1) A marijuana cigarette. 2) One's home. See CRIB. 3) Prison. These three uses have crossed over. 4) A gun. 5) A song, record, music video, single performance, that is impressive or outstanding. A "Spike Lee Joint" is a Spike Lee film; "Foxy Brown's video was the joint!"

JONES

1) A strong, overwhelming desire for anything you indulge in or acquire and never get enough of—money, sex, chocolate, gambling, clothes, etc. Originally referred to addiction to heroin or cocaine. 2) Penis.

JOOK

A partying place (shack, house, tavern) for dancing, drinking, gambling, drugs; an AFTER-HOUR JOINT. In the Old South, a place with a jukebox, a "low dive," a house of ill repute. From the Wolof language, *dzug*, to act disorderly, unruly; also related to the Bambara language, *dzugu*, wicked. An older term that surfaced in a song by the late Rapper Notorious B.I.G., who narrates a tale about "crooks" who "caught a jook" in his "Niggas Bleed" jam from *Life After Death*, 1997.

JORDANS
Any of several brands of Nike gym shoes named for B-BALL superstar Michael Jordan, who retired from the Chicago Bulls in January 1999.

JUBILEE
Traditional Black Church term for period of restoration and renewal.

JUICE
1) Power. 2) A gun. 3) Liquor; older meaning that has crossed over. 4) To trick or swindle; to con someone. 5) To kill.

JUICED
Excited.

JUMP
See JUMPSTREET.

JUMP BAD
To become aggressive, ready to fight and do battle, either verbally or physically.

JUMP SALTY
To get mad or angry. See also SALTY.

JUMP SHARP
To get dressed up in the latest fashion. "We have always loved to jump sharp! Back in the day, we reveled in styling from head to toe" (*Essence*, September 1998).

JUMPSTREET
The start; the beginning point of something. Also *Giddyup/Giddayup, Git-Go, Jump, Rip*. See also FROM JUMPSTREET.

JUNETEENTH
The day, usually in mid- to late June, when African Americans celebrate emancipation from enslavement; originally June 19, 1865, the date enslaved Africans in Texas learned that they had been freed. Although Lincoln's Emancipation Proclamation be-

came effective January 1, 1863, the status of enslavement continued, on some plantations for more than two years, because
many plantation owners did not inform their slaves of Lincoln's
order. When ex-slaves in Texas got the news, they instituted this
annual celebration. *Juneteenth* is currently celebrated in some
two hundred cities across the nation. The late writer Ralph Ellison chose *Juneteenth* for the title of his long-awaited second
novel, published posthumously in 1999.

JUNGLE FEVER

Among African and European Americans, an obsession with a
person of the opposite race based on racial myths and stereotypes and intensified by the lure of the unknown, due to continued racial separation. The concept was depicted in Spike Lee's
1991 movie *Jungle Fever*.

KEEP ON KEEPIN ON

A familiar expression in the Oral Tradition, a statement of encouragement to continue struggling and striving to reach a goal;
despite adversity, setbacks, and failures, the triumph is in continuing to struggle, to *keep on keepin on* against the odds. Originated in the Traditional Black Church.

KEEPIN IT REAL

1) Being true to the Black Experience and the Black Tradition. 2)
Being true to yourself and your roots.

KENTE (pronounced *kin-tee*)

A fabric imported from West Africa, styled in a variety of ways
and worn as ornamental dressing by African Americans; the
garment of royalty in traditional Africa.

By permission of the artist, Craig Rex Perry, and *Young Sisters and Brothers Magazine.*

KEY

Kilo, kilogram of weight, used in the drug game.

KIBBLES AND BITS

1) Cheap food. 2) Used in reference to a man who is not well endowed, not HUNG.

KICK

1) To inform, to convey the facts about something. "Let me kick some knowledge about the situation"; "Let's kick the ballistics," that is, Let's look at the facts I'm going to present to you. 2) To do something intensely and with high energy.

KICK BACK

To relax; take it easy. In the process of crossing over. Also *chill, chill out.*

KICK BUTT

To outdo a person or a team in a competitive endeavor; to excel over others. "Those lil seventh-grade Brothas at Malcolm X Academy kicked butt on the state math exam last year." Crossover expression.

KICK DOWN

To establish a person in the drug business.

KICK IT

1) To RAP, to use strong talk. Also *kick it live.* 2) To have an affair

outside of one's monogamous relationship. Also *kick it around* (older usage).

**KICK IT AROUND**

See KICK IT.

**KICK IT LIVE**

See KICK IT.

**KICK THE BALLISTICS**

See BALLISTICS, KICK.

**KICK TO THE CURB**

1) To reject someone who is trying to establish a relationship, who is HITTin ON you. 2) To end an established relationship with someone. "My boy got kicked to the curb." 3) By extension, to reject a person for any reason, or to refuse to grant a request of any kind.

**KICKIN**

1) Doing something intensely and with high energy. 2) Superb, excellent, etc. See DEF. 3) Smelling loud, generally used in a negative sense.

**KICKIN IT**

1) Talking informally, engaged in general conversation. 2) Taking it easy, relaxing. Also *chillin.*

**KICKS**

Shoes.

**KID**

1) Used by a speaker to refer to her/himself in the third person. "The Kid ain down for that," meaning I don't approve of that. 2) A friend, associate, "yo dog." This use spreading rapidly from the East Coast.

**KILLIN FIELDS**

Area where homicides and random killings take place.

**KINKS**

See NAPS.

**KINKY**

See NAPPY.

KITCHEN

The hair at the nape of the neck, inclined to be the most curly (NAPPY) and thus the hardest part of STRAIGHTENed hair to keep from GOING BACK.

KNOCK

To criticize something or someone; to DIS a person, idea, or thing.

KNOCK BOOTS

To have sex. Possibly from taking *(knockin)* off one's lover's boots before engaging in sex.

KNOCKED OFF

Arrested; busted for a crime. A resurfacing and extension of the older general slang expression *knock off,* meaning "to kill."

KNOT

A roll of money.

KNOW GOD

Traditional Black Church expression, to know that one has been rescued (SAVED) from sin by the power of Jesus and his sacrifice; to have strong belief and faith in God; having knowledge of the various ways his power has been/is manifested. "Don't nobody don't know God cain't tell me nothin!" Deacon Johnson said.

KNOW WHAT UHM SAYIN?

A call for a response from the listener.

KNUCKLE UP

To fight.

KUFI (pronounced *koo-fee)*

A West African style of hat, worn by men, shaped like a low, small crown. Worn especially by AFRICAN-CENTERED Black Americans. *Kufi* (also *skufi, skufia)* is sometimes used in a generic sense to refer to all hats.

KWANZAA

An African American and Pan-African cultural—not religious or political—holiday, celebrated from December 26 through

January 1. Historically, the Kwanzaa celebrations in traditional
agricultural African communities were times of harvest, commitment, and celebration. The African American version of this
celebration was created in 1966 by Dr. Maulana (formerly
"Ron") Karenga, intellectual activist, theoretician, and philoso-
pher of African Culture, who is currently the Chair of the Department of Black Studies at California State University–Long
Beach. In 1997, the U.S. Postal Service released a Kwanzaa stamp
in commemoration of the holiday, which current estimates indicate is celebrated by as many as thirty million people of
African descent, not only in the United States, but around the
world. According to Karenga, "The celebration of Kwanzaa... is
a ceremony of bonding, thanksgiving, commemoration, recom-
mitment, a respectful marking, an honoring, a praising, and a
rejoicing... [It] has two basic kinds of celebrations, family-
centered and community-centered" (from *Kwanzaa: A Celebration of Family, Community and Culture*, by Maulana Karenga,
Los Angeles: University of Sankore Press, 1998). At the core of
Kwanzaa are Seven Principles—the Nguzo Saba—which identify core values: 1) Umoja (Unity); 2) Kujichagulia (Self-
Determination); 3) Ujima (Collective Work and Responsibility);
4) Ujamaa (Cooperative Economics); 5) Nia (Purpose); 6)
Kuumba (Creativity); and 7) Imani (Faith). The components of
Kwanzaa combine African and African American cultural elements and synthesize cultural practices from all parts of Africa.
The name "Kwanzaa" comes from the Kiswahili language,
*matunda ya kwanza,* where "matunda" means "fruits," and "ya
kwanza" means "first." According to Karenga, the additional "a"
at the end of "Kwanzaa" has become a "convention as a result of
a particular history": seven children in the Organization Us
wanted to do a presentation in which each would represent a
letter of Kwanzaa. Because the Kiswahili word "kwanza" only
has six letters, another "a" was added. Karenga explains that this
addition "did not essentially change the pronunciation and,

most important, it demonstrated our principle of *priority of the person in the context of community.* It also was an indication of the humanistic and value stress in Kwanzaa."

**L**

Marijuana rolled in cigar paper; from the "El" of El Producto, a brand of cigar often used for this purpose. Also *blunt.*

**LADY**

A male's female lover/girlfriend/partner.

**LAID**

1) Stylishly dressed. Also *clean.* 2) High on liquor or drugs.

**LaLa Land**

Los Angeles.

**LAME**

A thing, event, or person that is out of step, unable to keep up, thus un HIP, not with-it.

**LAMP**

To hang out. Possibly from the idea of hanging out under street lamps on urban corners.

**LAMPIN**

Relaxing, taking it easy, *chillin.*

**LARCENY**

Negative feelings, hostility toward somebody.

**LARGE AND IN CHARGE**

Prosperous, successful, on top of things, in control of oneself and in charge of the situation, whatever it happens to be. See also LIVIN LARGE, LIVIN HIGH OFF THE HOG.

. . . . . . . . . . . . . . . . . . . . . . . . . . . . . . . . . . . . . . . . . . . .

LATER

An expression used to indicate Goodbye; I'm leaving. "Okay, Kwesi will be there. Later." Also *Catch you later* (older expression which has crossed over, but *Later* has not); *Outtie 5000, outa here* (newer expressions).

LATER

Used to dismiss or disregard something or somebody. Referring to African American politicians and other officials who forget all about their people, the SISTA said, "See, once they get in office, they just act like 'later for y'all.'"

LAWD

Lord, in Traditional Black Church, AAL pronunciation.

LAWD, HAVE MERCY!

Response of affirmation or surprise.

LAY DEAD

1) To wait. 2) To keep a low profile.

LAY IT DOWN FOR ME

Make it plain, explain it to me. Also *lay it on me*.

LAY IT ON ME

See LAY IT DOWN FOR ME.

LAY OUT

An easy activity. "This job is a lay out."

LAY PIPE

A reference to what the male does during sex.

LAY UP

To relax, to lounge around; often used to refer to relaxing in bed with one's partner.

LAYIN IN THE CUT

Refers to something or someone that is hiding, surreptitiously waiting to catch or surprise you; lurking. "When they tell you yo cancer in remission, all that mean is that bad boy layin in the cut waitin for yo ass!"

**LEAN**

See GANGSTA LEAN.

**LEAVE SOMEBODY HANGIN**

To ignore a hand extended for a handshake or a FIVE.

**LED BY THE HEAD OF ONE'S DICK**

Used in reference to a man unduly influenced by sex, one whose judgment is clouded by his sexual desire.

**LEG**

See GIT SOME LEG.

**LEGIT**

Refers to anything that's authentic; real, not fake; describes something that's appropriate, in order, as it should be.

**LET THE DOOR HIT YOU WHERE THE GOOD LORD SPLIT YOU!**

Euphemism for "Get yo ass out of here!" (*split you* being a reference to "ass").

**LET'S HAVE CHURCH!**

In the Traditional Black Church, a call to the congregation to liven up, begin to praise and sing, show emotion, "make a joyful noise unto the Lord." See also HAVE CHURCH.

**LETTER FROM HOME**

Euphemism for "watermelon." The use of "home" is a reference to the watermelon as a fruit that originated in Africa; some Black seniors contend that the seeds were brought to the United States by Africans during enslavement. Because of historical characterizations of Blacks as childlike, lazy, the contented slave happily eating his watermelon, and the stereotypical association of the watermelon with Blacks only, there developed an ambivalence about the watermelon. The euphemism *letter from home* reflects this ambivalence. See also NIGGER APPLE.

**LIFTED**

Intoxicated, high on drugs or liquor. Also *blowed*.

**LIFTS**

Hydraulics on a car; installed usually on older cars, to elevate the car and make it possible for it to run on two or three wheels. "Drop the ass" refers to activating the *lifts* to lower the rear of the car and elevate the front, referred to as LOW RIDIN (which is illegal in most states). It costs from five to six thousand dollars to have *lifts* installed on a car. Popular among HIP HOPpers and car lovers of all ages. See also LOW RIDIN.

**LIGHT BREAD**

White bread.

**LIGHT INTO**

To confront someone verbally; to tell a person off, set them straight. Crossover expression.

**LIGHT-SKIN**

See FAIR.

**LIGHT UP**

1) To light a marijuana cigarette or crack pipe. 2) To dominate, especially in sports. "Michael Jordan lit up the Knicks for 54."

**LIGHTEN UP**

To reduce the verbal or psychological pressure.

**LIGHTWEIGHT**

Lacking in achievement; unimportant. "He wasn't nothin but a lightweight ball player noway." Crossover term.

**LIKE THAT**

Possessing whatever quality is suggested by a preceding statement. "You live in this fine crib?" "Yeah, cause I got it like that," that is, I am in possession of the finer things in life, such as a beautiful house; "Yo, Momma! Look at all that weight you lost since I last saw you!" "Yeah. It's like that, I got it like that," meaning, Yes, I have the discipline and fortitude to stick to a weight loss program and succeed.

**LIKE TO**

To have almost done something. "Momma like to drop the baby."

**LIKE WHITE ON RICE**
> See WHITE ON RICE.

**LIL BIT**
> Affectionate name for a petite woman.

**LIL MAN**
> A male child; the practice of calling male children *Lil Man* emphasizes that, though they are young boys, they are still men.

**LIL SOMETHIN SOMETHIN** (pronounced *sum-n sum-n*)
> A gesture or gift, "lil" or big, to show affection or recognition.

**LINE DON'T LIE**
> In B-BALL games in the HOOD, used in reference to a decision determined by the outcome of shooting from an agreed-upon line. In the absence of referees, whenever a player calls a foul, the opposing player can challenge the call. The conflict is resolved by SHOOTing THE DIE, that is, by the act of shooting from the agreed-upon line (usually a line roughly equivalent to the distance from the basket to the top of the key in regulation b-ball). If the player makes the basket, then the call was legitimate, and both teams accept that truth has been established because the *line don't lie*.

**LIP**
> A defensive verbal response when under attack or when resisting a command. "Do what I told you, and don't give me no lip!" Crossover term.

**LIPS**
> The vagina.

**LIQUID JUICE**
> Liquor.

**LISTEN UP!**
> A call to listen carefully, to pay attention because the speaker is about to KICK some knowledge.

**LIVE**
> See ALL THE WAY LIVE (older form).

## LIVER-LIPS

Reddish purple–colored lips, also usually BIG LIPS. A negative term; but see BIG LIPS.

## LIVIN HIGH OFF THE HOG

Having an opulent life style; living big in a material sense. Literally, eating the upper parts of the hog, that is, the ribs, pork chops, etc., rather than the lower parts, that is, CHITLINS, pig feet, etc. Crossover expression. Also *big-timin it; livin large* (newer term).

## LIVIN LARGE

See LIVIN HIGH OFF THE HOG.

## LIZARDS

Shoes made from lizard skins; expensive, and popular as a symbol of success, especially among African American males.

## LOCK CITY

The state of "locking up" men or women emotionally, such that their affections are reserved for their partner and their partner only. "Naw, we don't see my boy much no mo; when he met LaTonya, she took him to lock city."

## LOCK DOWN / ON LOCK DOWN

1) In prison. 2) In basketball, refers to a player who has been stopped from making baskets because of strong defensive pressure on him. "He only made two shots all day. Rodney got the nigga on lock down."

## LOCKER NUMBER

Beeper or voicemail number.

## LOCKS

See DREADLOCKS.

## LOKE

Messed up, mentally unbalanced, fanatical, "loco."

## LOKES

Sunglasses. Also *shades* (older term that has crossed over).

**LOOK FOR YOU YESTERDAY, HERE YOU COME TODAY**

Expression to convey disapproval of a person's timing and behavior, when he/she is not living up to expectations, not producing what is needed at the point or time it's needed.

**LOOSE CHANGE**

In basketball, when the ball is bouncing and rolling around after the dribbler has lost control of it. "Loose change, loose change, pick dat shit up!"

**LOOT**

Money. Older term resurfacing.

**A LOT OF NATURE**

Describes a person who has a high sex drive. See also HOT-BLOODED, HOT-NATURED.

**LOUD TALK**

To talk in such a way as to confront or embarrass someone publicly.

**LOVE**

Appreciation, recognition, respect. Also *give or show some love.*

**LOVE BONE**

See BONE.

**LOVE ME SOME**

Expression to show intense liking or deep love for something or someone. "I love me some greens" (from a person speaking about her love of turnip greens). "That girl love her some Robert" (referring to a woman who is deeply in love with "Robert").

**LOW**

Describes a person who is maintaining a low profile; not flashy. See also TAKE LOW.

**LOW FIVE**

A FIVE with the hands held low. Probably originated when the HIGH FIVE crossed over and too many white folks started high-fivin.

**LOW-LIFE**

Refers to the seamy underside of people, events, or places; "low-class"; unscrupulous, without morals or principles.

**LOW-LOW**

See DL, DOWN LOW.

**LOW RATE**

To downgrade something or someone. Also *rank*.

**LOW RIDIN**

Riding low; a car in which the suspension has been adjusted and hydraulic lifts installed to make it possible for the driver to bounce the car, sometimes very high in the air, or to drive it low, very close to the ground. LOW RIDER car shows, such as those held in Los Angeles or Detroit, feature these vehicles in creative, spectacular stunts. However, on the street it's a different story because most states have laws requiring automobiles to be driven with a certain amount of distance from the ground to the car; thus *low ridin* can result in the police ticketing the driver and/or impounding the car. See also LIFTS.

**LOW SICK**

Extremely sick.

**LP**

A long-playing, large phonograph record (33⅓), which has been replaced by the cassette tape and the compact disc. Originally a trademark label, made popular by African Americans; a crossover term. See also EL PEE.

**LUG**

A DIS; an expression of CAPPIN or SIGNIFYIN; may be said seriously or in fun. See also DROP A LUG.

**LYIN**

The art of telling stories and anecdotes, RAPPIN, telling jokes; general clever conversation using the African American Verbal Tradition. Some stories are fictional, that is, literally "lies"; others may have a kernel of truth; all are raised to the level of broad and imaginative exaggeration by a storyteller, who must have a good memory and be verbally adept, clever, witty, and funny to hold the listeners' attention during conversations that may go on FOR DAYS.

**MACARONI**

1) See MACK DADDY (newer term). 2) The name of a Midwestern gang, no longer in existence.

**MACK**

1) A man who can sweet-talk women. 2) A man who has lots of women; a PLAYA. 3) A man who manipulates women for money; a PIMP. 4) To hustle or exploit someone.

**MACK DADDY**

A man who has a lot of women and PLAYS them; a PLAYA. Also *Macaroni* (older term).

**MACKIN**

Refers to a man trying to HIT ON, GIT WIT, deepen his acquaintance with a woman to make her his.

**MAD**

A lot of; very much. Also *crazy*.

**THE MADISON**

See THE HUSTLE.

**MAIN MAN**

1) One's best friend. 2) Back-up; a person who GOT YOUR BACK.

**MAKE BANK**

To obtain money.

MAKE LIKE

See MAY LIKE.

MAKE SOMEBODY'S LOVE COME DOWN

To stimulate somebody sexually.

MAMMA JAMMA

Euphemism for MUTHAFUCKA.

MAN

1) A woman's boyfriend/husband/partner; used by males and females. 2) A form of address for any male. Crossover meaning. From the Mandinka language of the Mandingo people, *ce*, "man," used as a form of address.

THE MAN

1) The police. Crossover term. Also *five-O* (newer term that has not yet crossed over). 2) A male of distinction. "Michael Jordan is The Man." 3) The white man.

MANDINGO

A strong, usually big-built African American male; an allusion to the stereotype about the sexual powers of the Black man. Older term that was derogatory when used by those outside the Black speech community. Probably came into use from the fact that large numbers of Mandingoes, an ethnic group in West Africa, were brought to the "New World" as slaves.

MANNISH

Used to reprimand a young male who is acting too grown-up and too much like an adult. Females acting too grown-up are said to be WOMLISH or WOMNISH.

MANY WINDOWS

The local city bus. Older term.

MARINATE

To think deeply about something. Outkast raps: "United Parcel Service and the people at the post office didn't call you back because you had cloudy piss. So now you back in the trap...Gon and marinate on that for a minute" (from "Spottie Ottie Dopalicious" on the 1998 album, *Aquemini*).

**MARK**

A weak person, a pushover. Resurfacing and extension of older general slang term. "Musta thought I was sleazy or thought I was a mark cause I used to hang with Eazy" (from Dr. Dre's "Wit Dre Day," on his 1992 album *The Chronic*).

**MARY FRANCES**

Euphemism for MUTHAFUCKA.

**MARY JANE**

Marijuana.

**MARYLAND FARMER**

Euphemism for MUTHAFUCKA.

**MAX**

See CHILL.

**THE MAX**

The height of something; the supreme state of something; the ultimate. This meaning has crossed over. See also DO IT TO THE MAX.

**MAY LIKE**

To pretend ("make like") something is true when it isn't. "She may like she was sick, but she wadn't."

**MC**

The Rapper; literally, the "Master of Ceremonies." In RAP, the *MC*, not the DJ, does the RAPpin.

**ME AND YOU**

Used as a challenge to fight ONE-ON-ONE, HEAD-UP.

**MEAN**

See DEF.

**MECCA**

Harlem, in the vocabulary of the FIVE PERCENT NATION.

**MELLOW**

A very close friend. Older term.

**MEMBER**

Any African American; derived from the notion of racial bonding and solidarity of Blacks.

**MESS**

Nonsense; a bunch of crap; bullshit.

**MESS AROUND**

1) To take it slow, hang around, do nothing important. This use has crossed over. 2) To have an affair outside one's monogamous relationship. Also *play*. This use has not crossed over.

**MESS WIT**

To bother someone; to hassle or irritate a person. Crossover expression. *With* pronounced as *wit* in AAL.

**MESS WIT SOMEONE'S MIND**

To confuse someone through mental gymnastics; to unnerve or rattle a person emotionally or psychologically.

**MF**

Euphemism for MUTHAFUCKA.

**M.F.I.C.**

Muthafucka in charge. Detroit's late mayor Coleman A. Young, the longest-serving mayor in the city's history, was known for his bold and witty use of the Vernacular. He had a nameplate made up with the initials M.F.I.C., which sat on his desk. See also H.N.I.C.

**MICHAEL WHITE JACKSON**

The entertainer Michael Jackson; a reference to the ever-increasing lightening ("whitening") of his natural skin color, along with a perception that he rejects African features, which coincides with the plastic surgery he underwent to create a more European physical look. This view persists despite the revelation that he has the disorder vitiligo, which results in unnatural whitening of the skin.

**MICKEY D**

Any McDonald's restaurant.

**MICKEY MOUSE**

Petty, unimportant, small-time. Crossover term.

**MICKEY MOUSE IS IN THE HOUSE, AND DONALD DUCK DON'T GIVE A FUCK!**

An expression used at parties to suggest, Let's take the party to a higher level; let's party with abandon, drop all serious concerns, stressors, and the burdens of daily life.

**MICKEY T**

A woman who goes after men for their wealth and power.

**MIDNIGHT HOUR**

1) A Traditional Black Church reference to a time when a person is in search of answers through prayer, deep meditation, and reflection, usually late at night when the person is alone. 2) By extension, any low point in one's life, a period of depression when things have gone wrong and one is in search of solutions.

**MIND'S EYE**

The inner "eye" of the brain, perceived as the source of insight and foresight. Intuition, or the intuitive faculty, is believed to exist in all people, but spiritually developed, wise people are thought to have more acute "vision" in their *mind's eye*. Probably comes from Kemetic philosophy/Egyptology, once highly popular in the Black COMMUNITY and resurfacing today.

**MISS ANN**

See ANN.

**MISS THANG**

1) An arrogant woman, one who acts high and mighty. 2) A derogatory term for a gay male who, through dress and behavior, over-exaggerates his femaleness.

**MISSION**

See ON A MISSION.

**MISTA CHARLIE**

See CHARLIE.

**MISTA FRANKLIN**

Euphemism for MUTHAFUCKA.

MISTA WIND

See HAWK.

MO-MO

Motel.

MOANUHS' BENCH

A special pew set aside during a Traditional Black Church RE-VIVAL (usually an annual event of week-long church services). The unsAVED, seeking salvation, sit in this pew in order to receive special attention from the AMEN CORNER, the choir, the preacher, and others trying to bring on the Spirit and SAVE their souls. On this symbolic *bench,* they mourn *(moan)* their sinful existence and pray for deliverance. *Mourners'* is pronounced *moanuhs'* in AAL. See also REVIVAL.

MOBBIN

Riding in cars (cruising) in large numbers to locate a person or persons who are going to be BEAT DOWN.

MOJO

Originally, a magical charm. By extension, a source of personal magic that one can tap into, enabling you to work magic on something or to put somebody under your spell. "You got yo mojo workin, but it ain gon work on me!" Derived from *moco'o,* literally "medicine man," in the Fula language of West Africa.

MOLDED

Old.

MOMMA

A form of address for a woman, used by males and females, especially for a woman who is DOWN.

MOMMY

Form of address for a Latina (Hispanic female).

MONDO

Large; extremely big.

MONEY

A form of address for any male, as in "Yo, Money! Sup?" Also *G* (newer term); *man, Jack, Bo-jack, Bo-dick* (older terms).

MONSTA
    See DEF.
MORE COAL ON THE FIRE
    Used by women in reference to a sexually inept man, as in "Put
    more coal on the fire" or "You need more coal on the fire."
MORINEY (pronounced *muh-RHINE-ee*)
    Describes an African American who has a light complexion with
    reddish tones to the skin.
MOTHER
    1) A title and form of address for older women in the Traditional
    Black Church. 2) Euphemism for MUTHAFUCKA.
MOTHER HUBBARD
    Euphemism for MUTHAFUCKA.
MOTHER WIT
    Common sense, intuition; wisdom not taught in school or
    found in books.
MOTHERLAND
    Africa.
MOTHERLODE
    The core, the center, the main thing.
MOTHER'S DAY
    The day women on welfare/ADC get their checks.
MOTHER'S DAY PIMP
    A man who lives off—PIMPS off—women on welfare/ADC,
    and who collects their checks on MOTHER'S DAY.
MOTHERSHIP
    1) See MOTHERLODE. 2) The lead car in an automobile cara-
    van.
MOTOR
    See JET (newer term).
MOTOR CITY
    Detroit. Crossover term. See also D.
MOTOWN
    1) Detroit. Crossover term. See also D. 2) The sound or style of

music that originated in Detroit in the 1960s and spread around the world.

MOUF

Mouth; the act of talking in a boastful or derogatory and insulting manner.

MOURNERS' BENCH

See MOANUHS' BENCH.

MOUTHPIECE

Gold caps on the front teeth. Also *front, gold front.*

MUG

Euphemism for MUTHAFUCKA.

MUH-FUH

See MUTHAFUCKA.

MURDER MOUTH

To make wild, outlandish threats that you don't have the power or guts to execute. See also FAT MOUTH.

MURDERIN US

Term used in B-BALL when the opponents' play is very physical.

MURPHY

A deception (scam or con game), usually played on white men, often involving sex for hire.

MUTHAFUCKA

Used to refer to a person, a place, an event, a thing, either negatively or positively, depending on the context. It *never* refers to a person who has sex with his mother. "Now that's a bad muthafucka," referring to a beautiful car; "Michael Jordan is a muthafucka on the court," meaning Michael Jordan's basketball-playing prowess is extraordinary; "That James, he is one sorry muthafucka," that is, James is rather useless, good for nothing. Also used for emphasis: "You muthafuckin right I wadn't goin," that is, You are absolutely correct in thinking that I wasn't going. City University of New York linguist Arthur Spears argues that this usage, the use of other so-called "obscenities," and use of the term *nigga* have in the postmodern era entered the public dialogue resulting in what he calls UM (uncensored mode) language. Analyzing expressions such as "jive-ass fool," "that nigga kicked ass," and "muthafuckin bitch-ass nigga," Spears writes: "It is clear that there has been a shift over this century in the use of uncensored speech in the United States and in all similar modern, highly industrialized societies…What is new…is the presence of uncensored speech in the mass media in much greater quantities than before and its *normalization,* the use of uncensored expressions by some types of people in most social settings in an evaluatively neutral way, i.e., the expressions are not inherently negative or positive…they are neutralized: they are negative, positive, or neutral in force depending on how they are used. Many people who function exclusively or primarily in mainstream settings are not aware of this. In brief, neutralization across a wide range of social contexts, if not almost all, results in normalization" (from "African American Language Use: Ideology and So-Called Obscenity," in *African American English.* Salikoko S. Mufwene, et al., London and New York: Routledge, 1998). Also *muh-fuh.*

**MY BAD**

Used to convey an apology, acknowledge a mistake, to say "I'm sorry."

**N's**

Money. Possibly from "notes," i.e., the bank notes of paper currency. Also *scratch. Scratch* has crossed over, but *N's* has not.

**THE N-WORD**

Euphemism for **NIGGER**. Use of this phrase, instead of the word "nigger" itself, is becoming more common, even in instances in which someone is quoting the use of "nigger" in a literary passage or from another person. "They were acting outrageous, calling him the N-word and stuff."

NANA

Euphemism for PUSSY.

NAP UP

What STRAIGHTENed hair does when it returns to its original, tightly curled (KINKY, NAPPY) state.

NAPPY

Describes extremely curly hair, the natural state of African American hair, curled so tightly that it appears "wooly." In the Black Power Movement of the 1960s and 1970s, wearing one's hair in its natural, *nappy* state became symbolic of Black pride and rejection of white beauty standards. "Happy is nappy" became a popular slogan. Since that era, wearing the hair in its natural state has become as much a fashion statement as it was once a political statement. However, among some Blacks, "nappy" continues to be a name-calling word, and thus its use has double meanings, dependent on the context and the user's intent. A children's book, entitled *Nappy Hair* (written by African American Carolivia Herron, an English professor at California State University, Chico, and published by Alfred Knopf in 1997), celebrates the value of this different kind of hair in the human family. For this reason, a white teacher, Ruth Sherman, used the book to teach her Brooklyn, New York, students about the value of and tolerance for differences. The book celebrates the child's nappy hair as a symbol of the strong-willed spirit of SISTAS. However, Black parents protested, accusing Sherman of racism and/or poor pedagogical judgment, and Sherman, under attack and fearful, requested a transfer to another school. A self-described nappy-headed Sista, writer and economist Dr. Julianne Malveaux, writes: "Parents, a teacher, and a principal failed to use this nappy misunderstanding as a

growth opportunity…our community and society are so nar-
rowly focused that we are incapable of understanding that some
words have mixed messages and ought to be sensitively handled.
Let me make it personal. I wouldn't trade my nappy hair for the
stringy stuff if you paid me good money to do so. But I'd take
you to task in the harshest of terms if you called my hair nappy
as a criticism and not a compliment. Somebody needed to com-
municate the mixed meaning of 'nappy' to teacher Ruth Sherman before she started reading and teaching about nappy hair.
Then we could all have avoided the PC—as in 'politically correct'—blues that turned a classroom misunderstanding into a
national incident" (from "Just a Nappy-Headed Sister with the
PC Blues," *Black Issues in Higher Education*, December 24, 1998).

NAPS

The extremely tight curls of natural, unsTRAIGHTENed Black
hair. Also *kinks*. See also NAPPY.

NATHAN

Nothing.

THE NATION

The Nation of Islam, a Black Muslim group, today under the
leadership of Minister Louis Farrakhan. Founded in 1930 by
W. D. Fard; led by Elijah Muhammad for decades; the chief
spokesperson in the 1960s was Malcolm X. Stresses clean living,
self-help, respect for women, and African-Centered knowledge.
Applauded for resurrection of drug addicts, criminals, and
street people—especially males. Minister Farrakhan enjoys a
strong following among Black youth, and in a national poll of
adult Blacks, 70 percent thought he said things the country
should hear and 62 percent felt he was good for the COMMU-
NITY (*Time*, February 28, 1994).The religious theology is similar to, but with some adaptations from, the older, traditional
Islamic faith.

THE NATION

A generic name for a gang.

NATURAL

African American hair worn in its natural state, not HOT-COMBed or treated with chemical straighteners. Also *Afro*.

NATURAL HIGH

A state of excitement or exuberance induced by inner, spiritual forces; a BUZZ not due to liquor or drugs.

NATURE

A generic reference to a person's sex drive; one's libido. See also A LOT OF NATURE, NO NATURE.

NEARER, MY GOD, TO THEE

See GOOD HAIR.

NECK

See RED NECK.

NEGRO

A person of African descent; the term originally was not capitalized. From about 1930 to the 1960s, the preferred term among intellectuals and the middle class. However, many working-class Negroes never were quite comfortable with *Negro*, possibly because of the way it was often pronounced—"nigra," making it sound close to NIGGER. The term fell into disfavor during the Black Freedom Struggle of the 1960s and 1970s and came to be used for African Americans opposed to Black causes and/or those who identify with European Americans.

In the late 1990s, the term is reemerging as a euphemism for NIGGA. 1) Used in the sense of a generic label: "These Negroes round here is somethin, girl" (SISTA describing people in her HOOD). And: "Go to that person and say, 'Listen, Negro, you know you did me wrong, but I got to forgive you and love you'" (televised sermon by the Reverend Creflo Dollar, on the text of forgive and forget). 2) Used for women, in contrast to *nigga*, which is generally used for males: "Negro, do you want to get well?" (medical doctor to female patient refusing to take her medication). 3) Used for a friend: "What you should do is sit yo boy down and say, 'Now, Negro, have you thought bout what you finna do?'" (preacher in a sermon teaching that a real friend is one who advises his friend about his irrational actions). 4) Possible emerging trend in HIP HOP, used in contrast to *nigga,* who is real, hard-core, DOWN, whereas *Negro* lacks talent, comes up short, not *down,* just ordinary, or maybe even lacking: "For some, talking about the ghetto's ills remains necessary. The problem stems from ghetto negroes being handed the mic to address a larger audience than their skills merit"(from Donnell Alexander's "Bout It, Bout It," in *LA Weekly* magazine, September 5–11, 1997).

NEO-SLAVERY

Used by AFRICAN-CENTERED Blacks and activists to refer to the current state of African America: nothing has changed (or the more things change, the more they remain the same). The current condition of Blacks is viewed as simply a movement from legal slavery to a new form of enslavement, since Blacks are still powerless and whites powerful, as in the enslavement era. The term also links the African American situation to that of postindependence African nations, which are viewed as having moved merely from colonization to neocolonization.

NEW JACK

1) The new urban HIP HOP Culture. 2) In tune or in sync with the HOOD. 3) Culturally upscale.

NEW JILL

The female version of urban HIP HOP Culture. Conveys a new female assertiveness, branching out from NEW JACK and establishing the SISTAS' own thang.

NICE

High, usually on drugs or liquor.

NICKEL

1) Five dollars. 2) By extension, anything that is a "five" can be referred to as a "nickel." The first Black paratroopers in U.S. his-

tory dubbed themselves the "Triple Nickels," although the army called them the 555th Parachute Infantry. See TRIPLE NICK-ELS.

NICKEL N DIME

Refers to a small-time, petty idea, person, or event. "It ain nothin but a nickel n dime operation"; "I don't like for people to nickel n dime me." Crossover expression.

NICKEL SLICK

Petty, small-time; refers to a low-level attempt to manipulate people or situations; trying to be SLICK but falling short. "That nickel slick shit you pulled didn work, did it?"

NIGGA

Used with a variety of meanings, ranging from positive to neutral to negative. 1) "She my main nigga," that is, She is my close friend, my backup. 2) "Now that Brotha, see, he ain like them ol e-lights, he real, he is a shonuff nigga," i.e., He is culturally Black and rooted in Blackness and the African American Experience. 3) "That party was live; it was wall-to-wall niggas there," a generic, neutral use of the word, meaning simply that many African Americans were present at the party. 4) "Guess we ain gon be seein too much of girlfriend no mo since she got herself a new nigga," African American women's term for the Black man as lover/partner/significant other, here meaning simply that the woman in question has a new boyfriend. 5) *The Source* magazine, describing filmmaker Spike Lee and basketball super-star Charles Barkley: "Nineties Niggers...two outspoken Black men...Charles calls the ones that push and fight '90s Niggers.'" While with the NBA team the Philadelphia 76ers, Barkley answered the press about a bad shot he had made: "I'm a 90s nig-ger...*The Daily News, The Inquirer,* has been on my back... They want their Black athletes to be Uncle Toms. I told you white boys you've never heard of a 90s nigger. We do what we want to do" (*The Source,* December 1992). *Nigga* here refers to a

rebellious, fearless, unconventional, IN-YO-FACE Black man.
6) "A group of Brothas was buggin out, drinkin the forty ounce,
goin the nigga route," a clearly negative use of the word, meaning, Some Black males were on the street, partying, getting
drunk off malt liquor, and acting out the loud, vulgar stereotype
of a *nigga*, "disrespecting" the BROTHA's "Black Queen, holding their crotches and being obscene" (from former RAP group
Arrested Development's "People Everyday"). 7) In the late 1990s,
emerging as a term for *any* COOL, DOWN person who is deeply
rooted in HIP HOP Culture.

When used by whites, *nigga* has historically been used in a
negative sense, as a racial epithet, to CALL an African person
OUTA THEY NAME—and pronounced "nigger," not *nigga*
(which has become the preferred spelling as Hip Hop enters the
millennium). However, the frequent use of *nigga* in Rap Music,
on "Def Comedy Jam," and throughout Black Culture generally,
where the word takes on meanings other than the historical
negative, has created a linguistic dilemma in the crossover world
and in the African American community. Widespread controversy rages about the use of *nigga* among Blacks—especially the
pervasive public use of the term—and about whether or not
whites have license to use the term with the many different
meanings that Blacks give to it.

In the early 1990s, the term WIGGA / WIGGER emerged as a
label for a white *nigga*, a European American who strongly identifies with African American Culture. According to journalist
Robin D. Givhan, wiggers "don't just appreciate Black Culture,
they have absorbed it. They consider Black Culture their culture.... They've taken a racial epithet, reworked it and come up
with a word that is not an insult, just a description" (*Detroit Free
Press*, June 21, 1993). This terms appears to have had limited linguistic currency.

In keeping with the AAL pronunciation and meanings of

"nigger," the spelling "nigga" is becoming widespread. See also
BAD NIGGA, FIELD NIGGA, HOUSE NIGGA.

NIGGA MESS

Any messy personal or community affair of African Americans;
something that should be resolved in-house, within the COM-
MUNITY or Black "family."

NIGGA, PLEASE!

Expression of exasperation, impatience, social critique, or used
to dismiss the relevance or significance of what someone has
said.

NIGGA RICH

Used to describe someone who has come into a lot of money, a
lot, that is, for a "nigga," which is considerably less than what
would be considered a lot for whites, thus calling attention to
the wealth disparity between African and European Americans.

NIGGA-TOE

A type of nut, known as a Brazil nut. Because of the word *nigga*,
the term may cause offense.

NIGGAMATION

Used in reference to the practice of speedups on automobile and
other industrial assembly lines, where the majority of the workers are African American, in order to increase productivity
without having to pay workers overtime wages. This once-
widespread practice often led to serious injuries among Black
production workers, who charged that the industrial corpora-
tions increased productivity by exploiting Black labor, not by
using automation—thus *niggamation*.

NIGGAS AND FLIES

Negative phrase for Blacks, recalls stereotypes of incompetence,
laziness, irresponsibility, etc. From the folk rhyme in the Oral
Tradition: "Niggas and flies I do despise / The more I'm around
niggas, the more I like flies."

NIGGER

Racial epithet, used by whites to insult or offend a person of

African descent. Its various neutral and positive uses appear to still be off-limits to whites. As the white comic Gary Owen said on a "Def Comedy Jam" show, whites invented the word but can't use it. However, it has apparently found a "new home" at Web sites on the Internet, according to Nathaniel Sheppard, Jr. (*Emerge* magazine, November 1998): "A recent search on Yahoo! found 4,639 instances of the word, down from 5,500 hits 10 days earlier when Yahoo! was asked about its policies governing such posts. But Yahoo! turned out to be small potatoes. Infoseek identified 6,718 articles that contained the word; HotBot, 8,737; and AltaVista, 15,473. Samplings of these found a majority to be the works of apparently uncomplicated individuals who simply could not contain their hatred." (Sheppard also noted that the search engines had lumped several sites by or about African Americans — some of these espousing a positive mission — into the "nigger" category!)

NIGGER APPLE

A watermelon. Phrase developed by Southern whites; from stereotype of Blacks as lovers of the watermelon, a fruit which originated in Africa.

NINE

A nine-millimeter semiautomatic gun; can be purchased legally, but sold on the street for $500 to $1,000. See also THE WHOLE NINE.

NINETY-LEBEN

A lot of something, literally "ninety-eleven."

NIP

A small quantity of liquor; possibly derived from the *nipple* of a baby's milk bottle.

NITTY GRITTY

The core, fundamental essence of something. Crossover term.

N.O.

New Orleans.

NO COUNT

1) Of insufficient quality or durability; useless. "That chair he bought ain no count." 2) Describes a person who is not of any help. "When it's time to work, he ain no count."

NO LONGER THAN JOHN STAYED IN THE ARMY

A very short period of time.

NO LOVE

No appreciation or recognition.

NO NATURE

Describes a person who has a very low sex drive.

NOD

1) Sleep. "I think I'll cop a nod." 2) A state of semiconsciousness induced by heroin.

NOI

The Nation of Islam. See also THE NATION.

NOISE

Music, particularly instrumental music rather than vocals. See also BRING/BRANG THE NOISE!, SHUT THE NOISE!

NONE

No sex; used by males or females. In the 1998 Gospel play *Mr. Right Now,* one character says: "The reason you cain git married is cause you a nun. You ain nevah had none, you don't want none, and you ain nevah gon git none." See also SOME.

NONE-YUH

None of your business; stop DIPPIN.

NOOKIE

Euphemism for PUSSY.

NOSE JOB

A person who is deeply in love with someone, so much so that he/she is vulnerable to exploitation, is said to have received a *nose job*. See also NOSE OPEN.

NOSE OPEN

Literally, a nose that is open. Used to describe a person who is vulnerable, helplessly and hopelessly in love with someone. Derived from the notion of the scent or smell of sex; it is that which "opens the nose." The person who is the love object is said to have "got" the other person's "nose open." *Got his nose open* was used by former D.C. mayor Marion Barry in a conversation with his ex-girlfriend Rasheeda Moore. Noting the expensive watch she was wearing, which she had gotten as a present from her new boyfriend, Barry said to her, "You got his nose open, huh?" The FBI, which recorded the conversation and was gathering evidence for their case against Barry, misinterpreted the statement to refer to cocaine use.

NOT TRYIN TA

An expression used to dismiss what somebody is saying, to disregard an option or course of action that the person is proposing; in short, "I'm not even listening."

NUMBER GAME

See NUMBERS.

NUMBER MAN

See NUMBERS.

NUMBER ONE

Urination. Crossover term.

NUMBER TWO

1) Bowel movement. Crossover use. 2) Something rank, wrong, deceptive, unethical, or immoral, in the sense of SHIT. This use has not crossed over. "Many of these elected officials are full of number two"; "Liberals [white liberals] will give you a whole lot of number two if you don't watch them."

NUMBERS

A once highly popular illegal betting game, played in communities across the nation; similar to today's state lotteries. Betting was referred to as PLAYING THE NUMBERS. An entire culture, employment industry, and lexicon developed around the *Numbers*. Many *Number men* (chiefs who *backed the Numbers,* i.e., guaranteed and paid off the bets) were respected leaders and business people in the COMMUNITY. With the advent of state lotteries, the community's *Number Game* declined considerably, although it still exists on a smaller scale in many communities today.

NURSE

Traditional Black Church term for the spiritual nurse who administers to those who SHOUT and, on occasion, lose consciousness as they become overwhelmed by the SPIRIT and filled with the HOLY GHOS. These *nurses* dress in all-white uniforms, shoes, and hats, but they do not play a physical role, i.e., as medically licensed nurses (although occasionally one or two members of the Church nursing staff might be registered nurses). The cultural style of Black Church funerals allows for open grieving and heavy emotional displays; thus nurses are in great abundance at funerals. A European American, unfamiliar with this Africanized cultural practice, in attendance at such a funeral, commented after the service: "I've never seen so many nurses at a church before. Was there some problem or somebody who needed medical attention?"

NUT

See GIT A NUT.

NUT OUT

See NUT UP.

NUT ROLL

A great deal of money; a big bankroll carried by a person.

NUT UP

1) To become enraged, so much so as to lose control. 2) To get mad and ready to fight. Also NUT OUT.

NUTS

Testicles. See also BUS ONE'S NUTS.

**OAKTOWN**

Oakland, California.

**OD**

1) To overdo anything; to do something to excess. "I ODed on the chitlins." 2) To overdose on drugs (older usage). This use has crossed over.

**O.E.**

Olde English 800 malt liquor. Also *Eight Ball.*

**OFAY**

A reference to any white person; no longer derogatory, but originally negative. Probably from PIG LATIN for "foe" (enemy) and West African language sources, in words such as *ofaginzy,* literally "white man." Also *fay.*

**OFF**

To kill somebody.

**OFF THE HOOK**

Exciting, lively, fun-filled social event, usually a party. Also *off the hinges, off the heazy.*

**OFF THE WALL**

Inadequate, insubstantial, incomplete, not up to par. Older term.

**OG**

Original Gangster; a gang member who has earned PROPS because of his bold actions.

**OIL**

Liquor.

**OKAY**

All right, "OK." From the form *kay* in several West African languages, meaning "yes," "of course," "indeed." Wolof, *waw Kay/waw Ke;* Mandinka, *o-ke;* Fulani, *eeyi kay.* Crossover term.

OKE-DOKE (pronounced *OH-key-DOHK*)

A scam, con, deception. "I ain goin for the oke-doke."

OL BIRD

One's mother. Older term resurfacing in HIP HOP.

OLD HEAD

An older person; generally suggests the person is not only older but wiser.

OLD SCHOOL

1) The style of RAP Music in its early days, beginning in the 1970s. Exemplified by such Rappers as Grandmaster Flash, The Sugarhill Gang, and Afrika Bambaataa. 2) Anything from the 1960s and 1970s. "Bell-bottom pants, platform shoes, that's Old School." 3) A reference to the status of a seasoned veteran or a person highly experienced in something (older usage); probably derived from African Americans' stress on the significance of life and living as a teacher, the "school" of experience.

OLDE ENGLISH

See O.E.

ON[1]

See DEF.

ON[2]

See IT'S ON.

ON A MISSION

Staunchly dedicated to achieving an objective.

ON E

Empty, lacking something; generally, but not necessarily, used to refer to being out of money. Derived from the "E" on the gas gauge of a vehicle.

ON FULL

Having plenty of something; generally, but not necessarily, used in reference to having plenty of money—"plenty" being whatever an individual considers it to be.

ON IT

In control; on top of a situation.

ON IT LIKE A HONET

Very much in control, on top of a situation. "Hornet" rendered as *honet* in AAL.

ON OVERRIDE

Describes the fact that a person remains quiet and low-key, displays no reaction to an explosive or emotional situation, or maintains his or her cool in the face of a DIS or other negative statement or action. Older use of the term possibly derived from the function of the "overdrive" in older cars, which was used to drown out or "override" engine noise, keeping it quiet. Current use possibly derives from "override" in computer technology, referring to the act of bypassing a program, utility, or computer instruction that is in place in order to perform some other operation desired by the user.

ON POINT

Doing something exactly, perfectly, as sharp as a needle point.

ON SOMEBODY'S CASE

Nagging or harassing a person about a situation or matter. "My momma is on my case about school," that is, She is fussing at me about my situation at school. This use has crossed over. See also CASE, GIT OFF MY CASE.

ON SOMEBODY'S SHIT LIST

Indicates anger at or disapproval of a person; relegating that individual to the group *(list)* of people who are out of favor with someone.

ON T

See ON TIME.

ON THE BLOCK

Used to refer to a prostitute who works the streets.

ON THE CASE

Taking care of business; on top of a situation. "When I need my taxes done, I go to Girlfriend cause she be on the case."

ON THE FLY

Living or acting in a dazzling, ultra-hip manner.

ON THE GOOD FOOT

See GIT ON THE GOOD FOOT.

ON THE OUTS

1) Angry or feuding with somebody. 2) Released from prison.

ON THE PIPE

1) Addicted to crack. 2) The act of FREEBAS in cocaine.

ON THE RAG

Menstruating. Crossover expression.

ON THE STRENGTH

An expression used to reinforce or reaffirm the seriousness of something; indicates something that is noteworthy. Probably a resurfacing and variation of STRONG.

ON TIME

At the appropriate natural, psychological moment, regardless of "clock" time. Probably from the Traditional Black Church expression associated with the story of Job. "He [God] may not come when you want Him, but He's right on time."

ONE-EIGHT-SEVEN (1-8-7)

To murder somebody. From the California Penal Code for homicide.

ONE-ON-ONE

1) Refers to a popular style of playing basketball involving only two players. 2) By extension, used in reference to any hard, HEAD-UP competition or confrontation between just two individuals.

ONE MO ONCE

Expression used when something has to be repeated, done or said again, maybe for the nth time. Conveys impatience and a certain air of disgust that the thing has to be done or said all over again because it should have been right the first time.

ONE TIME

1) Exactly, that's right, on the money. 2) The police.

**OPB**

> Other people's brand (of cigarettes); said in reference to some-
> body's needing a cigarette and having to borrow it and smoke
> whatever brand the other person is smoking.

**OPP**

> Other people's (sexual) property; originally, other people's
> PUSSY. Used in reference to a person involved in a sexual affair
> with someone else's MAN or WOMAN. A resurfacing and exten-
> sion of OPB.

**OPRAH**

> To dredge intimate facts from a person. Derived from the name
> of talk show host Oprah Winfrey, who built her career using this
> strategy with dramatic effect, getting people to reveal innermost
> information about their lives on national television. Term not
> used as frequently as it was in the 1980s and early 1990s, proba-
> bly due to the late 1990s shift in the *Oprah* show's format.

**OREO**

> An African American who is Black in skin color but white in
> thinking and attitudes; like the cookie, black on the outside,
> white on the inside.

**OUT BOX**

> From the beginning.

**OUT COLD**

> Out of order, out of control.

**OUT OF ORDER**

> Inappropriate or inadequate way of talking (or acting) in a situ-
> ation, out of step with the requirements of the situation. "He
> was up in there, just runnin his mouth, didn't know what he was
> talkin bout, all out of order" (referring to a BROTHA during a
> court proceeding).

**OUTA HERE**

> Gone; goodbye; I'm leaving. Crossover expression in the form
> "I'm outa here." Also *Outtie 5000* (newer term); *Later, Catch you
> later* (older expressions). See also UHM OUT.

**OUTA SIGHT**

Crossover term. See DEF (newer term).

**OUTSIDE KID**

A child fathered by a man who is not married to the child's mother but to someone else.

**OUTTIE 5000**

I'm gone; goodbye. AAL version of "Audi 5000." Also *Later, Catch you later* (older expressions), and *outa here* (newer term).

**OVAH**

See GIT OVAH, GIT OVAH ON, GO OVAH.

**OVERRIDE**

See ON OVERRIDE.

**OVERSEER**

The police.

**OVERSTAND**

AFRICAN-CENTERED term referring to profound knowledge and insight, over and beyond that of mere "understanding." Formed by FLIPPING THE SCRIPT. Sanyika Shakur, author of *Monster: The Autobiography of an L.A. Gang Member* (1993), writes: "Language is a very important factor in the establishment of national identity...Overstand...is a term coined and popularized within the New Afrikan Independence Movement after contemplating the negative connotations of understand. Simply put, to 'understand' implies an inferior viewpoint of comprehension, i.e., to 'stand under'...Yet, to flip that up and get over it would certainly afford one a greater view with which to glean knowledge. Hence, overstand" ("From the Kamps: For Y'all Who Don't Be Knowin' (Part II)," *The Source,* April 1998).

P

1) A reference to anything in its pure, unadulterated state, such as drugs. 2) Euphemism for PUSSY.

PACKER'S CLUB

Used in reference to any woman involved with a man unable to maintain an erection during sexual intercourse; such women are said to be "members of the *packer's club*." See also PACKIN CHITLINS.

PACKIN

1) Refers to a person carrying a gun. "Be cool; he's packin." 2) Refers to a man who has a large penis. "Check that out. Is the Brotha packin or what?" 3) What the male does during the sex act.

PACKIN CHITLINS

Used by women to refer to a man whose erection during sex is not hard, or who is unable to maintain an erection. See also PACKER'S CLUB.

PAD

House, apartment, condo, etc., where a person lives. Term dates to 1930s, when, according to Cab Calloway's *Hepster's Dictionary* (1938), it meant "bed."

PADDY

Any white person; a neutral, generic term by now.

PAID

Getting money, a significant amount, whether by legitimate means or not. Could refer to a paycheck but one that is substantial (i.e., minimum wage does not qualify as "paid"). The person who is getting the money may be described as "gittin paid," or simply "paid," as in "He paid," meaning he is making money. The person who is making a great abundance of money may be described as "so paid." SISTA asked, "Would you have a man who wasn't paid?" That is, would you have as your significant other someone who was not making very much money?

**PAPER**

Money. See also BIG PAPER.

**PAPER CHASE**

The pursuit of money, by any means, legitimate or not. From the use of the term PAPER for money. See also PAPER ROUTE.

**PAPER ROUTE**

A person's job or other source of income. See also PAPER, PAPER CHASE.

**PAPERS**

Divorce summons and divorce settlement documents.

**PAR-TAY**

A party, pronounced *par-tay* to suggest a lively, high-spirited event, as in "The par-tay was live!" Also *to par-tay,* as in "We got to par-tay tonight, Jack."

**PARANOID**

1) Suspicious, anxious, constantly on guard against a racist statement or behavior, or a European American pulling a fast one. 2) Concerned about the possibility of getting killed, especially while in the HOOD. For African Americans, being *paranoid* is not characteristic of mental imbalance but a survival strategy.

**PARLAY!**

Slow it down. As this term settles in, it is moving closer in meaning to CHILL.

**PARTNER**

1) One's close friend or associate. 2) One's lover or "significant other."

**PARTY**

See PAR-TAY.

**PASS**[1]

Euphemism for "died." "His mother has just pass." AAL pronunciation of "passed."

**PASS**[2]

To pass oneself off as white; to live life as a European American. Obviously only possible for very FAIR Blacks with hair and other physical features that are NEARER, MY GOD, TO THEE.

**PAY DUES**

1) To pay the cost of living one's life; from a belief that life exacts a price—in the form of emotional and/or physical hardships—that is, *dues*. Everybody has to pay this cost; nobody gets life for "free"; *paying dues* is an inevitable obligation of the human condition. Crossover meaning. 2) Originally, the dues-paying referred to hard times as a result of oppression and white racial supremacy. 3) Occasionally used in the sense of retribution and punishment—*payment* of *dues*—for wrong deeds done in the past. Older term still in current use; dates from the jazz scene of the 1940s.

**PAYBACK**

The return of something negative to the person who initiated the negativity, reaffirming Blacks' belief in the philosophy WHAT GO ROUND COME ROUND.

**PCP**

Phencyclidine, an animal tranquilizer, used as an illegal street drug; induces a psychedelic effect. Also *angel dust*.

**P.E.**

Public Enemy, pioneer Rap group from the 1980s. Politically conscious HIP HOP innovators; contributed soundtracks for Spike Lee films, most recently *He Got Game* (1998).

**PEACE**

Goodbye. Popularized by the FIVE PERCENT NATION. Also *Peace out*.

**PEACE OUT**

See PEACE.

**PEANUT BUTTER**

Anal sex.

**PECK**

See PECKAWOOD.

**PECKAWOOD**

1) Any white person. 2) A lower-class white person. 3) According to Zora Neale Hurston, a "poor and unloved class of Southern whites" (from her 1942 "Glossary of Harlem Slang"). A derogatory term. AAL pronunciation of "peckerwood." Probably derived from the association of the color of the woodpecker—red—with whites; the word was reversed to preserve its value as part of the coded semantics of Ebonics speakers. Nowadays used primarily by Black seniors; possibly dates to the 1830s, according to Clarence Major (*Juba to Jive*, 1994).

**PEEL A CAP**

See BUS A CAP.

**PEEP**

1) To discover someone or something that one wasn't expected to. 2) To observe someone or something.

**PEEP THINGS OUT**

To see what's going on.

**PEEPS**

1) Your "peoples"; can refer either to biological kin or people who are just as close as one's biological family. 2) Your partner, husband/wife, man/woman, significant other.

**PEN**

Penitentiary; prison.

**PEOPLE OF COLOR**

Generic term for BLACKS, Chicanos/Hispanics/Latinos, Asians, Native Americans/Indians, and other "nonwhite" peoples, especially in the United States, but also around the globe. See also COLORED PEOPLE.

**PERM**

Refers to the process of STRAIGHTENing hair using chemicals,

By permission of the artist, Craig Rex Perry, and *Young Sisters and Brothers Magazine.*

as well as to the resulting hairdo. The natural tight curl is RE-LAXed, and a straight style or less tightly curled style is imposed onto the natural hair. From "permanent."

PERP

Perpetrator; one who is pretending, faking it.

PERPETRATIN

Acting like something you're not; pretending, faking, fronting. Also *perpin.*

PERPETRATOR

See PERP.

PERPIN

See PERPETRATIN.

PHAT

See DEF. Probably derived from "em-*phat*-ically"; also a play on the word "fat," in the sense of "fat" describing someone who is well fed, rich, successful.

PH.D.

Playa hata degree. A SIGNIFYIN phrase to symbolize the highest level of *playa hatin.* Describing a person who has such a "degree" because he/she has become an expert in the "field" of *playa hatin,* that is, in displaying envy and jealousy of the success or accomplishments of another person. See also PLAYA HATA.

PHILLY

A cheap cigar used for smoking crack or marijuana. Also *Philly blunt*.

PHILLY / PHILADELPHIA BANKROLL

A lot of one-dollar bills wrapped underneath a hundred-dollar bill to make it appear that a person has a lot of money.

PHILLY BLUNT

See PHILLY. Also *Vega*.

PICKED YO POCKET

In B-BALL, when the offensive player steals the ball from the defensive player, or when he causes the defensive player to lose the ball, he is said to have "picked" the "pocket" of the defensive player. Also *raped*.

PICKIN IN HIGH COTTON

Doing well financially. Older expression.

PICK-UP GAME

In basketball, an informal or impromptu game, with players not known to one another or who do not generally play together; very popular on the outdoor ("official" or "homemade") courts of urban areas.

PICK-UP LADY / MAN

A person who collects the NUMBERS bets in the community and turns them in to the NUMBER MAN (the man BACKIN THE NUMBERS). The winning combination is made up of three digits, but it is possible to bet on only one digit. If the *pick-up lady/man* collects bets on one digit only, she/he is referred to as a *single action lady/man*.

PICTURE

A movie. "Did y'all see the picture wit my girl, Janet, in it yet?" (a reference to Janet Jackson in John Singleton's 1993 film *Poetic Justice*).

PIE

Euphemism for PUSSY. Older term.

**PIECE**

> 1) Sex with a woman; euphemism for PUSSY. See also STRAY PIECE. 2) A gun. This meaning has crossed over.

**PIG**

> Police. Older term that resurfaced among activists in the Black Struggle of the 1960s and 1970s to refer to racist police. Still used to some extent today.

**PIG LATIN**

> A coded form of English in the Black Verbal Tradition. Once very popular, but now fading. To speak it, move the first letter of a word to the end of the word and add *ay.* Thus *boy = oybay; girl = irlgay; foe = ofay.* If a word begins with two consonant sounds, then shift both letters. Thus *store = orestay; Black = ackblay.* Although not heard as frequently today among youth as in the previous generation, middle-aged Blacks occasionally use *Pig Latin,* especially some women who incorporate and code "cuss" words this way in their informal speaking style. For example, a prominent African American woman college administrator recently said to a small group of women: "You see, Sistas, I let the good white folk know in my own way that I was not going to take their *itshay.*"

**PILL**

> A basketball.

**PIMP**

> 1) A man who lives off the earnings of a prostitute; not to be confused with the pimp as a procurer or solicitor. This meaning of *pimp* is one who "rest, dress, and request." Older meaning. 2) A man or woman who lives off the earnings of another person in an exploitative relationship. 3) A man who has a lot of relationships with women. Newer meaning. Also *playa, balla.* 4) To exploit someone or something. "He's pimpin religion," that is, He is using the church as a front for some kind of personal gain, such as money, popularity, political advantage, etc. 5) To dominate one's competition in sports.

PIMP SLAP

An open-handed slap across the face.

PIMP STRUT

See GANGSTA LIMP.

PIMP WALK

See GANGSTA LIMP.

PIMPED OUT

Well dressed.

PINK TOES

A white woman; the color pink suggesting softness, delicateness, and tenderness, reflecting the stereotype of the soft, delicate quality of the white woman's body. Older term.

PIPE

See LAY PIPE, ON THE PIPE.

PITCH A BITCH

To complain; to create conflict through loud, confrontational, argumentative talk.

PLAY

1) To be involved in affairs outside one's main relationship. 2) To deceive someone; to put something over on people, to outsmart them. "We all got played" is how a BROTHA characterized the split decision in the federal trial of the police officers involved in the 1991 Rodney King beating in Los Angeles (two officers found guilty; two acquitted). 3) Attention, special favor, signals of interest, in the romantic or sexual sense. "When I first met her, she gave me a lil play, so I decided to call her." 4) Acknowledgment, endorsement, support. "I went by the fish fry, gave 'em a lil play" (said in reference to purchasing a fish dinner at a church group's "fish-fry" fundraiser).

PLAY BROTHER / SISTER / COUSIN / AUNT

A person who is not one's biological kin but who is so close and shares so much history and experience that he/she attains the status of biological kin. In an interview story by *Rap Pages* music editor P. E. Cobb (December 1998), Mystikal refers to Snoop Dogg as his "play cousin."

PLAY LIKE
To pretend. "She play like she sleep when he come in."

PLAY OUT
1) To lose value, usefulness, or effectiveness; also, to lose the attraction or interest of someone; can be used with reference to a thing or a person. "This little machine is bout to play out." (The speaker is talking about her answering machine, which is no longer working properly.) "My man was in there for a minute, but he done played out now." (The speaker is referring to a male friend of his who has lost his woman's interest.) Also *run out.* 2) To become outdated. This meaning has crossed over.

PLAY PAST
1) To miss an opportunity, usually because you were unprepared or your business/GAME wasn't TOGETHA. "I think the man was gon offer the Brotha the job, but the Brotha kept goin on about some dumb shit and played right past it." 2) To avoid confrontation or having to deal with or talk about something by diverting attention to something else.

PLAY PUSSY AND GIT FUCKED
Used as a warning or threat; if you present a PUSSY, you can expect it to be fucked. That is, if you do or say a certain thing, be prepared to suffer the consequences.

PLAY SOME BID
See BID.

PLAY SOMEBODY CLOSE
To test a person's will, seeing how far you can go in trying to manipulate the person before getting caught.

PLAY SOMEBODY FOR HIS / HER REACTION
To say something to test out how a person reacts to it.

PLAY SOMEBODY LIKE A PIANO
To deceive someone, to put something over on them smoothly

and completely, doing so with the ease and smoothness of playing the piano, hitting all the keys.

PLAY THAT

Used in the negative, "I don't play that," meaning, I don't like what you said or did, or are about to say or do, and I will not accept it.

PLAY THE DOZENS

See THE DOZENS.

PLAY THE NUMBERS

To place a bet on the number one believes will FALL OUT. See also NUMBERS.

PLAYA

1) A man or woman who has many women or men and PLAYS them. 2) A flamboyant, flashy, popular man or woman, who may or may not have many women or men in his or her life.

PLAYA HATA

1) A person who displays envy or resentment of a man or woman who has many relationships, a person who is jealous of a PLAYA. 2) By extension, resentment of a person who is successful in any endeavor. See also PLAYA HATE.

PLAYA HATE

1) To exhibit envy or resentment of a man or woman who has many relationships, jealousy of a PLAYA. 2) By extension, envy or resentment of another person's success in any area of life. See also HATE ON SOMEBODY / SOMETHING, HATA.

PLAYER

See PLAYA.

PLAYER HATE

See PLAYA HATE.

PLAYER HATER

See PLAYA HATA.

PLAYIN FOR BLOOD

Used in reference to serious, aggressive, hard play in cards, basketball, Nintendo, or any other competitive activity, such as a debate, an argument, etc.

PLUCK

Wine. Possibly derived from *pluck,* meaning "courage"; in earlier years, wine was often drunk before gang fights. Today's *pluck* is the FORTY.

PLUMBING

What the male does during sexual intercourse.

PO-LICE

The police. AAL pronunciation. Also *one time, po-po, five-O.*

PO-PO

Police. Possibly from older term for police, *pig,* as pork, thus PO-PO.

POINT GAME

In PICK-UP basketball GAMES, the stage toward the end of the game when one team is leading by a point, and there is only one more point to be scored for that team to win. (Based on this style of B-BALL, there is a set number of points which constitutes victory, regardless of the amount of time played.)

POINT UP

In PICK-UP basketball GAMES, the stage toward the end of the game when the score is tied, and only one point remains to be scored; whichever team scores that point wins. (Based on the concept of winning as determined by a set number of points to be achieved.)

POISON

Drugs.

POONTANG

Euphemism for PUSSY.

POOT

To pass gas.

POOT-BUTT

1) A small-time, unimportant person. 2) Someone who isn't motivated to strive or work toward a goal.

**POOTENANNY**

See PUNANY.

**POP**

1) To shoot someone. 2) To steal. 3) To have sex.

**POP A CAP**

See BUS A CAP.

**POP A CAR**

To steal a car.

**POP SOMEBODY**

To deceive, lie, manipulate, GIT OVAH ON a person.

**POPPY**

Form of address for Latino (Hispanic male).

**POSSE**

Associates, friends; one's social group. Also *crew*.

**POUNDIN**

1) Drinking large amounts of liquor rapidly. 2) A male performing very hard, vigorous sex is said to be *poundin*.

**PP**

Personal problem; used to dismiss or discount a person's complaint about something.

**PRAISE HIM**

Traditional Black Church expression calling out in exclamation and acknowledgment of God. See also REJOICE.

**PRAISE HOUSE**

1) A place of worship, not necessarily a conventional church building. 2) Reference to the church during a period of intense rejoicing.

**PRAYER MARCH**

See ALTAR CALL.

**PRESS**

To STRAIGHTEN the hair by using a HOT COMB.

**PRESSED**

Concerned.

PRIMO
1) Excellent, high-quality, powerful marijuana. 2) See FIFTY-
ONE.

PROCESS
See CONK.

PROFILE
To assume a pose of confidence and COOLNESS. See also
STYLIN AND PROFILIN.

PROGRAM
1) A verbal strategy, a scheme or plan of verbal action for handling any situation. "Girlfriend working her program." Similar
to GAME, in the sense of a story or RAP used to obtain a desired
end. However, runnin a *program* can be positive or negative,
whereas runnin a *game* is deceptive and manipulative. 2) The established routine or pattern of something—an organization, an
event, an activity, etc. "Yo, git wit the program, baby!" (said to a
member of an aerobics class who has slowed down during an
exercise session). 3) The way you operate, your life style, your
way of doing things. "Any dude that ain wit my program can go
right back where he came from cause I'm not havin it."

PROMISED LAND
Any place north of the Mason-Dixon Line. The failure of Reconstruction ended the "freedmen's" dream of equity and first-
class citizenship in the South. The death of Reconstruction was
symbolized by the 1877 compromise that elected Rutherford B.
Hayes to the presidency, the politicians' agreement to return
home rule to the Confederates, and the withdrawal of federal
troops from the South. From 1877 until the 1960s Freedom
Struggle, African Americans believed that the northern United
States was free of segregation and racism. Thus, like the He-
brews in the Old Testament, they "escaped" in massive numbers
out of "Egypt" (the Jim Crow South), fleeing to the "Promised
Land" (the North). The explosion of this myth was given liter-

ary voice in *Manchild in the Promised Land* (1965), writer Claude Brown's autobiography.

PROPERS

1) Respect. 2) Recognition for doing or saying something. Also *props* (newer term).

PROPS

See PROPERS (older term).

PSYCH / PSYCH OUT

1) To use clever deception to persuade a person to think or act the way you want him/her to. 2) To fake out or fool someone using one's mental powers.

PUFFER

See CRACKHEAD.

PULL A TRAIN

Refers to several males having sex with one female at the same time. Also *run a train.*

PULL SHIT

To do something low-down, treacherous, and mean to someone.

PULL SOMEONE'S COAT

To enlighten someone; to HIP a person to something.

PULL SOMEONE'S HOLE (pronounced *ho*) CARD

To put somebody on the spot, embarrassing them by referring to some aspect of their personal business. OLD SCHOOL PLAYAS' and HUSTLERS' term "hole card" resurfacing; derived from poker and similar card games wherein one card always remained facedown ("in the hole"); this mystery card could turn the game in one's favor.

PUMP IT UP!

1) See BRING / BRANG THE NOISE! 2) By extension, to intensify anything; to up the energy and power level of something. Also *Pump up the volume!*

PUMP UP THE VOLUME!

See BRING / BRANG THE NOISE!, PUMP IT UP!

**PUMPIN**

See DEF.

**PUNANY**

Euphemism for PUSSY. From Jamaican patois. *The Source,* a HIP HOP magazine, reports on the formation of an Oakland, California, group of artists who named themselves the Punany Poets. Using "spoken word and performance art," combined with erotica, the group seeks to promote safe sex and AIDS awareness "in a cool way" ("Hip-Hop Erotica," by Eric K. Arnold, April 1998). Also *pootenanny.*

**PUNCHY**

Stupid or ignorant.

**PUNK**

1) A cowardly, passive person; a nonfighter. 2) A gay man (derogatory reference). 3) Someone who backs down, knuckles under to a stronger, more aggressive force. See also PUNK OUT.

**PUNK OUT**

To turn someone into a passive person who knuckles under and backs down from his or her position.

**PUSH COME TO SHOVE**

Expression indicating a turning point in an event or situation, a decisive stage when things have come to a head and some kind of action must be taken. Can be applied to small, as well as major, events. "If push come to shove, you-ah eat dem lil beans 'n' rice cause I ain cookin no mo today." That is, if "push come to shove" in the form of a hunger attack, you will eat what I have cooked even though you are rejecting it now. Older term.

**PUSH UP ON**

1) See HIT ON (older term); GIT WIT (newer term). 2) To make romantic moves on a person for sex. 3) To intimidate someone.

**PUSSY**

1) Sex from a female. 2) The vagina.

PUSSY-WHUPPED
Describes a man who lets his WOMAN boss him around because of her sexual power over him. Crossover term. The female version is DICK-WHUPPED, which has not crossed over. Also WHUPPED.

PUT A BABY ON A MAN
1) To have a child without the father's knowledge and/or consent.
2) To claim as the father of your child a man who is not the father.

PUT IT ON HIM / HER
1) To draw on all of one's creative energy and power and apply it in a variety of situations—to "put it on" one's partner in dancing, to "put it on" one's adversary in competitive play, sport, argument, etc. 2) To give the maximum sexual performance to please one's partner.

PUT ON WAX
See WAX.

PUT OUT WITH SOMEBODY OR SOMETHING
Annoyed or exasperated with someone, something, or an event, to the point of no longer associating with the person or thing or participating in the event.

PUT SHIT ON SOMEBODY
To take advantage of somebody; to manipulate or con a person.

PUT SOMEBODY IN CHECK
See CHECK.

PUT SOMEBODY ON FRONT STREET
See FRONT².

PUT SOMEBODY'S BIDNESS IN THE STREET
To make public someone's personal affairs, personal experience, or some aspect of their personal situation by openly discussing it with others.

PUT THE IG ON
To DIS somebody by applying the *ig*, that is, by refusing to acknowledge their presence or ignoring them. See also IG.

**PUT THEY MOUTH ON YOU**

The act of someone talking negatively about you, generally in your absence; the talking motivated by intent to cause you harm of some kind. Cause for concern lies in the belief that the mouth (words) can cause events to happen.

**PUTTIN ON A CLINIC**

In B-BALL, when opponents are scoring from every angle, as if putting on a seminar or clinic teaching all facets of the game.

**PWT**

Poor white trash, derogatory term for lower-class white person.

**Q**

Barbecued ribs.

**QUICK, FAST, AND IN A HURRY**

Refers to doing or understanding something extremely fast.

**QUIET AS IT'S KEPT**

Here's the little-known truth about something.

**QUO VADIS**

A male hairstyle, cut short and combed to the front; popular from the 1950s to about the mid-1960s and the advent of the NATURAL hairstyle. Probably derived from the 1951 film epic *Quo Vadis,* set in Rome thirty years after the death of Jesus Christ. *Quo Vadis, The Robe,* and other big-screen historical religious epics of this era portrayed Christians and Romans, some wearing this hairstyle. Also *caesar,* newer term.

RACE MAN / WOMAN

A person who is devoted to, DOWN FOR, the race, who promotes African American Culture, and who staunchly defends Blacks; for example, historically, Dr. Carter G. Woodson, founder of Black History Month in 1926 (then it was "Negro History Week"). The concept and term both date back to the early 1900s, when being a *race man* or *woman* was a full-time preoccupation, engaged in by self-conscious Blacks who worked ordinary jobs for survival and took on racial promotion activities, usually for no monetary benefit or personal gain. Other *race men* of this early era were Marcus Garvey, J. A. Rogers, W E. B. Du Bois, and Monroe Trotter. A significant *race woman* of the time was Ida B. Wells, who risked her life to conduct extensive investigations into the lynchings of Black men. *Race men/women* in the 1990s included people like Dr. Johnetta Cole, the former president of Spelman College; the late Judge A. Leon Higginbotham; Dr. Mary Frances Berry, chairperson of the U.S. Civil Rights Commission; and Dr. Henry Louis Gates of Harvard University (who in a 1990 *New York Times* cover story described himself as a *race man*). HIP HOP *race men/women* are artists such as Public Enemy, Tribe Called Quest, Speech and his former group, Arrested Development, Queen Latifah, Ice Cube, and Lauryn Hill.

RADA

An Eldorado Cadillac, once a very popular status symbol among PLAYAS, preachers, and the FLY.

RAG

1) A gang member. 2) To talk disparagingly about, to DIS someone. 3) To criticize a person harshly. 4) To make fun of someone.

**RAGAMUFFIN**

A down-to-earth person. Probably from the Jamaican style of music that combines Rap and reggae to convey messages about ordinary people, their problems, and their politics.

**RAGAMUFFIN TIP**

An ordinary, down-to-earth status or situation. See also TIP[1].

**RAGGEDY**

Not up to par; unHIP, uncOOL. "Yo shit is raggedy," that is, In this area of life (whatever it happens to be), your behavior or BIDNESS is dysfunctional and ineffective.

**RAGS**

Stylish clothes. Older term.

**RAISE**

To leave. Also *raise up*.

**RAISE A HYMN**

Spontaneously breaking into song in the Traditional Black Church, often during a particularly climactic break within the sermon.

**RAISE CAIN**

See RAISE SAND, the more common expression in the COMMUNITY. *Raise Cain* derives from the Old Testament story of Cain, Adam and Eve's son, who murdered his brother Abel and was banished from the community. To "raise Cain" is to make enough noise or fuss to raise up Cain.

**RAISE SAND**

To talk loud, engage in provocative, argumentative behavior. Also *raise Cain*.

**RAISE UP**

See RAISE.

**RANK**

1) Describes something that is in poor taste. 2) See LOW RATE.

**RAP**

1) Strong, aggressive, highly fluent, powerful talk on a sociopolitical or moral topic. Crossover meaning. 2) Conversation de-

signed to win a woman's sexual favor. Older meaning that has not crossed over. 3) To talk in a clever, charming style to win a woman's affection. Older use of the term, has not crossed over. 4) To talk in a strong, aggressive style on any subject. Crossover meaning. Originally, *rap* referred to creative conversation from a man to a woman for purposes of winning her affection and ultimately for getting sex. When the term crossed over into the white mainstream, it lost its sexual association.

RAP

Musical style rooted in the Black Verbal Tradition—talk-singing, SIGNIFYIN, blending reality and fiction. A contemporary Black response to conditions of joblessness, poverty, and disempowerment; a rebellion against what a cultural critic from the "front lines of the White Struggle" calls "white America's economic and psychological terrorism against Black people—reduced in the white mind to 'prejudice' and 'stereotypes,' concepts more within its cultural experience" (Upski, "We Use Words Like 'Mackadocious,'" *The Source,* May 1993).

RAP ATTACK

1) Listening to a lot of RAP Music at one time. 2) Nonstop, strong, aggressive talk; can't stop RAPpin.

RAPED

In basketball, when the ball has been stolen from the ball handler, he is said to have been *raped.* Also *picked yo pocket, stole yo lunch.*

RASPBERRY

A male who sells himself to other men for drugs or money to buy drugs. A female who does the same is a STRAWBERRY.

RASTA

A follower of RASTAFARIA.

RASTAFARIA

A cultural and religious movement of resistance to enslavement in the early years and to white racism and domination after Emancipation. Originated in Jamaica; its spiritual base is the

Ethiopianism of Haile Selassie, whose former name was Ras (in the Amharic language, "prince") Tafari (Amharic, "to be feared"). *Rastafarians* have often been misunderstood because of their cultural practices—wearing DREADLOCKS, smoking GANJA/the Chillum Pipe, and their strong, rebellious reggae music. Yet RASTA men such as the late Bob Marley promoted the drum as a tool of communication with working-class Jamaicans and other Africans in the Caribbean and used reggae for social and political commentary. "The Rastafari has dramatised the question that has always been uncomfortable in Caribbean history, and the question is where you stand in relation to blackness" (George Lamming, quoted in *Rasta and Resistance,* 1987).

RASTAFARIAN

A follower of RASTAFARIA.

RAT

An ugly person.

RAT PACK

1) A group that gangs up to BEAT DOWN a person. 2) Any informally organized clique or group that socializes together.

RAW

1) Refers to the actual truth or status of something, the "real deal." 2) See DEF. 3) Refers to having sex without a condom. 4) Describes cocaine without any additives.

RAW DOG

Sex without a condom. Also RAW.

READ

To tell someone off in no uncertain terms and in a verbally elaborate manner. See also TAKE A TEXT.

READY

Excellent, superb, great. "The catfish was ready."

REBELLION

A term used by activists and AFRICAN-CENTERED folk to describe a mass display of dissatisfaction with the system. *Rebel-*

*lions* have occurred throughout African American history, for instance, during the 1960s and 1970s and in South Central Los Angeles in 1992 following the trial of the police officers who brutalized Rodney King. The social disruption and upheaval are perceived as manifestations of a people in struggle, in contrast to the perception of European Americans and the media, who refer to these uprisings as "riots."

RECOGNIZE

See BETTA RECOGNIZE.

RECRUITING

Refers to males on the lookout for females, especially attractive ones.

RED, BLACK, AND GREEN

A color combination suggesting strong identification with Blackness and the Black Experience. "What red, black and green Afrikan B-boy wouldn't want to go over to this twentysomething, Brooklyn flygirl's crib?" (Louis Romain, "A Rose Grows in Brooklyn" [interview with Rosie Perez], *The Source,* July 1993). Derived from the colors of the flag of the "Black Nation," red for blood, black for the people, and green for the land. One of the first proponents of the idea of African Americans as a separate nation was Marcus Garvey (1887–1940), founder and leader of the Universal Negro Improvement Association and of the first mass "Back-to-Africa" movement.

RED EYE

A long, hard stare, usually directed at a person.

RED NECK

Any white person; also, a lower-class white person; a derogatory term. Also *neck.*

REEFER

Marijuana. Crossover term.

REJOICE

Traditional Black Church practice of responding with a

SHOUT, or some expression of praise, in acknowledgment of the presence of the Spirit. See also PRAISE HIM.

RELAXED

Refers to hair that has been STRAIGHTENed using a RE-LAXER, a chemical treatment that *relaxes* the hair from its natural, tightly curled state, creating either a totally straight look or a loosely curled style, such as the JHERI-CURL. Before the 1970s, females used the HOT COMB method and males used the CONK method to straighten their hair.

RELAXER

See RELAXED.

RENT-A-NIGGA

A derogatory reference to private security guards in COMMU-NITY stores and shops, who sometimes insult the Black shoppers and treat them with brutal disrespect. Although perceived as modern-day overseers protecting the white man's property, many guards, who are very often males, indicate that they are desperate and driven to seek this kind of work because no other jobs are available.

REP

A reputation for being powerful or highly accomplished in a field.

REPRESENT

To exemplify a group, position, cultural style; to reflect what Hip Hoppers call the FLAVA of something or someone; a model example of the group or thing being represented. Commonly expressed in HIP HOP as simply "Represent!" Can be used with or without an object, and expressed as "represent for." A DJ hosting a party on the club scene asks one of the party people: "What side of town you representin tonight?" She answers: "I'm representin the South Side." SISTA talking about the Million Man March: "Girl, did you see the Brothas? They was representin!" BROTHA to DJ on call-in radio show: "I'm representin for the Red Dogs" [his local B-BALL team]. DJ: "WJLB, 98.7

representing Lauryn Hill," that is, reflecting the style or flava of the Hip Hop DIVA.

RE-UP

To replenish a crack supply for the purpose of ROLLIN.

R-E-S-P-E-C-T

Title of 1967 megahit song by DIVA Aretha Franklin, became something of an anthem. When people wanted it understood that they were serious about demanding respect, they would spell it out as SISTA REA did in the JAM. Enjoyed long linguistic currency throughout the 1970s and into the 1980s; can still be heard occasionally today.

REVIVAL

An extended Church service, usually a week, devoted to two main purposes: 1) to "revive," reignite the spirit, to rejuvenate and renew the congregation's religious commitment, and 2) to SAVE souls and bring new Christians into the fold. Generally, *revivals* are held once a year, but twice-yearly (i.e., spring and fall) *revivals* are also held in some church congregations. During the week, there are nightly services of preaching, singing, and prayer. See also MOANUHS' BENCH.

RIDE

1) A car. 2) One's transportation to any place. 3) To have sex; from the male viewpoint, to *ride* a woman, or, from the female viewpoint, to "mount" and *ride* the penis.

RIDE DOWN ON

1) To track somebody down in your vehicle in order to confront the person. 2) In gang terms, to travel by vehicle to a rival gang's territory in order to confront or attack them.

RIDE FOR

To be loyal to your man/woman, your family, your DOGS, to be willing to support them in whatever they do. Rapper Foxy Brown says, "I have been in a lot of situations where...I was ridin' for niggas, like no matter what, that's *my nigga*." Commenting on this, writer Danyel Smith says, "When she says *I ride for my niggas,* she means she will go with them wherever, whenever, for whatever. She means loyalty. And she's serious about it" (from "She Got Game: Foxy Brown Is the Illest," *Vibe,* December 1998/January 1999).

RIDE ON
See RIDE DOWN ON.

RIDE SHOTGUN
To ride in the front passenger seat of a vehicle. From the Wild West practice of having a guard armed with a shotgun ride beside the driver of a stagecoach, which usually transported money as well as people.

RIGHT HAND OF FELLOWSHIP
The extending of a handshake to new or newly converted members of the Traditional Black Church congregation; the ritual involves the entire congregation shaking hands with the new members. The various Black Power handshakes used as greetings in the 1960s and 1970s derived from this ritual. See also SOUL SHAKE.

RIGHT ON T
Right on time. See ON TIME / ON T. The response "Right on!" was derived from *right on T* and popularized by the Black Panther party (a political revolutionary organization of the 1960s and 1970s).

RIGHTEOUS
Excellent, especially referring to somebody or something that is on the political and/or social activist TIP. "The BROTHA is righteous."

RINKY DINK
Inadequate, insignificant. Crossover term.

RIP
See JUMPSTREET.

RIP IT
To have a rousing good time, to party hard, ROCK THE HOUSE, TEAR THE ROOF OFF THE SUCKA.

RIP OFF

1) To kill someone. 2) To take unfair advantage of someone. 3) To rob someone of his or her material valuables or ideas. Crossover meaning.

RIPPED

1) Exceptionally unattractive. 2) Intoxicated from liquor; drunk. Crossover meaning. 3) In B-BALL, the act of the ball being stolen right out in open court, usually in a face-off between the player dribbling the ball and the player CHECK in him. "He can't handle that rock so good. I ripped him a few times."

RISE

See HOPS (newer term).

ROACH

A marijuana cigarette butt; often used to roll a new marijuana cigarette or a COCKTAIL. Crossover term.

ROAD DOG

A HOMEY who always rides around with you.

ROBO COP

A hard-core, rigid, gung-ho type of police officer.

ROCK¹

1) A basketball. 2) Cocaine, with no fillers or additives. Crossover meaning.

ROCK²

1) To jolt, excite extremely. "I'll rock your world." 2) To play exceptionally live music that will get everybody dancing and *rock the house.*

ROCK N ROLL

1) Music, dance, and cultural styles begun by African American musicians in the 1950s. Crossover term and meaning; however, ROCK N ROLL in its original Black meaning referred to sexual activity. 2) To fight. 3) To compete. 4) To leave. Also *roll.*

ROCK STAR

See CRACKHEAD.

**ROCK THE HOUSE**

See ROCK².

**ROKEE**

Jeep Cherokee.

**ROLE**

In the NUMBERS, refers to an object, event, idea, etc., from a dream or an inspiration that comes to you. The term is always used in combination with another word, as in *dead role, shit role, house role.* Each *role* is symbolized by a number, located in the DREAM BOOK, that one can place a bet on.

**ROLL**

1) To leave. Also *rock n roll.* 2) To drive a car.

**ROLL EM UP**

1) To roll marijuana cigarettes. 2) To beat somebody up.

**ROLL UP ON**

To arrive at a place discreetly, in order to come upon someone inconspicuously, with the intent of confronting the person and/or doing them harm.

**ROLLER**

A person who sells crack (and other drugs).

**ROLLIE**

A Rolex watch.

**ROLLIN**

1) Selling drugs. Also *dealin* (older term). 2) Associating with, hanging around with a person or group. 3) Laughing hard. "That crazy-ass Chris Rock [popular 1990s comic] had me rollin." 4) Describes a person who has a nice car (older usage).

**ROULIE**

See FIFTY-ONE

**RUG RATS**

See CRUMB SNATCHERS. Also *table pimps.*

**RUN**

Something you have to leave the house and do. "I got to make a run" could refer to a simple errand or to something more major that one has to go and do.

RUN A BOSTON

In the game of BID, to win every round of play; to turn all the books (see TURN A BOOK). Also *Boston.*

RUN A DRAG ON

See DRAG.

RUN A TRAIN

See PULL A TRAIN.

RUN AND TELL THAT!

A sarcastic statement reflecting on the tendency of some African Americans to "squeal" to European Americans about their BROTHAS' and SISTAS' plans. The expression probably dates from enslavement, when traitors within the race would *run and tell* "Ole Massa" about the slaves' schemes and plans for escape.

RUN IT DOWN

See BREAK IT DOWN.

RUN ONE'S MOUTH

To talk, usually not about anything important.

RUN OUT

See PLAY OUT. "That group used to sang good, but they done run out now."

RUN THE STREET

To be away from home a lot, partying, "good-timing," HANGin OUT.

RUN WILD

To live an unconventional life, in the fast lane, without any checks or balances on one's behavior.

RUNNIN

Busy; having to make a lot of RUNS. "I been runnin for the last hour," meaning, I've been busy; "He got a lot of runnin to do tomorrow," meaning, He'll be very busy and on the go tomorrow.

**RUNNIN OFF AT THE MOUTH**

1) Talking excessively. Crossover meaning. Also *jaw jackin,* which has not crossed over. 2) Gossiping.

**RUSH**

To jump on somebody; to beat somebody up.

**SACK CHASER**

HIP HOP term for GOLD DIGGER.

**SADIDDY**

Snooty, uppity-acting; acting like "yo shit don't stank." Also *dichty* (older term).

**SALTY**

Angry, mad. Term in use since at least the 1930s (listed in Cab Calloway's *Hepster's Dictionary,* 1938).

**SAM**

A derogatory reference to an African American male, possibly from Sambo in *Little Black Sambo.*

**SANCTIFIED**

SAVED, set apart from the secular world.

**SANG THE SONG**

Sing the song, an encouraging response to Traditional Black Church singers.

**SAPPHIRE**

A derogatory reference to a Black woman; from a character named Sapphire in the "Amos 'n' Andy" radio program (and later television sitcom), who was the stereotypical EVIL, loud, complaining, emasculating Black woman.

SATURDAY NIGHT SPECIAL

A gun. Originally any small, easily concealed gun, carried only on weekends when trouble might start at a party or out in the street. Crossover term.

SAUSAGE

Euphemism for DICK.

SAVED

Refers to a person who has been rescued from the world of sin and now belongs to a special national community of individuals united in Christ and religious spirit.

SAVIN

Action of a man or woman who tries to keep a person in a relationship with money and material things. "James sign his whole check over to 'em; boy be just savin broads."

SAY WHAT?

A response questioning the validity of what somebody has said. Crossover expression.

SCAG

Low-grade heroin that has been diluted (CUT) with something, such as baking powder.

SCANDALOUS

Describes a ruthless or low-down person.

SCANK

See SKEEZER (newer term).

SCARED OF YOU

A response celebrating someone's accomplishment, achievement, skill, or verbal adeptness.

SCHOLAR

Any person with a college education.

SCHOOLED

Describes a person who has learned a lesson through defeat.

SCHOOLGIRL / SCHOOLBOY

Any person, of any age, going to school or college.

**SCIENCE**

Knowledge, information, true facts.

**SCOPE**

1) To watch closely. 2) To keep tabs on somebody through sur-
veillance.

**SCOPE SOMETHING OR SOMEBODY OUT**

To observe something or someone in order to analyze or evalu-
ate it or that person. Crossover expression. Also *check it/this/
him/her/etc., out.*

**SCOREBOARD**

In B-BALL, the score. "What's scoreboard?" Or sometimes, simply "Scoreboard?" meaning, What is the score?

**SCOTTY**

Crack (or other drugs, but especially crack); used to show the
controlling nature of crack use. "She's in bad shape. Scotty got
her." On "Star Trek," Scotty operates the machine that beams
Kirk and company up and away. *Scotty* is in control.

**SCRATCH**

Money; older term that has crossed over. Also *N's,* which has
not crossed over.

**SCREAM ON**

To put someone down; to DIS a person.

**SECOND HEAD**

Euphemism for DICK.

**SEEDS**

One's children; rarely used in the singular.

**SELL A WOLF TICKET**

See WOOF TICKET.

**SELL A WOOF TICKET**

See WOOF TICKET.

**SELL-OUT**

1) An African American who isn't DOWN WITH the Black
cause, one who betrays the race and compromises the COMMU-

NITY's principles, usually for personal gain. Also *sell-out Negro.* 2) By extension, anyone who GOES FOR SELF and abandons his or her group's collective mission. This use has crossed over. 3) See CHOKE.

SELL-OUT NEGRO

See SELL-OUT.

SELLING BLESSINGS

The selling of good fortune, usually by preachers, using candles and other objects which one receives and for which one in turn leaves a donation. A blessing could be in the form of a winning number buried within the candle or object that the person could play; the good fortune is received when the number FALLS.

SEMI-BLACK

An African American who exploits the Black cause for his/her own purpose, but who doesn't identify with the race; Black only when it's convenient and serves one's own self-interest.

SEND

To excite someone in a romantic/sexual sense. Resurfacing of a term from the popular 1958 recording "You Send Me," by the late Sam Cooke.

SENEGALESE TWIST

A large, intricate braided hairstyle reported to have been adopted from contemporary Africa.

SENT UP

Incarcerated; sentenced to time in prison. "All of them got sent up."

SERIOUS

Superb, excellent; describes something or someone to be taken seriously because of profound quality, impressive accomplishment, or depth. "That is a serious car," that is, It is a beautiful, well-made car; "That was a serious cake," meaning, That was a very delicious, superb cake. Crossover term.

SERIOUS AS A HEART ATTACK

Describes someone's degree of seriousness about a particular issue or statement; also the degree of severity of a condition or thing.

**SERIOUS BIDNESS**

See SQUARE BIDNESS.

**SERVE**

1) To provide sexual favors. "I just want to be the one to serve you." 2) To be outdone by a competitor. "He got served." 3) To beat up.

**SET**

1) A gang or group. 2) Neighborhood. 3) A party or social gathering, usually small and intimate. 4) To defeat in the game of BID. "We set yall every game." That is, We defeated you in every single game we played.

**SET BOOK**

In BID, the cards played at the moment of victory; also used to refer to the card or cards in a player's hand that will be played to clinch the opposition's defeat. "Come wit it, I got yo set book right here."

**SET IT OFF**

1) To cause trouble. 2) To start something.

**SET IT OUT**

See COME WIT IT.

**SETTIN HAND**

In BID, the cards in a player's hand that will constitute defeat for the opposition when played. As the SISTA said, "Yeah, Baby Sis, this settin hand is jes waitin for yo ass!"

**SHADE TREE**

See JACKLEG.

**SHADES**

Sunglasses. Crossover term. See LOKES, newer term that has not crossed over.

**SHAKE AND BAKE**

1) In basketball, a set of moves where the offensive player with

the ball tries to elude *(shake)* the player guarding or CHECK in him/her by executing a series of skillful movements, such as going from side to side on the court, faking, stop-and-go dribbling, etc. 2) By extension, any act of artful dodging.

SHEIK

A scarf worn by males over the hair and tied in back; suggests toughness/BADness.

SHERM

A long, brown cigarette dipped in PCP. From Nat Sherman's cigarettes, an old, established brand, more expensive than other cigarettes, made of all-natural tobacco, with no chemicals or additives.

SHINE

A derogatory reference to a Black male; possibly derived from the shiny appearance of ebony skin. The hero of the toast "Shine and the Sinking of the *Titanic*" is given this name. ("Toasts" are rhyming, epic-like Black folk stories, usually raw and racy, that celebrate Blacks.) The model for Shine is believed to have been the first Black heavyweight champion, Jack Johnson. According to Black folk legend, Johnson tried to book passage on the *Titanic,* but because of racism, he was refused. In this legendary mythical tale, Shine is the only survivor of the *Titanic* disaster of 1912, and Jack Johnson is thus vindicated. In the toast, Shine is the stoker on the *Titanic.* Though looked down upon by the white world, he ends up surviving because of his MOTHER WIT. He is the only one who realizes that this technological marvel is sinking, and he abandons ship. While he is swimming away from the ship, the captain and other passengers, finally realizing that the *Titanic* is going to go down, come out on deck and beg Shine—who now becomes "Mr." Shine—to save them. After a few choice words refusing their offers (of sex, money, etc.), Shine proceeds on his way. His strength enables him to swim to shore (some twelve hundred miles from the point where the actual *Titanic* went down). He fends off sharks and whales during this long journey, and, "when news reached land that the great *Titanic* had sunk, Shine was down on the corner halfway drunk."

SHIT

1) Can refer to almost anything—possessions, events, etc. "He had on some bad shit," meaning, He was wearing stylish clothes; "We wasn't goin for they shit," that is, We refused to accept their abuse. See also CHICKEN SHIT, FULL OF SHIT, ON SOME- BODY'S SHIT LIST, PULL SHIT, PUT SHIT ON SOME- BODY, SHOOT THE SHIT, SLICK SHIT, TAKE SHIT, TALK SHIT, UP SHIT CREEK, WEAK SHIT. 2) A filler with no meaning, just used to complete a statement.

THE SHIT

A person who is the ultimate; most powerful; above all others; top dog.

SHIT FROM SHINOLA

See ASS FROM A HOLE IN THE GROUND. "Oh, no, I ain no fool by a long shot. I can tell shit from Shinola." "Shinola" is a brand name for an inexpensive and very strong-smelling liquid shoe polish that once was widely used because it was cheap.

SHIT HIT THE FAN

A reference to the start of an incident, commotion, disturbance, argument, or conflict precipitated by some critical statement, important action, or significant event. "Then my momma said she didn't give a care who they was, and that's when the shit hit the fan." Crossover expression.

SHIZ OUT

See SHOUT OUT.

SHO YOU RIGHT

Expression of affirmation in response to what someone has said or done. "Sure, you're right," pronounced according to AAL rules as *Sho you right*.

SHOOK

Scared.

SHOOT DICE

To play craps, a gambling game. Older term.

SHOOT SOME HOOP

See B-BALL, HOOP.

SHOOT THE DIE

On urban B-BALL courts, where there are no referees, to shoot from an agreed-upon line in order to determine various outcomes, as in deciding which team gets the ball at the beginning of the game, resolving disagreements about fouls, etc. For example, if a foul is called and the opposing player disagrees, the player who called the foul shoots from this line, and if he makes the basket, then the alleged foul was an actual foul, but if he doesn't make it, then the alleged foul was not a foul. *Shooting the die* is viewed as impartial, unbiased. Derived from the older expression SHOOTing DICE. See also LINE DON'T LIE.

SHOOT THE GIFT

See SHOOT THE SHIT. The *gift* refers to the "gift of gab."

SHOOT THE SHIT

To engage in general conversational talk; to chitchat. Also *shoot the gift* (newer term); *talk shit* (older term); *buck whylin* (older term, resurfacing).

SHOOTIN THE ROCK

Playing basketball.

SHORT

A car. Older term.

SHORTY

Generic, positive term for a female.

SHOT CALLER

One who calls the shots; the person running things; the authority.

SHOUT

1) To express religious/spiritual ecstasy, a state of deep emotion

brought on by a religious experience; may be in the form of hollering, whooping, moaning. See also GIT HAPPY, GIT THE
SPIRIT. 2) By extension, in the secular world, especially during
performances at concerts, clubs, and in other places of entertainment, to express high emotion brought on by the musical
entertainment, GITtin THE SPIRIT from the music.

SHOUT OUT

A greeting, a "hello," sent out to one's associates, friends, or supporters, often via the media. "Ima give a shout out to the posse
over at Douglass High School" (from a call-in to a local radio
DJ). Also sometimes *shiz-out*.

SHOW

1) To exhibit the state of pregnancy, to be visibly pregnant. "She
was six months before she started to show." That is, the woman
was six months pregnant before her body exhibited any sign of
pregnancy. 2) The movies or a movie.

SHOW AND PROVE

1) To speak very articulately. 2) To provide hard, concrete proof
of something.

SHOW SOME SIGN

Expression referring to the importance of demonstrating and
verbalizing one's religious fervor and the power and spirit of
God by praising, REJOICing, moaning, SHOUTing.

SHOWBOAT

See GRANDSTAND.

SHUCKIN AND JIVIN

Putting someone on, deceiving a person. A useful strategy for
accomplishing an objective when you are in a subordinate position without power. Enslaved African Frederick Douglass
learned to read by *shuckin and jivin,* that is, by pretending that
he already knew how to read and thereby tricking some white
schoolboys into teaching him to read.

SHUT THE NOISE!

A response of strong agreement or affirmation, meaning the opposite of what it says, that is, Keep on with the noise, Talk on, I'm wit that! Also *Shut up!*

SHUT UP!

See SHUT THE NOISE!

SICK

Describes a person who is very funny, gets lots of laughs from telling jokes, humorous commentary, and acting CRAZY. Also *ill.*

SIG / SIG ON

See SIGNIFY / SIGNIFY ON.

SIGGIN

See SIGNIFYIN.

SIGNIFICATION

See SIGNIFYIN.

SIGNIFY / SIGNIFY ON

See SIGNIFYIN. Also *sig/sig on.*

SIGNIFYIN

1) Ritualized verbal art in which the speaker puts down, needles, talks about *(signifies on)* someone, to make a point or sometimes just for fun. *Signifyin* depends on double meaning and irony, exploits the unexpected, and uses quick verbal surprises and humor. When used as social critique, it is characterized by nonmalicious and principled criticism. Malcolm X once began a speech with this bit of *signifyin:* "Ladies and gentlemen, friends and enemies." Also *signification.* 2) The act of *signifyin.* Also *siggin, sig on, signify on.*

SILK

A reference to a white woman; derived from the stereotypical notion of the softness and silkiness of white hair.

SILLY

Foolish, lacking in good judgment.

SIMP

See LAME, SQUARE (older terms); GEEK[1] (newer term).

SINGLE ACTION

A reference to PLAYING THE NUMBERS by betting on a single digit of the winning combination.

SINGLE ACTION LADY / MAN

See PICK-UP LADY / MAN.

SISSY

A derogatory term for a gay male.

SISTA

Any African American woman. Derived from the Traditional Black Church pattern of referring to female members of the Church "family" as *Sista*.

SISTA REA

Singing DIVA Aretha Franklin.

SKEEZE

To engage in a sexual orgy; done by RAP groupies.

SKEEZER

A person who has sex indiscriminately, especially a groupie. Also *scank* (older term).

SKILLZ

1) Ability to flow, BUS A RHYME. 2) By extension, high ability in any area. A person who has such ability "got skillz."

By permission of the artist, Craig Rex Perry, and *Young Sisters and Brothers Magazine.*

By permission of the artist, Craig Rex Perry, and *Young Sisters and Brothers Magazine.*

SKIN

See GIVE SOMEBODY SKIN / SOME SKIN.

SKINNIN AND GRINNIN

Refers to a person who is happy and showing it, GIVING FIVE *(skinnin)* and smiling from ear to ear *(grinnin)* because everything's all right in his/her world.

SKINS

1) Females. 2) Euphemism for PUSSY. See also GIT SKINS, IN THE SKINS. 3) Cigarette papers for rolling marijuana cigarettes. 4) Fried pork rinds. 5) Drums; the term dates from the 1930s but is still in use by musicians today. 6) Shoes made from animal skins, such as alligator and lizard.

SKUNK

A low-down, no-good person; someone who is treacherous, LOW-LIFE.

**SKY**

See HOPS (newer term).

**SLACK**

See CUT SOMEBODY SOME SLACK.

**SLAIN IN THE SPIRIT**

To have one's worldly self symbolically discarded ("slain") when making the transition from the secular to the spiritual world.

**SLAM**

To have sex. See also SLAMMIN PARTNER.

**SLAM-DUNK**

1) To dump the basketball into the basket from over the rim with aggressive power and force, usually using both hands; harder and more powerful than a DUNK. 2) By extension, to make any aggressive, powerful move. A Black debater referring to a recent debate competition between university forensics teams: "Yeah, I beat em; just slam-dunked they asses."

**SLAMMIN**

1) Dumping or DUNKin the basketball in a strong, powerful, aggressive way; short for SLAM-DUNKin. 2) See DEF.

**SLAMMIN PARTNER**

One's sex partner; a partner in a relationship for sex only.

**SLANG**

1) Young people's talk. 2) To sell crack and cocaine.

**SLANGUAGE**

Slang language.

**SLAVE**

See HAIM.

**SLEEF**

See FIFTY-ONE.

**SLEEP**

To overlook or miss something, to forget something, generally used in the past tense. The Sista said: "Dog, I slept the lottery today, out there trying to git my lil garden together." (I was doing yard work, not watching the time, and missed/"slept" the deadline for going to the corner store to play my number in the state Lotto.)

SLICK

Clever; describes a person capable of manipulating people and situations to his/her advantage. Often grudgingly admired for this ability; however, see NICKEL SLICK.

SLICK SHIT

A clever move designed to get what you want.

SLIDE

1) To let a person off the hook; to excuse somebody. 2) To leave.

SLIPPIN AND SLIDIN

1) Sneaking around; doing something under cover. 2) Sly behavior or camouflaged talk designed to mask one's real intentions or motives.

SLOB

An insulting name used by the Los Angeles gang the CRIPS for their former rivals, the BLOODS. Also *blob*.

SLOPE

To take a person down; to DIS someone.

SLOW JAM

A slow dance song.

SLOW YOUR / MY / HIS / HER ROLL

To reduce the momentum of something.

SMACK

1) Low-grade cocaine, adulterated with fillers. 2) Heroin (older usage). 3) Drugs in general. 4) Negative talk about somebody, referred to as TALKIN SMACK.

SMASH

The act of sex.

SMELLIN UP BEHIND SOMEBODY

Pursuing someone you're interested in sexually/romantically.

SMOKE

1) Marijuana. 2) To outdo someone in a competition. 3) To beat someone up. 4) To kill someone. 5) To ingest crack cocaine.

**SMOKER**

See CRACKHEAD. Also *puffer, rock star.*

**SMOKIN**

1) Performing excellently; doing something superbly. "Luther 'nem [singer Luther Vandross and other entertainers] was smokin at that concert." 2) Smoking crack, commonly done in a small pipe. "My man done start smokin again," meaning, The speaker's partner/significant other has gone back to using crack (after having been off it for some time).

**SMOOTH**

Dressed stylishly; looking good.

**SNAKE**

1) A sneaky person. 2) An informant; a snitch.

**SNAPPER**

A male's term for superb sex from a woman, specifically referring to intense, vigorous vaginal muscle movements during lovemaking. See also BITE.

**SNAPPIN**

Engaged in playing the game of talking about people or their mother or relatives, playing the game of ritual DISsin. HIP HOP term for older term PLAYIN THE DOZENS. *Snappin* includes both THE DOZENS and SIGNIFYIN; however, in OLD SCHOOL play, these were two distinct styles of verbal play.

**SNAPS**

The discounts, the ritual taunts, playful "insults," or DISses, in the game of SNAPPIN. See also THE DOZENS / PLAYIN THE DOZENS, SNAPPIN, SIGNIFYIN, YO MOMMA.

**SNATCH**

Euphemism for PUSSY.

**SNORT**

To ingest cocaine, or sometimes heroin, by sniffing it into the nostrils. Crossover term.

**SNOW**

A white person.

SNOW BUNNY

A white female.

SOLID

A response of affirmation or agreement. Crossover term.

SOME

Sex, used by males or females. "She was actin all evil; girl musta need some."

SOOKI-SOOKI

Expression indicating that something is good, usually said in reference to high-powered dancing. DJ: "Git it, girl, ah, put it on him—sooki-sooki!" Sexual overtones. Came out of the Blues Tradition.

SOONER

1) A person or thing that is cheap, shabby, not prime. 2) A mongrel dog, not a purebred; a dog that would "soon as be one thing as another."

SORRY

Useless, ineffective, inadequate. "That lil party was the sorriest thing I ever been to."

S.O.S.

The phrase "Stuck on stupid." Describes someone who makes silly, stupid mistakes all the time.

SOUL

The essence of life; feeling, passion, emotional depth—all of which are believed to be derived from struggle, suffering, and having participated in the Black Experience. Having risen above the suffering, the person gains *soul*.

SOUL BROTHA / SISTA

A generic reference to an African American man/woman, a member of the community of SOULful folk.

SOUL CLAP

A three-beat rhythmic unit of overlapping claps, with one regular clap on the beat rapidly followed by two quick claps off the beat.

By permission of the artist, Abdel Aziz Ramzah, and *Ebony* magazine, October 1991.

*Living in the suburbs has its disadvantages.*

SOUL FOOD

Cuisine characteristic of African Americans, such as red beans and rice, CHITLINS, greens, crackling bread, black-eyed peas, etc.

SOUL SHAKE

An intricate handshake to demonstrate solidarity; very popular during the 1960s and 1970s. Also known as the "Black Power handshake." Probably from the Traditional Black Church concept and practice of extending the RIGHT HAND OF FELLOW-SHIP. The *soul shake* has a number of complex variations on the basic structure, which is executed by juxtaposing the right thumbs, placing your thumb first to the right of the other person's thumb, then to the left, next grasping the other person's fingers in your palm, followed by your fingers being grasped in his palm.

SOUL SOUND

Music that is SOULful and rooted in Blackness and the African American Experience; the term is applied particularly to Rhythm 'n' Blues and the music of the 1960s and 1970s. An older expression, resurfacing along with OLD SCHOOL music in HIP HOP. "The...R & B, hip hop soul sound of songstress Mary J. Blige [who has] redefined R & B...by bringing in elements of hip hop and soul...Mary's unique blend of old school groove, hip hop and jazzy vocals have shot *What's the 411?* straight to the top" (from "Real Love: The Mary J. Blige Story," in *Word Up!*).

SPADE

A reference to any African American; a derogatory term.

SPIRIT

See GIT THE SPIRIT.

SPLEEFER

See FIFTY-ONE.

SPLIB

A generic reference to any Black person; a fairly neutral term.

SPONSOR

A man who supports, or contributes significantly to the support of, a woman in exchange for sexual favors; a man with a "kept woman."

SPOOK

A derogatory reference to an African American.

SPORT

1) To dress stylishly and attractively. 2) To spend money on someone; usually said about a man of means spending money on a woman (older usage).

SPOT

1) In the jazz world, a nightclub; term dates to the early 1900s according to Clarence Major (*Juba to Jive,* 1994). 2) Updated in HIP HOP to refer to any popular social gathering place.

SPRINGS

See HOPS

SPRUNG

Hopelessly in love; out of emotional control.

**SQUARE**

1) A person who is uninformed, lacking in sophistication, unHIP. This meaning has crossed over. Also *lame, geek, simp.* 2) A cigarette. This meaning has not crossed over.

**SQUARE BIDNESS**

A phrase tacked onto a statement to indicate that a statement or action has integrity, is serious, appropriate, sincere, on the up-and-up. "My boy gon do the work, square bidness." Derived from the Masonic tradition, in which the compass and the square are essential tools for a Mason. An upright man is a "square" man, who acts and deals with integrity, which is what the Masonic tradition teaches. Also *serious bidness.*

**SQUASH**

1) To argue. 2) To fight.

**SQUASH IT**

1) Resolve the matter once and for all. 2) Forget it, disregard it.

**STACY ADAMS**

A popular, high-fashion brand of shoes for men; used for STYLIN AND PROFILIN.

**STALLION**

See FOX.

**STANK**

Nasty, very bad, the action or person stinks, generally because of the person's attitude or some unprincipled thing the person has done.

**STAR**

See FOX.

**STATIC**

Confusion, trouble, conflict; something you don't want to hear.

**STAY IN THE STREET**

To be away from home a lot, always on the go.

**STAY UP**

Keep yo head up, stay in good high spirits.

STAYING ON THE PLACE

Domestic workers living in the home where they work, cooking, cleaning, taking care of the employer's children, etc. Once a common arrangement for African American women who worked for white families. In most instances these Black women had a home and family of their own but were able to see them only the one day a week they were off from work. Older term used by Black seniors.

STEADY

Indicates something done frequently and continuously. "Them fools be steady hustlin everybody they see."

STEAL

To sneak up on someone, to catch them off guard and harm them.

STEP

1) To perform fraternity or sorority marching moves, a style with intricate patterns or steps. Portrayed in Spike Lee's film *School Daze.* See also STEP SHOW. 2) To leave.

STEP OFF

GIT OUT MY FACE; leave me alone.

STEP SHOW

A type of marching art involving intricate steps and movements performed by fraternities and sororities. See also STEP.

STEP TO

To challenge someone to a fight.

STEP UP

1) To face a challenge, to rise to the occasion and take responsibility for getting the job done, whatever it is. 2) To engage in a confrontation.

STEPPIN

1) Walking, often with a decisive purpose; applies to males or females. From Sonia Sanchez's poem "Queens of the Universe": "Black women/ the only Queens of the Universe/ though we be stepping unqueenly sometime." 2) Walking on indoor skates, not gliding in the usual way, but walking in slower, albeit intricate, steps.

**STICK**

Any kind of cigar used to roll up marijuana.

**STICK IT**

Refers to what the male does during sex.

**STIFF**

A person who is stuffy, no fun.

**STOCKING CAP**

A head covering made by cutting off the lower part of a woman's nylon stocking; fits tight and keeps the hair in place.

**STOLE YO LUNCH**

Basketball term. See RAPED, PICKED YO POCKET.

**STOMP**

To beat up; to hurt someone badly.

**STONE**

Added before a word for emphasis, as in *stone fine*, meaning very beautiful; *stone tired*, meaning extremely tired. See also COAL (newer intensifying term).

**STONE TO THE BONE**

Describes a person who has all positive qualities in great abundance.

**STOOPID**

Also *stupid*. See DEF.

**STOREFRONT CHURCH**

A church located in the front part of a building, on the ground floor, in a space generally used for a small store. Generally these are churches which have been recently established and whose membership is small and financially struggling. There may be several such churches in a COMMUNITY.

**STORY**

An explanation, usually elaborate and extended, to account for something or justify one's behavior; generally fictionalized and exaggerated, but could also be a *story* with a kernel of truth that gets blown up in the telling.

STRAIGHT

1) OKAY; all right; good; content; not needing anything. In an interview, former NBA superstar Magic Johnson was asked about his relationship with his wife. He replied, "Oh, it's straight." The talk show host said, "I know you're straight. I just wanted to know how things were going." 2) Describes a person who has drugs for sale (older usage). "If you lookin, Bo's straight."

STRAIGHT UP

Directly, straightforwardly, honestly, frankly; stating the honest, unmitigated truth; boldly expressing one's thinking and/or feelings. Crossover expression.

STRAIGHTEN

To treat hair with a chemical RELAXER or to use a HOT COMB on it to remove the natural tight (KINKY) curls.

STRAIGHTEN UP AND FLY RIGHT

1) Get serious, stop playing around. Older meaning. This use has crossed over. 2) Come out of the streets, stop running around, and settle down.

STRAP

Carrying a gun. "Strapped" pronounced according to AAL rules. "My boy strap." That is, He is carrying a gun.

STRAPPED

See STRAP.

STRAWBERRY

See HEAD HUNTER. For the male version, see RASPBERRY.
*See strawberry shortcake below*

STRAY PIECE

A sexual encounter, usually a one-time event, with a female other than a male's wife or steady WOMAN. See also PIECE.

STREET WEAR

HIP HOP style of dressing—baggy clothes, with pants hanging low, oversized tops of sports teams, hiking boots, backpacks, body piercing, tattoos, short tops that reveal the midriff, etc.

STRENGTH

See ON THE STRENGTH.

*chocolate STRAWBERRY SHORTCAKE WHEN A GIRL IS SUCKING A BLACK MAN'S DICK AND HE PUNCHES HER IN THE STOMACH AND SHE CHOKES, AND BLOOD AND CUM COME OUT OF HER NOSE.*

**STRIDES**

Shoes.

**STRIDIN**

SOULful, rhythmic walking.

**STROKE**

The act of sex performed by the male.

**STRONG**

Describes a particularly bold or noteworthy assertion, one that shows mental toughness. "That's some strong stuff you talkin!" Related to, and probably the source of, the newer expression ON THE STRENGTH.

**STRONGER THAN RED DEVIL LYE**

Superstrong. Red Devil is the brand of lye that was used in CONKin men's hair during Malcolm X's era.

**THE STRUGGLE**

1) The collective struggle of Black people against the system and structures of racism and oppression, used with reference to the Civil Rights and Black Power Movements of the 1960s and 1970s (older meaning). 2) The struggle to survive on a daily basis as a Black man/woman in America (newer HIP HOP meaning).

**STRUNG OUT**

1) Addicted to drugs. Crossover meaning. 2) By extension, obsessed with or hung up on any person or activity. "My man is strung out behind this new lady he just copped."

**STRUT**

SOULful, rhythmic walking, especially done when one is G'D up and SHOWBOATin.

**STRUT YO STUFF**

To display your wares, knowledge, dress, or whatever; show 'em what you got. Crossover expression.

**STUFF**

1) Euphemism for PUSSY. 2) Anything extraordinary. 3) Crack cocaine. 4) To DUNK the basketball, to stuff it in the basket.

STUPID

Also *stoopid*. See DEF.

STYLIN AND PROFILIN

Adopting a cool, poised, confident posture, and usually dressed stylishly/FLY; appearing CHILLed and in control.

SUCKA

A weak person, a pushover, a chump.

SUGAR

1) A form of address for females; used by females or males, a neutral term, does not convey romance or intimacy. 2) Homosexuality. See also SWEET. 3) A kiss; term can be used with friends, lovers, relatives, small children. "Come here, Kwesi, and give yo Grandma some sugar" (said to a six-year-old).

THE SUGAR

Boxing legend Sugar Ray Robinson (1921–1989). Was welterweight champion (1946–1951), middleweight champion (1951–1952; 1955–1957; 1958–1960). Considered by many to be the greatest fighter, "pound for pound," in boxing history. Born Walker Smith in Detroit on May 3, took the name "Robinson" from another boxer's certificate so he could meet the age requirement. Called "The Sugar" because he was dubbed the "sweetest fighter."

SUP?

See WHASSUP?

SUPERFLY

Exceptionally upscale; ultra-exciting and with-it. From the 1970s film by that name.

SUPERMARKET CONVERSATION

Empty, meaningless chatter, i.e., like the music played in supermarkets.

SURE, YOU'RE RIGHT

See SHO YOU RIGHT.

SWEAT

1) To bother or hassle someone. 2) To proposition someone.

**SWEET**

1) Outstanding; very nice. 2) Refers to a gay male; not as derogatory as PUNK or *faggot,* but still bordering on the negative.

**SWEET-TALK**

A style of talk using words of endearment and promises for the purpose of persuading someone to do or think what you want them to; often a CONVERSATION or a RAP in male-female relationships.

**SWEETIE**

A form of address used by males to address any female; does not necessarily convey intimacy.

**SWEP**

Describes someone strongly in love, vulnerable due to the depth of their affections for another. From "swept," i.e., swept away by one's emotions, swept off one's feet, rendered in AAL pronunciation as *swep.* Also NOSE JOB, NOSE OPEN.

**SWEPT**

See SWEP.

**SWOOP**

To take someone else's man or woman in a short amount of time.

**SYSTEM**

The entire criminal justice system — jail, bail, parole, awaiting sentencing, probation, undergoing trial, etc. "Ain heard from Joe in a while. Hope he ain in the system." In the 1960s and 1970s, *system* referred to the dominant society and the Eurocentric political and economic realm of the United States. The resurfacing and narrowed meaning of the term reflects the deteriorating condition of working-class and UN-working-class African Americans since 1980, resulting in an astronomical increase in the number of African American males in various levels of the criminal justice system. In the age group twenty to twenty-nine, there are more Black men involved in the *system* than are enrolled in college. And in the age group fifteen to nineteen, in some urban districts, there are more Black men involved in the *system* than are graduating from high school.

A T

A precise and exact match or fit. "These shoes match yo hat to a
T"; "That dress fit you to a T."

TABLE PIMPS

See CRUMB SNATCHERS.

(LOOK AT THE) TAIL ON THAT WHALE

Expression of aesthetic appreciation for a SISTA who has a full,
round butt.

TAKE A CHILL PILL

See CHILL.

TAKE A TEXT

1) In a Traditional Black Church service, to announce the Scriptural reference and message of a sermon, a fairly elaborate ritual
with a set formula involving the reading of the Scriptural passage and a reinterpretation using a contemporary, cleverly
worded theme. 2) By extension, to *take a text* on a person is to
tell that person off in an elaborate, dramatic manner, using SIG-
NIFYIN and other forms from the Verbal Tradition. See also
READ.

TAKE CARE OF BIDNESS

To seriously attend to or complete something; to get on with
something, get down to business. Also *TCB*.

TAKE IT TO THE HOLE.

See TAKE IT TO THE HOOP.

TAKE IT TO THE HOOP

1) In B-BALL, to move the ball all the way to the basket and
make the shot. Also *take it to the hole*. 2) By extension, to go all
the way with something; to go down to the wire and succeed; to
perform something superbly.

**TAKE LOW**

To assume a posture of humility in order to defuse conflict and achieve an objective. "Take low and go," that is, Humble yourself, and you'll succeed in whatever you're trying to accomplish.

**TAKE OUT**

1) To outdo a competitor. 2) To kill. Crossover meaning.

**TAKE SHIT**

To accept abuse or mistreatment from someone. Crossover expression.

**TAKING NO SHORTS**

Not to be taken advantage of.

**TALK SHIT**

1) To talk nonsense, nothingness; to bullshit. This meaning has crossed over. 2) See SHOOT THE SHIT. See also BUCK WHYLIN.

**TALK SHOW SHIT**

A messy personal affair exposed to outsiders; a personal conflict over love, money, or other issues, in which knowledge of the sordid details has gone beyond the parties involved. From the practice on television talk shows of people airing their personal business and their differences, confronting each other, arguing, yelling, and sometimes even fighting right on national television. Expression popularized by the song "Talk Show Shhh!" (1998, by Rhythm 'n' Blues artist Shae Jones, with "shit" euphemistically represented in a variation on ISH, the emerging HIP HOP style). The song is addressed to her lover about an affair he is having with his "ex" girlfriend: "He say—she say / You got our business all up in the street / Everyone knows, it's like we're on T.V. / Is it her that you want to be wit? / Ya got me involved in some talk show shhh!"

**TALK THAT TALK**

To use the forms of the African American Verbal Tradition in an intense, creative, dynamic, energetic style; an expression indicating the speaker is RAPpin in a powerful, convincing manner.

TALKIN HEAD

Someone who is arguing and wants to fight.

TALKIN IN TONGUE

In the Traditional Black Church, speaking in a secret, coded language while SHOUTin and undergoing spirit-possession.

TALKIN OUT THE SIDE OF YOUR NECK / MOUTH

Lying, deceiving; TALKIN SHIT

TALKIN SMACK

Talking junk, nonsense; bullshitting. See also SMACK.

TALKIN TO

Dating someone.

TALKIN TRASH

1) The art of DISSin one's opponent during competitive play (as in basketball, Nintendo, BID) so as to erode their confidence, get them rattled or distracted so they'll make poor plays and lose the game. 2) The art of using strong, rhythmic, clever talk and forms in the African American Verbal Tradition—e.g., SIGNIFYIN, WOOFin—to entertain, to promote one's ego, to establish leadership in a group, or to project an image of BAD-ness.

TALL PAPER

See BIG PAPER.

TAP IT

To have sex.

TAP THAT ASS

See TAP IT.

TARRYING SERVICE

A prayer service for those awaiting the HOLY GHOS, waiting to feel the power and be SAVED.

TASTE

Liquor or wine.

TCB

Take care of business. See TAKE CARE OF BIDNESS.

TEAR THE ROOF OFF THE SUCKA!
> To PAR-TAY; to have BIG FUN.

TELEPHONE NUMBER
> A long prison sentence.

TELL IT!
> See TELL THE TRUTH!

TELL THE TRUTH!
> An enthusiastic response affirming what someone has said or done. Also *Tell it!*

TENDER
> A young, desirable female or male. Also *tenderoni*.

TENDERONI
> See TENDER.

TENT MEETING
> A REVIVAL meeting, held outdoors, under a tent, generally in the summer.

TERRIBLE
> See DEF (newer term).

TESTIFY
> 1) In the Traditional Black Church, to give affirmation to the power and truth of something; when GITTIN THE SPIRIT, people often *testify*. 2) By extension, to celebrate through verbal acknowledgment the greatness of anything, or one's strong feelings about something.

TG
> In gang terminology, a young member; literally, Tiny Gangster.

THAT HOW YOU LIVIN?
> Why are you acting like that?

THAT YOU?
> Is the item, person, song, whatever, yours or your type of thing?

THAT'S ALL SHE WROTE
> An expression used to refer to the end of something; can be something that leaves either good or bad memories. After eating

a huge, delectable serving of CHITLINS, Ralph said, "Well, that's all she wrote!"

### THAT'S MIGHTY WHITE OF YOU!

A SIGNIFYIN expression referring to someone patronizing you or making up your mind for you; from the perception that whites typically do this to Blacks.

### THERE IT IS

A response meaning "That's how it is," "That's the way it goes"; conveys a sense of surrendering to the finality and inevitability of an event or situation. The expression dates from the 1960s; now resurfacing and expanding meaning in HIP HOP, as in the 1993 moneymaking hit JAMS by two different RAP groups, Tag Team's "Whoomp! (There It Is)" and 95 South's "Whoot, There It Is."

### THICK

1) See DIESEL (newer term). 2) Describes a large penis. 3) Describes a voluptuous female. 4) Describes an intimate, close friendship.

### THICK LIPS

See BIG LIPS.

### THIRD STRUGGLE

The struggle against sexual weaknesses and unprincipled sexual affairs, in the vocabulary of activists.

### THIRTY-EIGHT

A .38-caliber gun.

### THOUGHT LIKE LIT

A response to a person trying to explain away or excuse an error. From the first line of the familiar little rhyme from the Oral Tradition:

You thought like lit
Thought you farted,
but you shit.

**THREADS**

1) Stylish clothes or outfit. 2) Clothes in general. Crossover meaning.

**THREE-SIX-NINE (3-6-9)**

Euphemism for *shit*. Older term still in use today. The SISTA said, "You know men, they always comin up with some 3-6-9, jes when you least expect it." From the numerological symbol for the *shit role* (listed, for instance, in older and current DREAM BOOKS). Favorite expression in the Blues Tradition: "I'm gon tell yall women and please understand/Don't start no 3-6-9 with my man" (Lil Johnson, "New Shave 'Em Dry," 1936; quoted in Paul Oliver, *Aspects of the Blues Tradition*, 1968). Used for its symbolic significance in Ralph Ellison's classic work, *Invisible Man* (1952), where the home of the main character became an underground sewer with 1,369 lightbulbs.

**THREE-SIXTY-FIVE (3-65)**

Refers to something done on a continuous basis; literally, 365 days a year.

**THROUGH**

1) Exasperated, annoyed with someone or something. 2) Emotionally exhausted, outdone, completely taken aback by an action or statement. See also ALL THE WAY THROUGH.

**THROW / THROW DOWN**

1) To do something vigorously, to the limit. This meaning has crossed over. To *throw down* at a party is to have an exceptionally good time, BIG FUN. *Throwin down* in school is excelling at one's studies. 2) To have sex. 3) To fight.

**THROW A BRICK**

To commit a crime; do something wrong or illegal. "Money been so hard to come by I'm thinkin about throwin a brick."

**THROW BONES**

1) To play dominoes. 2) To shoot dice.

**THROW THE D / THROW THE P**
To have sex.

**THROW THE GIFT**

To talk to a person romantically in order to captivate that person's heart. The *gift* refers to the "gift of gab." See also HIT ON.

**THROW UP A BRICK**

In basketball, to miss the basket and hit the backboard or rim with an ugly sound. Not to be confused with THROW A BRICK.

**THUMP**

To fight.

**TI-IS**

To tell it like it is; speak the truth in a frank, forthright manner.

**TIGHT**

1) Describes a relationship between people that is close, intimate. "We done kinda drifted apart, but we was tight back then" (said of a teenage friendship between two women whose lives took different pathways in adulthood). 2) Describes a situation, business, event, which is well organized, in place, the way it's supposed to be. "The Alphas [Alpha Phi Alpha fraternity] had it togetha. The program was tight." 3) Describes a negative, uncomfortable situation (older meaning). "What? You mean he busted my girl with Frank? Oooo, that's tight!" (said about a woman whose live-in partner caught her with her outside lover).

**TIGHT AS DICK'S HATBAND**

Extremely stingy. Also *tight as Jimmy's hatband* (newer version).

**TIGHT AS JIMMY'S HATBAND**

See TIGHT AS DICK'S HATBAND.

**TIMBOS**

Boots or shoes by Timberland. Popular in HIP HOP style of dressing.

**TIME**

A reference to the political or psychological state or mood of things. *What time it is* refers to the real deal, the truth, the real story, what's actually occurring at the moment; not a fantasy. If you know *what time it is,* you're UP ON IT, HIP, knowledgeable, a survivor.

**TIP**

1) A person's GAME, one's own Thang, some aspect of you that makes you *you.* Legendary singer James Brown in his "I'm Real" JAM chides all the HIP HOP Rappers who are sampling freely from his old hits, telling them to get off his *tip.* 2) Often used in combination with another word suggesting association with that word. "Everybody out there is on some kinda gangsta tip." Meaning, Everybody there is GANGSTA-like. "Yeah, we was kinda on the boyfriend-girlfriend tip for a minute." Meaning, Our relationship was like that of boyfriend-girlfriend for a brief period. 3) To have an affair outside one's monogamous relationship.

**TIRED**

Stale, old hat; inappropriate, PLAYED OUT. "Yo shit is tired." A popular term among women.

**TLC**

Tender, loving care. Crossover term.

**TO PUT SOMEBODY ON ICE**

B-BALL term for cooling off an opponent's game, reducing his level of play, his ability to move or shoot the ball.

**TOE OUT THE FRAME**

Torn out of the frame. High, drunk.

**TOE UP**

AAL pronunciation of torn up. 1) Intoxicated; drunk. 2) Homely, ugly.

**TOGETHA**

1) Describes any place, event, idea, or thing that is great, effec-

tive, in order. 2) Describes an accomplished individual, some-one who has *got it togetha* (see GIT IT TOGETHA), which has crossed over, although *togetha* has not.

TOKEN

An African American placed in a job or social position, usually due to pressure or demands from Blacks. However, the person does nothing to promote the Black cause and, in fact, has been put in the position only to showcase a Black presence and quiet African American protest. The term came into widespread usage in the COMMUNITY during the Black Freedom Strug-gle of the 1960s and 1970s, wherein a few African Americans were moved into the economic mainstream as a result of marches, sit-ins, and other forms of Black activism and RE-BELLION.

TOM

A negative label for a Black person, suggesting that he/she is a SELL-OUT, not DOWN WITH the Black cause. *Tom* comes from the character Uncle Tom, in Harriet Beecher Stowe's nine-teenth-century novel *Uncle Tom's Cabin,* who put his master's wishes and life before his own. *Dr. Thomas* SIGNIFIES ON an educated *Tom.* The terms *Aunt* and *Uncle* recall the Southern custom of whites addressing *all* Blacks as "aunt" or "aunty" and "uncle," a practice resented by Blacks. Also *Uncle Tom, Uncle Thomas;* for women, *Aunt Thomasina, Aunt Jane.*

TOO THROUGH

See ALL THE WAY THROUGH.

TOP OF MY / HIS / HER GAME

Someone at the pinnacle of his or her career, GAME, whatever it happens to be. Crossing over.

TORN UP

See TOE UP.

TOTALED

1) Ugly. 2) All messed up.

**TOUCH IT UP**

To have sex.

**TREY EIGHT**

A .38-caliber gun.

**TRICK**

1) A person who can be easily manipulated. 2) A customer of a prostitute. Crossover meaning.

**TRICKERATION**

The act of PLAYing on, deceiving someone; manipulation to lead someone astray.

**TRICKIN**

Selling sex; prostitution.

**TRICKNOLOGY**

European American technological innovations, viewed as things to be distrusted, as often being not technology, but *tricknology*. Popularized by THE NATION.

**TRIFLIN**

Describes a person who fails to do something that he/she is capable of doing; irresponsible; inadequate.

**TRIM**

Sex from a woman; euphemism for PUSSY.

**TRIP / TRIPPIN**

1) To talk or behave in an irrational way. 2) To do or say something outside the norm or outside one's usual pattern.

**TRIP SOMEBODY OUT**

To cause an unusual or surprise reaction in someone; could be positive or negative.

**TRIPLE NICKELS**

The 555th Battalion, which began as a test platoon of sixteen handpicked Black soldiers, the first Black paratroopers in U.S. history. The time was World War II and the still segregated U.S. Army was pressured to utilize its seven hundred thousand Black soldiers for the war effort instead of the cooking and cleaning the army had assigned them to. The army grudgingly formed this group, calling it the 555th Parachute Infantry, but these BROTHAS named themselves the *Triple Nickels*. They made history at Fort Benning, Georgia, on January 24, 1944, with the first jump ever by Black soldiers. The first *Triple Nickels* lived in the "Colored" section of the post and rode in the back of the bus. They suffered the taunts and insults of U.S.-style apartheid, not the least of which was the belief, even from their white peers among the paratroopers, that they lacked the courage to jump. Some of their accomplishments included parachute firefighting techniques; the first army unit to pioneer and develop real and experimental firefighting techniques; the first unit to make a mass parachute jump from a glider; the first parachute group to train U.S. Navy pilots in ground-support combat operations; to date, the only airborne unit to have a bridge named after it, the Triple Nickel Bridge in Ettrick, Virginia; the first Black airborne unit to have its emblem enshrined at Arlington National Cemetery. One member of the original 555th group, seventy-six-year-old retired Lieutenant Colonel Roger Walden, still refers to himself as a "Triple Nickel" (from "History of the Triple Nickels," *Eclipse*, Vol. 36, No. 1, January-February 1999, and "One Fell Swoop" by Neal Rubin, *Detroit Free Press*, February 13, 1998).

TRUCKIN

1) Running fast. See also JET (newer term); MOTOR, FLY (older terms). 2) Going somewhere; moving forward with a purpose.

TRUTH BE TOLD

An expression of validity; usually occurs at the beginning of a statement, emphasizing the truth of the statement. "Truth be told, boyfriend done run out of DUCKETTES," meaning, It may not be widely known, but the fact of the matter is that this man has run out of money.

TRYIN TO MAKE A DOLLA OUTA FIFTEEN CENT

Long-standing expression from the Oral Tradition used to convey the continuing difficulty of making it as a Black man/woman in white America, especially in terms of the economics of THE STRUGGLE. In the 1990s, Tupac Shakur rapped, "I'm just another Black man caught up in the mix / Tryin to make a dolla outa fifteen cent." In his 1968 collection of folk material (some of which dates back to enslavement), J. Mason Brewer includes this expression in the group of "Jeering and Taunting Rhymes."

TUDE

1) An aggressive, arrogant, defiant, I-know-I'm-BAD pose or air about oneself. 2) An oppositional, negative outlook or disposition. Also *attitude*.

TURF

1) Your street or HOOD. Crossover meaning. 2) By extension, any endeavor or topic of conversation that you know well and lay claim to. "They up there tryin to talk about math and numbers, that's yo girl's turf."

TURKISH

Heavy, elaborate, flashy gold jewelry.

TURN A BOOK

In BID, to win a round of play.

TURN SOMEBODY OUT

1) To introduce a person to something new and profoundly different, often something not in their best interests. 2) To have sex with a person that goes beyond the ordinary, to give them pleasure that they have not experienced before.

TURN SOMETHING OUT

1) To create a scene, causing people to vacate a place. 2) To party aggressively, loudly, and with wild abandon, partying until the place is emptied out.

TWENTY CENTS

1) Twenty dollars. 2) A quantity (BAG) of marijuana selling for twenty dollars. Also *twinkie*.

TWENTY-FOE-SEVEN (24-7)

Twenty-four hours a day, seven days a week; used to describe something that is continuous, that appears to be happening nonstop. "The only way we got ovah was that my daddy work twenty-foe-seven." Crossover term. AAL pronunciation of "twenty-four-seven."

TWINKIE

1) A twenty-dollar bill. 2) A quantity (BAG) of marijuana selling for twenty dollars. Also *twenty cents.*

TWISTED

Acting irrationally; not behaving like one's usual self; mixed-up.

TWO-MINUTE BROTHA

In Black women's talk, a man who performs sex only for a very brief moment and who is thus an undesirable partner.

UAW

You ain working; also, You ain white. Created by African American workers to put the United Automobile Workers, or UAW, on FRONT STREET for its racism and failure to protect the jobs of Black workers.

UHM OUT

I'm leaving; gone. Also OUTA HERE.

UNCLE THOMAS

1) Associate justice of the Supreme Court Clarence Thomas. 2) See TOM.

UNCLE TOM

See TOM.

UNDERGROUND HIT

1) A record that is a hit in the COMMUNITY and out in the street, but doesn't make it to the mainstream. 2) A record not made in a studio, not professionally recorded.

UP ON IT

Well informed, highly aware of something; sophisticated; HIP.

UP SHIT CREEK

In serious trouble; vulnerable to exposure or defeat; in danger of losing something. Crossover expression.

UP SOUTH

The Northern part of the United States; coined by Malcolm X to correct the Black perception of the North as the PROMISED LAND and to emphasize the existence of racism in the North as well as the South. See also DOWN SOUTH.

UPS

See HOPS.

UPSIDE YO / THE / HIS HEAD (also GO / HIT / SLAP / KNOCK UPSIDE YO / THE / HIS HEAD)

Describes act of hitting or slapping somebody on the head, which could effectively knock the person down. On the origin of the term, the legendary comic genius Redd Foxx (who finished out his very long career in the television sitcom "Sanford and Son") offers the following: "While there doesn't seem to be any written explanation of how the phrase 'up side yo' head' got started, it is generally agreed that it is a variation on the term upside down. In other words: "I'll put yo' head where yo' feet is, turkey!" (from Redd Foxx and Norma Miller, *The Redd Foxx Encyclopedia of Black Humor,* Pasadena, Calif.: Ward Ritchie Press, 1977).

UPTIGHT

1) Full of anxiety; stressed out about something. Crossover meaning. 2) Everything is all right, excellent, all is in good order (older meaning).

USG

United States Ghetto. A SIGNIFYIN characterization speaking to the racism of the system that has created "inner cities," concentrations of African Americans of the working, and increasingly UN-working, class in every major U.S. city. Fredro Starr of the RAP group Onyx: "We're from New York but we're in LA and it's still the ghetto. You go to Washington, it's ghetto, everywhere it's ghetto... We don't represent the USA, we represent the USG... You got the USA and we got the USG. We ain't really from the USA because we really ain't got no props in the USA, so we relate our shit to the USG" (from *The Source*, June 1993).

VAMP

To leave, to go away.

VAPORS

1) An opportunistic desire for someone who was previously shunned, but who now has status or material possessions. "It wasn't until I got that recording contract that she caught the vapors." 2) Jealousy. 3) Crack smoke.

VEE-IN

An initiation ritual used by gangs.

VEGA

Brand of cigars used for smoking marijuana. See also PHILLY BLUNT.

VERDICT

1) Something that's going to happen; the plan. 2) The final word about a subject; the outcome. "So what is the verdict? Are we goin to the show tonight or what?"

VIBE

1) Carrying yourself a certain way, your RAP, your style, especially when relating to the opposite sex. "I wanna see you… wanna meet you and see how you vibe." 2) To date or maintain a relationship with someone. "The Brotha and I been vibin for a couple of months now." 3) Intuition; a hunch. 4) The elusive, indefinable quality of something that can't be described, you have to feel it. This use has crossed over.

VICIOUS

See DEF.

VINE / VINES

A male's suit. Probably from the idea that when it really fits, it hangs as do vines in nature. Older term.

VISITATION OF THE SPIRIT

In the Traditional Black Church, referring to the Holy Spirit (HOLY GHOS) descending upon members or a member of the congregation, manifested by SHOUTin, cries of praise, REJOICin, holy dancing, and other manifestations of GITtin HAPPY. When the Spirit "visits," it reflects the power of God.

VOODOO

A religion with roots in West Africa; the belief system is polytheistic (many gods) and includes demons and the "living dead"; practices include the use of rituals, charms, herbs, and potions to control reality and events. The word *Voodoo*, meaning "protective spirit," comes from Dahomey (now Benin) in West Africa and is derived from *Vodu* in the Fon and Ewe languages. Members of this religious sect reside throughout the United States, but the largest concentration of members is still in New Orleans, the birthplace of *Voodoo* in North America. African American writer and anthropologist Zora Neale Hurston was initiated into the religion in New Orleans in the 1920s and presents detailed accounts in her writings.

Although *Voodoo* relies on a system of magic, which some scholars say is characteristic of all religions, this is not its fundamental aspect. In Africa it was used to unite groups to fight against a common enemy, and during enslavement in North America, it became a force to organize, rally, and strengthen those rebelling against enslavement. This was probably the primary reason for slave masters' attempts to suppress *Voodoo* as a religion by banning religious meetings and services. With the outlawing of the religious aspect, the magic aspect — the use of charms and herbal rituals, the creation of *Voodoo* objects, etc. — became more pronounced, since ole massa viewed the magic as only so much primitive hocus-pocus. In 1945 the World Order of Congregational Churches gave its official stamp of approval to *Voodoo* as a legitimate religion. However, the association of the religion with "primitive" magic, and especially the HOODOO MAN's manipulation and exploitation of the magic element for profit, widespread in the Black community by the 1940s, drove genuine *Voodoo* followers underground. However, George Brandon reports that an Orisha-Voodoo community was established in South Carolina in Oyotunji Village, which was founded in 1972 (from "Sacrificial Practices in Santeria, an African-Cuban Religion in the United States," in Joseph E. Holloway, ed., *Africanisms in American Culture*, Bloomington: Indiana University Press, 1990). *Voodoo* is fairly prevalent in Haiti, other parts of the Caribbean, and Brazil. Although not widely practiced in the U.S. Black community today, there still exists a belief that Blacks have supernatural powers, a belief that comes out of the tradition and religious system of *Voodoo* in the COMMUNITY. See also HOODOO.

**W's**

White folk. Generally generic, neutral reference.

**WACK**

Not with-it; undesirable; not good.

**WANNABE**

1) An African American trying to be white, acting white; in Spike Lee's *School Daze,* the *wannabes* opposed the Black-oriented "jigaboos." 2) By extension, a person trying to act as if he/she is a member of any group or has achieved a particular status that he/she does not have. 3) Someone trying to be a gang member.

**WASHED IN THE BLOOD**

Anointed, SAVED, symbolically having been cleansed ("washed") in the sacrificial blood of Christ.

**WASTE**

1) To kill. 2) To spill something. 3) See also GIT WASTED.

**WATCH DA BOWS**

Watch the elbows. In B-BALL, telling opponents to curb the rough, physical style of play.

**WATCH MEETING NIGHT**

New Year's Eve, when Traditional Black Church folk gather to "watch" the old year go out and the new one come in, giving thanks to God that they have made it through the year.

**WATERMELON HEAD**

A person who doesn't listen to reason, thinks he/she knows everything, is like the watermelon, full of nothing but water.

**WAVE NOUVEAU**

A chemically STRAIGHTENed hairstyle; gets curly when wet, but a controlled curl that doesn't NAP UP.

WAX

1) A record album or label. "To be put on wax" means to sign a recording contract. 2) To defeat someone in competition. "We waxed dem niggaz by 40 points" (refers to defeating the opposing team in B-BALL). 3) To do something energetically and strongly, to perform to the maximum.

WAX SOME ASS

To have sex.

WE BE CLUBBIN

Statement indicating that the group is partying hard, lively, at a club, and that they do this on a regular basis.

WEAK SHIT

1) Insufficient or inadequate action, words, or behavior. "Don't come in here with no weak shit, cause I ain goin for it," i.e., Please don't bother me with an insubstantial explanation because I won't accept it. 2) In sports competition, a subpar performance.

WEAK SIDE

1) A point of vulnerability in sports competition or in one's argument or ideas about something. 2) Refers to something that is in poor condition or cheap.

WEAR FACE

To use or apply facial makeup.

WEAR OUT ONE'S WELCOME

Used by senior Blacks to indicate that 1) a person has exhausted his or her acceptability in a group or situation; 2) a person has exceeded the limits of hospitality.

WEAR YOU / THEM / IT OUT

1) To have sex. 2) To outdo somebody in a competitive situation, such as cards or sports.

WEAVE

A female hairdo with synthetic or human hair braided into the natural hair at the roots, with the rest left loose for a long, full-looking hairstyle.

**WEED**

Marijuana.

**WEIGHT**

1) Blame. 2) Psychological or emotional pressure.

**WELL, ALL RIGHT!**

A response of affirmation or enthusiastic endorsement.

**WES SIDE!**

Said with elongation and elevated pitch of "side." 1) Exclamation proclaiming the power of the West Coast, or, by extension, the west side of one's town. 2) Also used as an exclamation in general.

**WHAM BAM, THANK YOU, MAM!**

An older expression resurfacing in HIP HOP, as in the RAP JAM "What's the 4 1 1?" by DIVA Mary J. Blige: "I don't have no time for no 'Wham bam, thank you, Mam!' / Gas me up, git me drunk, and hit the skins and scram." See BIP BAM, THANK YOU, MAM!

**WHASS CRACKIN?**

See WHASS HAPNIN?

**WHASS HAPNIN?**

A greeting pattern, "What's happening?" meaning, Hello, how are you? WHASSUP? and WHAT UP?, newer terms, are variations on this older pattern.

**WHASSUP?**

1) "What's up?" Also *Sup?*, *What up?* See also WHASS HAPNIN? 2) In Los Angeles gang usage, a generic password.

**WHASSUP WITH THAT?**

"What is up with that?," an expression requesting clarity or information on something, literally "What is the status of X?"

**WHAT GO ROUND COME ROUND**

A proverb that expresses perhaps the essence of traditional "root culture" Blacks' beliefs about life, that whatever has happened before will occur again, even if in a different form. In a study of over a thousand proverbs used by African Americans, this was found to be the most frequently used proverb in the African American community (study reported in Jack L. Daniel, Geneva Smitherman-Donaldson, and Milford Jeremiah, "'Makin a Way Outa No Way': The Proverb Tradition in the Black Experience," *Journal of Black Studies*, June 1987).

WHAT IT B LIKE?

1) A greeting among members of the L.A. gang the BLOODS. See also WHAT IT C LIKE? 2) A general greeting among non–gang members (older usage).

WHAT IT C LIKE?

A greeting among members of the L.A. gang the CRIPS.

WHAT SET YOU FROM?

What neighborhood are you from?

WHAT TIME IT IS

See TIME.

WHAT UP?

A greeting pattern that has not crossed over, unlike WHAT'S UP?, which has crossed over. *What up?* is AAL form of *What's up?*

WHAT UP, DOE?

"Doe," address for a friend, associate, relative, a variation of dog. See WHASS HAPNIN?, WHAT UP?

WHAT'S HAPPENING?

See WHASS HAPNIN?

WHAT'S UP?

See WHASSUP?, WHAT UP?

WHAT YOU ON?

Said to a person who has said or chosen something irrational, who isn't making sense; implies that the person must be on some kind of drug or mind-altering substance.

WHIP / DA WHIP

The ultimate, highest superlative of anything (older term). Also DA BOMB (newer term).

WHIS

See BID.

WHISSIN

Playing BID.

WHITE ON RICE

Describes someone who clings to or follows something or somebody extremely closely, tenaciously. "Five-O was on my man like white on rice."

WHITE WHITE

1) A EUROPEAN AMERICAN who acts extremely "white," in a cultural sense; one completely lacking in knowledge of the Black sensibility and devoid of COOLNESS. 2) A very racist European American.

WHITEMAIL

Activists' and AFRICAN-CENTERED folks' emerging term for "blackmail." Reflects an effort to reverse negative images of Blackness in the English language.

WHITENIZATION

A reference to the early historical process of Europeanizing the United States through promotion of Euro-American values, culture, politics, ideology, patterns of thinking, and social habits.

WHITEY

A derisive term for a white person. Also *honky*.

WHO YO DADDY?

Who is your father? Used in the sense of the father as traditional authority figure, meaning, Who is your boss? Who controls you? Used in 1990s competitive sports to taunt the losing opponent, a part of B-BALL "trash talk"; crossover phrase. However, it is often misunderstood by an older generation as implying that the opposing player is illegitimate, that he/she has "no father," as was the case in a February 1999 college basketball game when the legendary Indiana University coach Bobby Knight took offense, on behalf of his players, at the use of the phrase by Northwestern University fans and occasioned much national media attention.

**WHOLE LOTTA YELLA WASTED**

Used in reference to an unattractive light-complexioned African American; usually a person who has light skin but African facial features and hair. The YELLA is "wasted" in the sense that this myth is based on light skin as a valuable commodity, but since the *yella* is ugly, the light skin is doing that person no good.

**THE WHOLE NINE**

Everything; all of something. AAL version of the general slang phrase "the whole nine yards." Crossing over.

**WHORE**

See HO.

**WHUPPED**

See DICK-WHUPPED, PUSSY-WHUPPED.

**WIFEY**

A steady girlfriend in a monogamous, heterosexual relationship.

**WIFIN**

Playing the wife role, in the traditional sense.

**WIGGA**

A white NIGGA; emerged in the late 1980s and early 1990s as a positive term for white youth who identify with HIP HOP, RAP, and other aspects of African American Culture. In the late 1990s, the term is losing linguistic currency. Throughout U.S. history, there have always been *wiggas*, particularly in the twentieth century. In the 1950s, white writer Norman Mailer dubbed them "white Negroes." Their numbers are significantly larger in the 1990s than in previous generations because of the exposure to African American Culture made possible by mass media. See also NIGGA.

**WIGGER**

See WIGGA.

**WILD**

See RUN WILD.

**WILDERNESS**

The North American continent, especially the United States.

WILLIE

See BIG WILLIE.

WINDY CITY

Chicago. Crossover expression. Also *Chi-town,* which has not crossed over.

WIT

Indicates approval of something; in favor of a thing, person, idea, or action. "I ain't wit being broke; I'm wit money." AAL rendering of "with."

WIT THE PROGRAM

Agreeable to a plan of action, activity, idea, or event.

WITH

See WIT.

WITH THE PROGRAM

See WIT THE PROGRAM.

WITNESS

1) To give testimony, bear "witness," to God's power. 2) A person who can testify to the wonders of God's power.

WOLF

See WOOF.

WOMAN

A man's girlfriend or wife; used by men and women. See also LADY.

WOMANISH

See WOMNISH.

WOMANIST

An African American feminist; also used to refer to Black feminist thought. The term was popularized by Alice Walker, author of several works, including *The Color Purple* (which won a Pulitzer Prize for literature and was made into a film by Steven Spielberg). A *womanist* is rooted in the COMMUNITY and committed to the survival and development of herself and the community at the same time. In keeping with her emphasis on the importance of using language that is "organic" to the African

American community, Walker appropriated the term from the AAL word WOMNISH. She writes: *"Womanist . . .* From the Black folk expression of mothers to female children, 'You acting womanish, i.e., like a woman...Wanting to know more and in greater depth than is considered 'good' for one...Acting grown up...Interchangeable with another Black folk expression: 'You trying to be grown.' Responsible. In charge. *Serious"* (from *In Search of Our Mothers' Gardens,* published by Harcourt Brace Jovanovich, 1983).

WOMLISH

See WOMNISH.

WOMNISH

Also rendered in AAL as *womlish.* Acting like a grown, adult woman; often used to reprimand young girls who are acting too grown-up for their age. See also MANNISH.

WOOD

1) A white person; see PECKAWOOD. 2) A Cadillac car, Fleet-wood model, once a popular symbol of LIVIN LARGE.

WOOF

To threaten by using boastful, strong language; the *woofer* may or may not intend to execute the threat (usually doesn't intend to). One who believes the *woofin* may challenge the *woofer,* in which case the person is said to have *bought the woof ticket.* Once thought to have been derived from the word "wolf," pronounced according to AAL rules as "woof," the term may have come from the sound of dogs barking for no reason, or from a conflation of the two words "woof" and "wolf." In 1935, Black woman anthropologist and writer Zora Neale Hurston wrote: "Woofing is a sort of aimless talking. A man half seriously flirts with a girl, half seriously threatens to fight or brags of his prowess in love, battle or in financial matters. The term comes from the purposeless barking of dogs at night" (from *Mules and Men*).

**WOOF TICKET**

A verbal threat, which one *sells* to somebody; may or may not be real. Often used as a strategy to make another person back down and surrender to what that person perceives as a superior power.

**WOOFER**

See WOOF.

**WORD! / WORD UP!**

A response of affirmation. Also *Word to the Mother! Word Up* is also the title of a music magazine that was published in New Jersey. See also WORD IS BOND!

**WORD IS BOND!**

An affirmative response to a statement or action. Also *Word!, Word up!, Word to the Mother!* A resurfacing of an old, familiar saying in the Black Oral Tradition, "Yo word is yo bond," still heard among many Black seniors. Popularized by the FIVE PERCENT NATION in its early years, *Word is bond!* reaffirms strong belief in the power of the word, and thus the value of verbal commitment. One's word is the guarantee, the warranty, the *bond*, that whatever was promised will actually occur. Sometimes expressed as "Word is born!"

**WORD TO THE MOTHER!**

A response of affirmation. See also WORD IS BOND!, WORD! / WORD UP!

**WORK**

1) To do something forcefully, completely, with high energy, and persuasively. 2) Used in reference to making something *work* for you with others. "Girlfriend working her program," meaning, She is expertly handling some situation or potential conflict. Also *work it*.

**WORK A SPOT**

To sell drugs or sex in a certain location.

WORK IT

See WORK.

WORK SOMEONE'S NERVES

1) To get on somebody's nerves; to aggravate or irritate a person.

2) To cause emotional stress to a person.

THE WORLD

The nonspiritual part of life. The secular world, outside the Church. A negative term.

WORLDLY

Describes things or people of a nonspiritual nature. A negative term.

X

1) A reference to Malcolm X, 1960s political theoretician and hero. Born Malcolm Little, he adopted the "X" after he joined the Nation of Islam. 2) Used as the last name of any member of THE NATION. From its inception, THE NATION has followed the practice of substituting an "X" for its members' last names, to symbolize the unknown and lost ancestry of Africans in America and to symbolize rejection of the slavemaster's surname, which was commonly adopted by ex-slaves.

XXL

New HIP HOP magazine. Not just "large," in the sense of excellent, superb, but double extra large.

**YACUB**

According to THE NATION, Yacub was a brilliant Black scientist whose curiosity and inventiveness got out of hand and led to the creation of the white man. See also DEVIL.

**YAH-YO**

Cocaine.

**YAK**

Cognac.

**YALL**

"You" plural. Probably derived from the practice in African languages of differentiating between the singular and plural forms of "you." Unlike English, African languages have different forms for this second-person pronoun. For instance, Wolof *yow* ("you" singular) vs. *yeen, yena* ("you" plural).

**YANG**

Gibberish, nonsense.

**YELLA / HIGH YELLA**

Describes a very light-complexioned African American; praised in some quarters, damned in others. COMMUNITY ambivalence stems from *high yellas'* close physical approximation to European Americans. To the extent that white skin is valued, as was the case, for example, in the 1940s and 1950s, then being *yella* is a plus. On the other hand, to the extent that a *yella* African is a reminder of whiteness/the "enemy," as was the case in the Black Power Movement of the 1960s and 1970s, for instance, or in the case of *yellaness* being a reminder of the historical rape of Black women by white men, then being *yella* is a minus. Also *yelluh.* See also COLOR SCALE, COLOR STRUCK, WHOLE LOTTA YELLA WASTED.

YELLOW

> See YELLA.

Yo!

> 1) A greeting, meaning simply "Hello." 2) Used to get someone's attention, instead of saying "Hey!" or "Hey you!" Possibly from African American military men in the 1950s, who would answer "Yo!" at roll call, whereas their European American counterparts would answer "Yep!"

YO

> "Your," as in "your house," pronounced *yo* following AAL rules. The basketball player who said "Yo ball" was telling his opponent that it was his turn to get the ball; he was not greeting or talking to the ball, as a confused European American onlooker mistakenly perceived.

YO BOY / GIRL

> Friend, associate, or someone you admire.

YO MAN / WOMAN

> Lover, significant other, partner, boyfriend or girlfriend.

YO MOMMA

> Your mother; the standard formulaic expression used in ritualized "insults" in the verbal game of PLAYing THE DOZENS. See also THE DOZENS, SNAPS.

YO THANG

> See DO YO / HIS / HER OWN THANG.

YO WORLD

> Expression used in B-BALL, urging player to create conditions to make a basket, that is, handle it, it's all yours.

YO-YO

> A weak, stupid person.

YOU DON'T HEAR ME, THOUGH

> Expression to indicate that a person isn't heeding what you are saying; they may be pretending to listen, but the person is actually ignoring you. "Uhm tellin you not to do that, but you don't hear me, though."

# Z

**Z's**

Sleep. Crossover term.

**ZILLIONS**

Braided hairstyle, with numerous—"zillions"—of tiny braids; worn by women or men.

# TEXT CREDITS

•••••••••••••••••